PROTEST

WITH CHINESE CHARACTERISTICS

PROTEST
WITH CHINESE CHARACTERISTICS

DEMONSTRATIONS, RIOTS, AND PETITIONS IN THE MID-QING DYNASTY

HO-FUNG HUNG

COLUMBIA UNIVERSITY PRESS *New York*

Columbia University Press
Publishers Since 1893
New York Chichester, West Sussex

Paperback edition, 2013

The author and Columbia University Press gratefully acknowledge the support of the Chiang Ching-Kuo Foundation for International Scholarly Exchange in the publication of this book.

Library of Congress Cataloging-in-Publication Data
Hung, Ho-fung.
Protest with Chinese characteristics : demonstrations, riots, and petitions in the Mid-Qing Dynasty / Ho-fung Hung.
p. cm.
Includes bibliographical references and index.
ISBN 978-0-231-15202-0 (cloth : alk. paper)—ISBN 978-0-231-15203-7 (pbk. : alk. paper)—
ISBN 978-0-231-52545-9 (ebook)
1. Protest movements—China—History—18th century. 2. Riots—China—History—18th century. 3. Demonstrations—China—History—18th century. 4. Petitions—China—History—18th century. 5. China—Social conditions—18th century. 6. China—History—Qing dynasty, 1644–1912. I. Title.
HN733.H86 2011
303.48'4095109033—dc22
2010053571

Columbia University Press books are printed on permanent and durable acid-free paper.

This book is printed on paper with recycled content.
Printed in the United States of America

Cover image: Songqingtang Zhuren ed. 1915. Xinhai Sichuan Lushi Jilue *(Chronology of Protecting Railroad Movement in Sichuan). Chengdu: Qiangfu Gongshi (Courtesy of National Library of China)*
Cover design: Shaina Andrews

To **GIOVANNI**

CONTENTS

FIGURES

TABLES

PREFACE

THIS PROJECT ORIGINATED about ten years ago, when I was introduced to the debate on Eurocentrism while pursuing my Ph.D. Contrary to the standard view that modernity emerged in Europe in early modern times (c. 1500–1800) and then spread to the rest of the world in the nineteenth and twentieth centuries, anti-Eurocentric historiography postulated that in Asia—and China in particular—modernity flowered independently in the sixteenth through the eighteenth century, with robust commercial growth and political centralization that paralleled, and perhaps dwarfed, Europe's. The literature on this topic portrays the current rise of China as a resurgence of its political and economic vitality in the Ming-Qing period. The pervasiveness of this intellectual current notwithstanding, it has been until now not much more than a celebration of China's early modern might and has focused more on macrostructures than on human actions. Like social historians intrigued by how ordinary people reacted to the sweeping economic and political changes in early modern Europe, as well as social scientists concerned about the growing conflicts unleashed by the current Chinese economic miracle, I am curious about the ways in which the subjects of the Chinese empire lived through and responded to the rise of early modernity. How were their responses different from the responses of their counterparts in early modern Europe? Did these responses constitute a lasting pattern of action that continued into the twentieth century and beyond? These are the questions that this study, which focuses on popular protest in the eighteenth and early nineteenth centuries, sets out to answer.

This decade of research has been supported by numerous institutions and individuals. A J. Brien Key Graduate Research Grant from the Krieger School of Arts and Sciences at the Johns Hopkins University enabled me to do pilot research and to establish initial contacts with scholars in Beijing and Taipei, who guided me to the Qing archives there. An International

Field Dissertation Fellowship from the Social Science Research Council, with funds provided by the Andrew Mellon Foundation, and a Dissertation Improvement Grant from the National Science Foundation supported further research in the archives. After the completion of my dissertation, which dealt only with two decades, the 1740s and the 1830s, I continued to enrich and expand my analysis to the period between those two decades by going back to the archives regularly. These trips were supported by a faculty research grant from the Chinese University of Hong Kong and a faculty summer fellowship and research grant from Indiana University.

Research and writing are painstaking endeavors that are impossible to complete without the advice, support, and friendship of mentors and colleagues. My dissertation adviser Giovanni Arrighi, who unfortunately passed away in 2009, contributed invaluably to my work, with his high standards and relentless critiques. His acute intellect and encyclopedic knowledge always kept me on course in the ocean of historical materials available to researchers. He kept me from losing sight of the larger structural context and analytic significance of every case of protest that I encountered. I hope this book would have made him proud. Mark Selden introduced me to the debate on Eurocentrism in his East Asian seminar at SUNY Binghamton and helped shape my research through his critical comments on earlier drafts of the dissertation proposal. Seminars and conversations with Immanuel Wallerstein were always intellectual feasts and opened my eyes to the world-historical and interdisciplinary perspectives on long-term, large-scale social changes.

At Johns Hopkins University, Beverly Silver and Mel Kohn helped me with methodological issues. Bill Rowe guided my exploration of the historiography of early modern China, updating me on the latest works in the field and educating me on the relevant primary materials. His assistance was essential to my gaining access to the archives in Beijing. At Indiana University, I am surrounded by a wonderful team of colleagues with diverse disciplinary backgrounds and substantive research interests. They never hesitated to read and critique manuscripts of various works developing from this project. They include Klaus Mühlhahn, Lynn Struve, and Jeffrey Wasserstrom from the history department; Gardner Bovingdon from Central Eurasian studies; Sara Friedman from anthropology; Scott Kennedy from political science; and Art Alderson, Liz Armstrong, Tim Bartley, Stephen Benard, Tim Hallett, Jennifer Lee, Paulette Lloyd, Ethan Michelson, Brian Powell,

Fabio Rojas, Brian Steensland, Qunicy Stewart, Leah Vanwey, and Melissa Wilde from sociology.

Generous comments and encouragement from fellow historical social scientists and China specialists at different stages of my research helped me identify the gaps and highlight the theoretical significance of my findings. They include Julia Adams, Richard Biernacki, Kai-wing Chow, Christopher Chase-Dunn, Randall Collins, Arif Dirlik, Joseph Esherick, Richard Louis Edmond, Rebecca Emigh, Ivan Ermakoff, Jack Goldstone, Gary Hamilton, Eiko Ikegami, Richard Lachmann, Tobie Meyer-Fong, Ng Kwai, Patrick O'Brien, Ravi Palat, Frank Pieke, Sarah Schneewind, Alvin So, Sidney Tarrow, Charles Tilly, Bin Wong, Yang Fenggang, and Dingxin Zhao. I also appreciate the insights that I gained from the participants in various colloquia and seminars at Northwestern University, Purdue University, SUNY Albany, UC–San Diego, the University of Illinois at Urbana-Champaign, Yale University, and panels at different professional meetings, where I presented the findings of this research.

The kind assistance, advice, and hospitality of Gao Xiang, Huang Ping, and Lu Aiguo from the Chinese Academy of Social Science; Qin Guojing and the archivists at the First Historical Archive of China; and the librarians in the Ancient Book Section of the National Library of China were invaluable to my fieldwork in Beijing. Chiu Peng-sheng, Ka Chih-ming, and Wu Jen-shu from the Academia Sinica, librarians at the Fu Ssu-nien Library at the Academia Sinica, and Zhuang Jifa and the staff of the National Palace Museum were immensely helpful while I worked in the archives in Taipei. The professionalism of Liu Wen-ling, the East Asian librarian at the Herman B. Wells Library of Indiana University, contributed significantly to the last stage of my research.

I am thankful for the support and advice of Anne Routon at Columbia University Press. Her incisiveness and efficiency make her one of the best editors an author could find. The detailed suggestions by the anonymous reviewers greatly facilitated my efforts in sharpening the arguments and clarifying some conceptual and methodological issues. I appreciate the professionalism of Robert Fellman and Roy Thomas at the press in the production process. Amy VanStee, my copy editor, meticulously combed through two successive drafts of the manuscript. I thank Boxun media and 64 memorial, which granted me permission to reproduce some photos in their archives, and the Ancient Book Section of the National Library of China, which made watermark-free copies of a number of late nineteenth- and early twentieth-century cartoons for inclusion in the book.

I thank my parents and sister for their patience and confidence in me during my lengthy pursuit of an academic career. Above all, I am most indebted to my wife Huei-ying, who has been by my side throughout this study, from its conception in Baltimore and Binghamton to its completion in Bloomington. Without the intellectual insights, emotional support, and sacrifice of Huei-ying, who is pursuing her own academic career, I would have been unable to get over many hurdles. Her humanity and humility, as well as our separate yet shared experiences in the student movement, make me remember the initial idealism that motivated me to choose sociology, a science that not only interprets the world but also seeks to change it. Our children, Henry King-heng and Helia Man-lai, came in time to witness the fruition of this project. The fun and challenges they offered never failed to refresh me from the frustration and stress during the writing process. When they grow up and read this book, I hope they will find that all the time I missed spending with them in order to complete this project was worthwhile.

PROTEST

WITH CHINESE CHARACTERISTICS

INTRODUCTION

Today's China is perhaps the most rapidly changing society in the world. With double-digit GDP growth during most of the last two decades, its social and cultural fabric has undergone a profound transformation, at a speed unprecedented in world history. Yet just as it was becoming popular with social scientists who hope to glean from China what the new century will look like, traditional forms of collective action began to rise as significant means for the underprivileged to make claims on political authorities. Two leading scholars on modern Chinese contention are surprised to find that "significant strains in contemporary popular protest can be traced back to Imperial and Republican era precedents" (Perry and Selden 2000, 8).

One example is the practice of petitioning the central government to attend to local injustices. In Qing times (1644–1911), a common remedy for powerless subjects abused by local officials was to travel all the way to Beijing to appeal to the emperor as their grand patriarch, hoping that he would sympathize with their plight and penalize corrupt local officials. The petition process was often emotionally charged and involved dramatic displays of desolation, such as kneeling upon both knees, collective public weeping, and knocking one's head upon the ground (*koutou*). From the 1980s to the 2000s, similar petitions proliferated, as grassroots citizens throughout the People's Republic traveled to Beijing to lodge plaints against tyrannical local officials (Michelson 2007; Minzner 2006; O'Brien and Li 2006). It is not certain whether government officials equate the power center of the Communist state with an emperor, but these petitioners apparently do. They acted in the same way as their imperial predecessors did, by kneeling and weeping in front of central-government offices. This parallelism is so conspicuous that a New York–based human-rights organization noted that

> China's petitioning system is a unique cultural and legal tradition with deep historical roots. . . . In China's last imperial dynasty, the Qing (1644–1911), petitioners traveled to Beijing and sometimes waited outside the gates of the emperor's palace on their knees, or tried to intercept imperial processions, to present their appeals. Today, their descendants stage sit-ins in front of Zhongnanhai, the Beijing compound where China's leaders live and work, and try to push their petitions into their limousines. Thousands of others throng Beijing's streets in front of national petitions offices, holding up signs that describe their cases.
>
> (HUMAN RIGHTS WATCH 2005, 3)

This traditionalist, submissive posture toward a supposedly paternalist state is not restricted to protests among less educated citizens. During the 1989 student movement, traditional protest repertoires were practiced along with radical antitraditionalist languages and actions. The act of three student representatives presenting a petition letter to the authorities by kneeling in front of the Great Hall of People was one of the most memorable moments of the movement. The moralistic tone taken by the students was more reminiscent of the loyal moralism that scholar-officials employed to constrain the emperor's behavior in imperial times than it was of the liberal ideology of popular sovereignty that the students purported to espouse (Esherick and Wasserstrom 1990; Zhao 2001).

Another auspicious example of the revival of traditional forms of Chinese protest is the Falong Gong movement of the 1990s. The movement employs very modern means of mobilization and information dissemination, such as text messaging and Internet Web sites. But its core convictions—that Falong Gong practitioners can attain invincibility and that the corrupt world will soon be cleansed by horrific disasters and replaced by a happy new epoch—clearly originated with the heterodox Buddhist sects that flourished during the Qing dynasty and intermittently rebelled against the state (Ownby 2008).

In the countryside, outbursts of collective violence against tax collectors, enforcers of unpopular policies (such as the one-child policy), and land-appropriating developers are on the rise. These rural unrests are always localistic. They rarely seek to change the larger system; rather, they tend to consider individual or local officials as the alleged sources of injustice. Attacking corrupt cadres or besieging government buildings or officials' residences or vehicles are nearly standard acts of resistance. As a historian of Chinese protests observes, this type of retributive violence, which personalizes injustice, constitutes "the most significant continuity" between today's China and the "peasant troubles linked to the centuries-long preindustrial old world" (Bianco 2001, xv, xvii, 251).

To be sure, China is also witnessing the emergence of novel protest forms and strategies. One example is the increasing use of legal means and languages in collective claim making. Another is the increasing prominence of internationally linked NGOs in the organization of protest. The rise of a contentious Internet-based public sphere among technologically savvy youngsters is also impressive (Lee 2007; Yang 2005, 2009). But the rise of these new forms does not mean that we can conveniently dismiss the traditional forms of protest as residue from the past that will automatically fade away. Their noteworthy survival despite the revolutionary ferment of the early twentieth century and the three decades of Maoist efforts to eradicate traditions once and for all suggests that they are far more resilient than commonly supposed. We should, in fact, treat these "traditional" repertoires as constitutive parts of China's "modern" protests. The persistence of traditional protest forms and ideologies is by no means unique to China: religious millenarianism around the world is on the rise, and in Latin America, the structural-adjustment reforms of the 1990s saw the proliferation of food riots, a protest type that was supposed to have gone extinct with the advent of the Industrial Revolution (e.g., Auyero and Moran 2007; Rude 1980, 33–108; Wickham 2002).

This persistence of past protest forms in China and elsewhere undermines the long-standing paradigm through which we have understood the historical rise of modern protest, social movements, and democratic politics. According to this paradigm, most protests and revolts in the premodern world, East and West, were "reactive," "backward looking," and "parochial." These reactive protests invariably aimed to resist change and to protect participants' traditional rights and subsistence from outside and nascent forces such as the centralizing state. In early modern Europe (c. 1600–1800), the irreversible rise of centralized national states and market capitalism fundamentally transformed parochial and reactive protests into cosmopolitan and proactive ones. The proactive protests usually involved cross-regional organizing and demanded new, universalist rights through engaging the state, not resisting it. This transformation heralded the rise of modern social movements and the democratic politics of nineteenth-century Europe. The historical development of protest in non-Western latecomers to "modernization," such as China, is argued to be nothing but a reprise of the European path.

Surging traditional protest forms and appeals in today's China raise questions that challenge this historical paradigm. Does Chinese protest manifest a distinct conception of rights, justice, and political authority, one that has persisted from past to present and that diverges from the supposedly "generic" modern protests that originated in Europe? When and how did these distinct features of Chinese protest originate? Is the transformation of a reactive form of protest into a proactive one unidirectional and inevitable? How do the dynamics and trajectory of the long-term historical development of protest in China differ from that of Europe?

In this book, I seek to answer these questions by drawing on the new historiography which posits that China's modernity, characterized by political and economic rationalization through state centralization and rise of an empire-wide market, did not begin with its nineteenth-century clash with Western powers, as has been previously supposed, but started earlier and spontaneously, around the sixteenth century. According to this framework, China's "early modernity," which was comparable to but different from European modernity, peaked during the eighteenth-century prosperity and stability of the Qing empire. Many "traditional" practices, institutions, and identities that continue today—such as lineage organizations and native place–based business networks—are in fact products of China's early modern development (e.g., Faure 2007; Hamilton 2006; Perdue 2005; Pomeranz 2000; Rawski 2004; Wong 1997; Woodside 2006). As Jonathan Spence once noted: "It is only by starting at this time [c. 1600] that I feel we can get a full sense of how China's current problems have arisen, and of what resources—intellectual, economic, and emotional—the Chinese can call upon to solve them" (1990, xx).

We shall see in this study that "traditional" protest forms and demands are likewise rooted in China's early modernity. The core of this book will describe the pattern, forms, and appeals of popular protests directed at the state in the heyday of China's early modernity: the mid-Qing period, from 1740 (during the great thrust of state centralization) to 1839 (on the eve of China's clash with Western imperialism, in the Opium War of 1839–1842). By connecting the dynamics of mid-Qing protests as unearthed in this study with those of the seventeenth century and the late nineteenth and twentieth centuries as documented extensively in the literature, I sketch the indigenous trajectory of the long-term historical transformation of protest from early modern to modern China. I then compare it with the Western trajectory, which has been erroneously presumed to be universal. I explore how and to what extent these early modern protests are related to large-scale rebellions, which have been more intensively studied (Bernhardt 1992; Bianco 2001; Perry 2002; Robinson 2001; Rowe 2007; Tong 1991). I also investigate how these protest forms survived the collapse of empire in 1911, perpetuated into today's China, and hybridized with Western forms of protest that have been introduced to China since the nineteenth century.

TELEOLOGICAL AND EUROCENTRIC VIEWS OF PROTEST

Most historical studies of protest have been premised on the general view that modernity started with the state centralization and transition to capitalism in sixteenth-century Europe and that modern historical developments outside Europe were only belated replications of Europe's development. This view has been recently criticized as "teleological" and "Eurocentric." Despite these assumptions, this established social historiography of modern protest is still an indispensable and useful conceptual apparatus for our investigation of mid-Qing protests. In this section and the next, I review the major themes of this historiography and its critics, deriving from them the analytic scheme and guiding questions of this study.

TELEOLOGY

According to the classical view, modern protests and social movements, as well as revolutionary and democratic politics, originated in eighteenth- and nineteenth-century Europe and then spread to the rest of the world in the nineteenth and twentieth centuries. This view was pioneered by classical sociologists such as Karl Marx and Max Weber, who saw the rise of modern protest as part of the unilinear progress of history.

In the ending section of the *Communist Manifesto*, Marx and Engels painstakingly attacked what they called "reactionary socialism," a type of political movement against the capitalist order by the aristocracy and peasants, who struggled to resist change and revive the precapitalist order. Given their conviction about the irreversibility and desirability of social progress, Marx and Engels declared that these backward-looking, "antiquarian" movements, owing to their "total incapacity to comprehend the march of modern history" (1972, 354–355), were doomed to fail, while the forward-looking revolutionary movement of the proletarians, who strived to bring about a more egalitarian and productive society, was destined to prevail. Marx's unilinear view is echoed by Max Weber, who discussed in *Economy and Society* the transformation of popular protest from "resistance to the market," such as food riots throughout antiquity and the Middle Ages, to "fight for access to the market," such as protests emerging from wage disputes. To Weber, the latter type of struggles "have been slowly increasing up into modern times" in the nineteenth and twentieth centuries (1946, 185–186).

By classifying opposition to the capitalist order into backward-looking and forward-looking movements and suggesting the inevitable evolution from the former to the latter in the "march of history," this Marxian or Weberian view had a significant effect on the historical study of popular protest in the New Social History. This scholarly movement has strived since the 1960s to bring historians' attention to the ordinary people at the bottom of society (see Sewell 2005, 22–80).

For example, Eric Hobsbawn (1959) painted in his *Primitive Rebels* a colorful picture of how banditry, mafias, urban mobs, and millenarian sects in southwest Europe constituted the "pre-historic stage" (10) of modern social movements. To Hobsbawn, the transition of these "archaic," "premature," "inchoate" movements into modern movements such as labor unionism and socialist-party politics was a drawn-out process of evolution through which the primitive rebels, who were "pre-political people who have not yet found . . . a specific language in which to express their aspirations about the world" (2), struggled to "adapt to the modern conditions" (8).

A similar evolutionary account of protest in terms of the "modernization" of protesters' consciousness can be found in Emmanuel Le Roy Ladurie's classic essay on the transformation of French peasant protest in the eighteenth century (1976 [1974]). For Le Roy Ladurie, French peasant protest in c. 1675–1788 witnessed a gradual transition from "past-based patterns" of protests in the seventeenth century, when peasants reacted to the newly imposed taxes from the modernizing state and yearned to return to the "good old way" through communal tax riots, to the "futurist patterns" of protest emerging after c. 1750, when peasants asked for a new and more just social order through humble petition to local authorities or the king against the old system of aristocratic seigneurial rights (442). This transition was inevitable and irreversible, as "there had been a modernization—ideological, cultural and social—of the peasant . . . [who increasingly] refused to go on living as it had lived in the past. . . . This kind of evolution could lead in no time at all to revolutionary consequences" (437). Hobsbawn and Le Roy Ladurie's delineation of protest transformation from "archaic" to "modern" forms fell far short of offering an explanation for such a transformation. Indeed, they seemed to assume, following in the footsteps of Marx, that this evolution was natural.

What is left unexplained in these pioneering works was elaborated in E. P. Thompson's study of the moral economy (1991). According to Thompson, grassroots society in precapitalist England was regulated by a moral economy, which is defined as a set of values and social relations that prioritized reciprocity and subsistence over market exchange and profit making. With the advent of market capitalism in the eighteenth century, local moral economies were disrupted when merchants shipped local grains away to sell them at better prices in distant markets. The subsequent subsistence crisis often unleashed reactions from the masses in the form of violent seizures of grain and attacks on greedy merchants or aloof local authorities. At the turn of the nineteenth century, the state increasingly espoused the market ideology, became further centralized, and cracked down on such food riots relentlessly. Facing ever tougher repression, food riots consequently died out in the course of the nineteenth century. They were replaced by more organized forms of anticapitalist opposition, such as labor unionism and socialist movements, which sought to influence or even control the state in their favor.

Thompson, like Marx, Hobsbawn, and Le Roy Ladurie, noted a unidirectional transition from parochial riots against the expanding market and state in the seventeenth century to organized protests or petition that sought to wrest control of the state in the eighteenth and nineteenth centuries. Thompson went further, linking the transition to the changing characteristics of the state apparatus. His work constitutes a crucial step toward the theoretically rigorous studies of Charles Tilly and Sidney Tarrow, who employ a large-scale survey of changing protest patterns in Western Europe and North America from the eighteenth to the nineteenth century to illuminate the macrohistorical dynamics underlying the unidirectional transformation of protest (Tarrow 1994; Tilly 1978, 1986, 1995).

Tilly classified protest repertoires in his earlier works into reactive and proactive categories. While reactive protests aimed to *defend* preexisting communal rights, proactive protests sought to *expand* the protesters' rights. Based on his catalogs of protest episodes in early modern France and England, Tilly converges with earlier scholars to observe a unidirectional transition of protest from eighteenth-century reactive violence, such as tax riots, to nineteenth-century proactive action, such as collective petitioning for legislative reforms.

Tilly later shifted to a more complicated terminology and characterized the transition as one from parochial, particular, and bifurcated protests to cosmopolitan, modular, and autonomous ones (Tilly 1986, 1995). Protests before the late eighteenth century were parochial, as they addressed local issues and expressed localistic identities. They were particular, as most repertoires were restricted to specific issues or localities. They were bifurcated, as protesters resorted to direct violence against local authorities while relying on the patronage of local power holders in making claims on higher-level authorities. In contrast, protests after the turn of the nineteenth century became more cosmopolitan, as protesters expressed more universal identities (e.g., citizens instead of villagers) and made more universalist demands (e.g., rights of political participation). They were modular, as protests converged on a few standard repertoires that transgressed localities and issues. They were autonomous, making their claim on higher authorities without any patronage or mediation of local authorities.

Rather than seeing this transition as natural and driven by some endogenous logic of protest, Tarrow and Tilly interpreted it as a function of the rise of market capitalism and the centralization of the national state, two structural processes exogenous to the development of protest. During the initial stage of state centralization, most protesters resisted the new demands imposed by the state, through reactive protests. As political centralization proceeded and appeared to be irrevocable, protesters shifted to engage the state proactively to ensure that it would act in their favor. Moreover, market expansion intensified interactions among people from distant communities, undermining localistic identities and cultivating more universal identities and claims—as well as standard repertoires of action. Concentration of political power in the national government and its increasing scope of social intervention eroded the relevance of local power holders as targets or patrons of protesters, who increasingly took on higher authorities directly.

The different accounts of the historical development of protest in early modern Europe from Marx to Tilly have been criticized indiscriminately as "teleological" (Sewell 1990, 2005). Though all of these accounts agree on the unidirectionality of protest development, lumping them together under the "teleology" label is far from accurate and fair. Teleology refers to the view that the development path of a certain entity and the final destination, or *telos*, of such development are predetermined by some inherent, evolutionary logic of the entity and are inevitable. Viewed in this light, the different accounts of the origins of modern protest from Marx to Tilly in fact manifest significant steps *away from* teleology. Marx's depiction of the transition from reactionary to revolutionary opposition to capitalism as an inevitable "march of history" is the most teleological. But Thompson, Tilly, and Tarrow explained the large-scale replacement of reactive protests by proactive ones in terms of exogenous political-economic changes, that is, the twin rise of market capitalism and the centralized state.

To be sure, their account would have implied a secondary teleology had it suggested that state centralization and market expansion, as the sources of the historical transformation of protest patterns, were inevitable and predetermined. But this is not the case. Although Thompson took the rise of market and state as given backgrounds, Tilly did meticulously explicate the twin rises in his other works. To Tilly, the protracted and costly war-making activities in the particular geopolitical terrain of early modern Europe encouraged European rulers to ally with the mercantile class, who financed the war in exchange for protection. This alliance between war-making states and profit-making capitalists heralded the advancement of centralized political institutions and the market economy (Tilly 1990). In other words, it was Europe's contingent geopolitical constellations that accounted for the unidirectional rise of states and markets, which in turn precipitated the unidirectional transformation of protest patterns there. This account does not hinge on any assumption that this direction is inevitable and universal (Tilly 2006).

More recently, cultural studies of protest downplay the role of political-economic processes in the rise of modern protest by looking at how its rise was in fact shaped by cultural changes. Agreeing with Tilly's and others' description of the unidirectional change in Western protest patterns at the turn of the nineteenth century, this literature interpreted this change not as an outcome of state centralization and market expansion but as a consequence of the replacement of corporate and localistic ideologies by new cultural idioms about popular sovereignty, rights, and nationwide collective identity (Chartier 1991; Hung 2009; Sewell 2005, 1990; Steinberg 1999; Young 2006). Despite their different emphases, both culturalist and political-economic theories agree that the unidirectional change in protest patterns in the early modern Western world was not inevitable but was determined by other contingent, exogenous processes.

It is therefore not impossible to imagine a non-Western case in which a different geopolitical or cultural context led to a different trajectory of macrohistorical development in protest. Nevertheless, so far few such non-Western cases have been discovered in the literature. The rarity of such cases, as we shall see, is not a function of reality but a manifestation of a problematic and deep-seated assumption that modern political, economic, and cultural developments in non-Western societies are nothing more than replicas of what had already unfolded in the Western world.

EUROCENTRISM

The above view of modern world history, criticized recently as being "Eurocentric," can be traced to the eighteenth century, when European philosophers increasingly identified Europe as a uniquely "progressive continent" with the dynamism for change and advancement, while the rest of the world sank in stagnation or decay. In this view, change would not occur spontaneously in the non-Western world until it was introduced directly or indirectly by Europeans. Once historical dynamism was injected from without, the argument goes, those non-Western societies would embark on such unidirectional changes as state centralization, marketization, and cultural modernization by repeating the path that Europe had undertaken spontaneously in an earlier period (Adas 1989; Blaut 1993; Hung 2003; Wolf 1982). Following this logic, transformation of protest patterns in the non-Western world should repeat the Western trajectory as well.

This Eurocentric view of non-Western protest was again pioneered by Marx, who saw China's Taiping Revolt, in the 1860s, as the first modern revolution in China's history and one that followed the same dynamics underlying European revolutions in the eighteenth century. He credited British imperialism for making such revolution possible by "[breaking] down the authority of the Emperor and forc[ing] the Celestial Empire into contact with the terrestrial world" after the Opium War, enabling "the finances, the morals, the industry, and political structure of China" to receive "their full development under the English cannon" (Marx 1951, 1).

This Eurocentric view was inherited by the modernization paradigm of the postwar social sciences. Though severely critiqued by a new generation of social scientists in the 1960s as being apologetic of imperialism, this view continued to haunt even the most brilliant and critical historical studies of Asian revolts in the 1970s and 1980s. For example, in his iconic study of Southeast Asia's peasant unrest in the colonial period, James Scott discussed how European colonialism shattered the unchanging equilibrium of the indigenous society and ushered in the rise of market capitalism and the centralized colonial state in the early twentieth century. These changes upset the peasants' moral economy, which had been undisturbed until colonization, and urged the peasants to rebel against the colonial order. Their resistance faded out under relentless repression by the colonizers. But it cultivated among the peasants a "dissident subculture" and "alternative moral universe," which became building blocks of the later rise of the communist revolutionary movement (1976, 240). What Scott saw in twentieth-century Vietnam was reminiscent of what Thompson saw in eighteenth-century England. The only difference between the two is that state centralization and market expansion, which were the origins of the resistance, unfolded spontaneously in England, while they were imposed by colonial rule in Southeast Asia two centuries later.[1]

Scott's analysis of how market expansion and state making unleashed peasant revolts is accurate and pathbreaking as far as the particular time period under scrutiny is concerned. The analysis, nevertheless, easily could lead us to assume that those peasant revolts were unprecedented and heralded a new era of modernity that should be considered a radical break from a tranquil and resistance-free past. Though Vietnam's precolonial state also taxed the peasants, according to Scott, it did not upset the rural moral economy and generate revolts, as "the ambition of kingly courts far exceeded their grasp . . . [and] their intelligence was limited, their 'bureaucracy' was porous to say the least . . . [and it] was a state with powerful thumbs but no fingers" (Scott 2000, 191). This characterization of Vietnam's precolonial countryside as a harmonious world left alone by the state is in discord with more recent findings concerning large-scale peasant revolts precipitated by precolonial state making and commercialization in eighteenth-century Vietnam. The Tayson Movement, in 1771–1802, is one intriguing case (Dutton 2006; Li 1998).

In another example, Lucien Bianco documented that modernizing reforms (such as new taxes for new schools and the eradication of opium growing), which the nascent nationalist elite promoted in late nineteenth and early twentieth-century China in response to imperialist pressure, triggered widespread resistance from peasants. Bianco remarked that China's peasant resistance during the first half of the twentieth century was identical to Europe's reactive violence against centralizing states from the seventeenth to the early nineteenth century. This time lag was "related to a universal process [of political centralization and industrial revolution] that has been spreading at an unequal pace in different parts of the planet" (2001, xviii). China's early twentieth-century resistances, just like their seventeenth-century European predecessors, were characterized by "the feeble class consciousness of the peasants and the defensive . . . characteristics of their activities" (2001, xiii). Only after 1927, when Westernized communist elites entered the countryside in full force and started to organize the peasants, was this parochial and reactive activism transformed into part of a universalistic and proactive revolutionary movement aspiring to build a new state and society for everyone.

In sum, this extension of the historical study of Europe's protests to China and other Asian societies suggests that (1) the unidirectional growth of centralized state power and markets in Asia, as landmarks of modernity, began at the turn of the twentieth century under the pressure of Western imperialism, constituting a replica of earlier Western development as well as a radical break from Asia's stagnant past and (2) that transformation of protest patterns in these societies since the early twentieth century has followed the same unidirectional path that Europe witnessed two centuries earlier.

These two assumptions were rejected recently by the literature on global early modernities that unveils the multiple and simultaneous origins of modernity across different Eurasian civilizations in the seventeenth and eighteenth centuries. These parallel and independent developments of early modernities are first and foremost the result of a global economic integration following the discovery of the Americas and the subsequent surge in silver circulation and hence expansion of commercial wealth across civilizations.

CHINA IN GLOBAL EARLY MODERNITIES

Since Marx, Weber, and Durkheim, modernity has been defined in the social sciences as a general process in which the parochial and traditional is replaced by the universal and rational (see Habermas 1985). It emerged in nineteenth-century Europe with the replacement of the local subsistence economy with market-oriented mass production, displacements of local patrons by centralized states, and the transition of regional loyalties to national identities grounded on the conception and institution of popular sovereignty.[2] The full-fledged development of modernity in the nineteenth century was preceded by the rise of early modernity, which began with the European colonization of the New World.

The colonization process generated a massive inflow of new resources to Europe in c. 1500–1800. While the introduction of New World crops such as maize and sweet potato led to a demographic upswing starting in the sixteenth century, the ample supply of precious metal fueled a price revolution, which in turn triggered the rise of market economies in Western Europe. The competition for access to these new resources exacerbated interstate conflicts, facilitating a centuries-long centralization of state power. Under the sponsorship of the rising bourgeoisie, intellectuals became more independent from courts and churches and increasingly courageous in debating radical ideas. These political, economic, and cultural changes in early modern Europe were the harbingers of the three pillars of modernity in the nineteenth century and onward: industrial capitalism, the nation-state, and democracy.

It has long been assumed that the above developments were confined to early modern Europe and that Asia was stagnant during the same period. In the past two decades, a spate of historical studies has challenged this thesis with solid new evidence. These studies reveal that not only Europe but also most other civilizations across the Eurasian continent benefited from the huge supply of New World silver, which flowed substantially to Asia, above all China, as an international currency that European traders used to purchase textiles, ceramics, spices, and the like. Frank (1998) estimates that China absorbed much more American silver than Europe did, making China the "sink of silver" and the center of the global economy in early modern times.

The abundance of silver precipitated an inflationary expansion of markets in China. When domestic and international trade blossomed, private merchant networks thrived, productivity surged, and the standard of living improved. Many quantitative and comparative studies of early modern socioeconomic performances converge on the view that China fared better than, or at least no worse than, most Western European economies. The shift to a simple silver standard in taxation and the general expansion of wealth enabled eighteenth-century Qing rulers to strengthen their centralized state power, which became more capable of reaching and delivering public goods to grassroots communities. The twin rises of the centralized state and market economy were in fact universal phenomena seen in most Eurasian civilizations in c. 1600–1800 (Arrighi 2007; Eisenstadt et al. 2001; Eisenstadt 2002; Frank 1998; Goldstone 2002; Hung 2008; Lee and Wang 1999; Lieberman 1999; Perdue 2005; Pomeranz 2000; Rawski 2004; Wong 1997; Woodside 2006; Zelin 2005).

Despite the parallelism between East and West, some studies also highlight the key differences in the political-economic trajectories of early modern Europe and China. For example, Kenneth Pomeranz (2000) and Jack Goldstone (2002) argued that toward the end of the eighteenth century, the dynamic economic expansions in China and Western Europe both hit serious ceilings because of mounting ecological constraints. These constraints generated widespread hardship, diminishing revenue of the state and proliferating unrest. What distinguished Western Europe from China was that it managed to transcend this ecological constraint to achieve further political centralization and ignite the Industrial Revolution, while China and most other Asian states plunged into prolonged economic crisis and political disintegration.

What enabled Western Europe but not others to overcome the ecological constraint is a topic of intense debate. For Pomeranz, it was Western Europe's direct access to the vast ecological frontier in the New World that set it apart from the rest of Eurasia. For Goldstone, the availability of engineering sciences, which had accidentally taken root in England in the sixteenth century, enabled England to weather the crisis by extracting its coal more efficiently and by boosting labor productivity through the use of machines. Either way, the twin rises of the centralized state and market in Europe perpetuated beyond early modernity into the nineteenth century, ushering in the age of full modernity and constituting a unidirectional trend over the long run. The same twin rises in China, on the contrary, were reversed toward the end of the eighteenth century, constituting a cyclical pattern.

In addition to this difference in trajectories, Western Europe and China also differed in the cultural milieus that encompassed the rises of state and market. Delving into the cultural aspects of early modernities, Shumel Eisenstadt and his collaborators (Eisenstadt et al. 2001) see that expanding commercial exchanges, increasing mercantile wealth, and centralizing political processes created new spaces for articulating nonconformist discourses and fostered the rise of large-scale territorial identities. These public spheres and quasi-national identities took diverging institutional forms and generated different cultural outcomes in different parts of Eurasia. For example, salons, as the most prominent form of the public sphere in eighteenth-century France, cultivated the radical universalist conceptions of popular sovereignty and identities of rational subjects, paving the way for the French Revolution (Giesen 2001; cf. Chartier 1991). In contrast, literati networks, which constituted the public sphere in early modern China, were immersed in statecraft, deliberating over pragmatic proposals that could improve the efficacy of the state. In the process, the literati maintained their collectivist, filial loyalty to the throne and repressed any individualist conception of the self (Wakeman 1998).

The global triumph of Western modernity in the nineteenth century and beyond never totally displaced the indigenous ideologies and identities that consolidated in the non-Western world during early modern times. The non-Western modules of early modernities were so resilient that many twentieth-century industrial modernities in Asia were indeed hybridizations of Western modernity and indigenous early modernities. One example of such hybridization is modern Japan's "honorific individualism," which was strongly influenced by early modern samurai culture and diverges from Western possessive individualism (Ikegami 1995; cf. Walthall 1986; Berry 2001). In a similar vein, many studies of the centralized paternalist mode of political power, the Confucianist-familial mode of business networks, lineage organizations in South China, and practices of criminal justice attest to the continuity between China's early modern (c. 1600–1850) and modern (1850–present) periods, despite the many twentieth-century transformations (e.g., Faure 2007; Hamilton 2006; Muhlhahn 2009; Walder 1988; Wong 1997). In this light, we can assume that a similar continuity exists in protest patterns as well.

This continuity, however, is never positively and rigorously verified, as the literature on China's early modernity is so far reticent about one of the most essential facets of Europe's early modernity: how the popular classes—as opposed to the elite classes such as French intellectuals and Chinese literati—increasingly shed their absolute subservience and expressed their claims on authorities through collective action. Popular claim making on power holders through protest is as important as elitist public spheres in early modern times in preparing the groundwork for the revolutionary movements of later periods. The question is as follows: how did the distinct trajectory of early modern state formation and market expansion, as well as the Confucianist orthodoxy circumscribing these processes, shape the forms and appeals of popular protests in early modern China?

THE HISTORICAL AND THEORETICAL SIGNIFICANCE OF MID-QING PROTEST

In this study, I combine the insights from, as well as overcome the limitations of, the theory of protest development and the historiography of early modernities to explicate the changing pattern, forms, and appeals of popular protest in the eighteen predominantly Han Chinese provinces in mid-Qing China from 1740 to 1839. The core questions that I derive from the above two literatures and that guide this study are:

1. Given the cyclical rise and fall of centralized state power and market prosperity in early modern China, in contrast to the unidirectional rise in Western Europe, did the historical change in popular protest patterns also follow a cyclical pattern, in contrast to the unidirectional change from reactive and parochial to proactive and universalist protests in Europe?

2. How did the specific cultural milieu of Qing China, as dominated by Confucianist ideology, shape the strategies and identities of Chinese protesters in comparison with their European counterparts? What are the historical legacies of these strategies and identities in early modern protests, and how did these legacies help shape the development of social and political movements in twentieth-century China?

This study first and foremost fills an important gap in both the historiography of eighteenth-century China at the apogee of its early modernity and the historiography of social unrest in early modern China. The former, while shedding new light on the dynamic development in state institutions, market networks, intellectual discourses, gender relations, etc. (e.g., Mann 1997; Perdue 2005; Pomeranz 2000; Rowe 2001), has been relatively silent on the topic of popular protest. In the meantime, existing historical studies of China's social unrest focus on large-scale peasant rebellions and are seldom interested in the mid-Qing period, when such spectacular upheavals were rare. This study shows that mid-Qing China was not free from social unrest. The plurality of mid-Qing protests, which included demonstrations, riots, and petitions, though less disruptive than large-scale rebellions, were more persistent, innovative, and widespread than previously assumed. They constituted lasting legacies that continue to shape the ideology, strategies, and identities of grassroots collective action in the twentieth century. As far as popular protests in contemporary China are concerned, the legacies of these mid-Qing protests are perhaps more relevant than those of large-scale revolts amid dynastic collapse, as the prosperous market economy and centralized state power of today's China is reminiscent more of mid-Qing China than of the dark days of the late Qing or late Ming period. Though the existing literature of revolutions assumes that large-scale rebellions were fundamentally different from localized protests (Goldstone 1991; Skocpol 1979), I show in this study how mid-Qing protests were connected to a number of rebellions in the era and to the revolutionary movements of the nineteenth and twentieth centuries. Rebellions and revolutions breaking out in extraordinary circumstances were usually not simply a sudden eruption of discontent out of nowhere but were the development and culmination of popular protest in ordinary times.

Second, this study enriches our global-comparative understanding of the dynamics of protest transformation. Mid-Qing China, as we will see in the next chapter, was one of the most politically centralized and commercially advanced states in preindustrial Eurasia. Yet the cyclical pattern of its political-economic development, in contrast to the more unilinear path of Western Europe, was among the most manifest in Asia. Mid-Qing China also experienced the enduring dominance of the conservative Confucianist ideology. This ideology was more distinct and isolated from European influences than were local cultures in other early modern Asian states, such as India, which started to be reshaped after the 1750s by British colonialism, and the Islamic world, which never ceased to intermesh with Europe through the intensive conflicts and exchanges between Europe and the Ottoman Empire. The general political-economic similarity, coupled with the diverging trajectories of political-economic changes and cultural contrast between China and Europe, makes China a particularly illuminating case for the study of protest transformation under diverse political, economic, and cultural conditions across Eurasia.

I choose 1740 as the starting point of my investigation because that year was in the wake of a wave of centralizing political reforms and liberalizing economic reforms of the 1720s and 1730s, under the Yongzheng reign (1723–1735). These reforms ushered in the peak of centralized state power and commercial prosperity in the 1740s and 1750s. They also instituted a centralized system of intelligence collection, rendering the documentation of protest episodes in the central-government archive more reliable and systematic from the 1740s onward. The year 1839 was chosen as the end point as it marks the beginning of the head-on collision between Chinese and Western powers in the Opium War of 1839–1842. By focusing on the hundred years between 1740 and 1839, we can depict the indigenous development of Chinese protest in its full-fledged form prior to its hybridization with Western patterns.

CHAPTER OUTLINE

In chapter 1, I outline the trajectory of the rise and decline of centralized state power and commercial prosperity in the mid-Qing period. I also delineate the conservative strain of Confucianism reinstated by the Qing state and how this orthodoxy conceptualized the empire's political hierarchy as a familial one grounded on the principle of filiality from below and paternalist benevolence from above. This orthodoxy not only constrained the empire's subjects but also subjected the emperor to the same rigid moral standard. I show how the moral legitimacy of mid-Qing emperors changed in a U-shaped trajectory under this self-imposed rigid standard. By taking the rhythms of political, economic, and cultural changes together, I partition the mid-Qing period into three subperiods: c. 1740–1759, when both centralized state power and commercial prosperity were at their peaks and the emperor's moral legitimacy was high; c. 1760–1799, when centralized state power unraveled, commercial prosperity continued, and the emperor's moral legitimacy was low; and 1800–1839, when both centralized state power and the market economy were in crisis but the emperor's moral legitimacy revived.

Chapter 2 discusses data and methodological issues, followed by a general overview and classification of all documented protests. These episodes were not distributed evenly over time but were clustered in three waves: 1740–1759, 1776–1795, and 1820–1839. These waves of protest correspond to the three political-economic and cultural constellations of the three subperiods discussed in chapter 1.

Chapters 3, 4, and 5 discuss the three waves of protest separately by looking at representative cases in great detail. The mid-eighteenth-century wave was composed mainly of state-engaging, or proactive, protests, in which protesters, through the performative expression of filiality toward the authorities, sought to expand their rights to universal care by the paternalist state and their rights to participate in the government's decision-making process. The late eighteenth-century wave, in contrast, saw mainly violent resistance against the state triggered by heightened tax levies and state repression of illicit activities. These state-resisting, or reactive, protests were prone to converging into large-scale uprisings aimed at overthrowing the Qing dynasty, which was deemed to have lost the Mandate of Heaven because of its moral decay. The early nineteenth-century wave was similarly characterized by violent resistance against the state. In this period, however, protesters ceased to be prone to recruitment by large-scale revolt, and they increasingly complemented their resistance against local officials with humble and direct petitions to the emperor, whose moral authority had recovered from its late eighteenth-century decline.

The first part of chapter 6 compares the three waves of protest with one another. The comparison shows that while the general political-economic contexts determined *whether* the protesters were more likely to engage or resist the state, the perceived moral legitimacy of the state delimited *how* exactly the protesters would engage or resist the state. This part of the chapter also compares the overall trajectory of mid-Qing protests with the contemporaneous Western European trajectory. It shows that the trajectory of protest development is generally shaped by the rhythm of macropolitical-economic change. While a long-term expansion of centralized state power in Europe fostered a unidirectional transition from reactive to proactive protest, the cyclical rise and fall of centralized state power in mid-Qing China entailed first the rise of proactive protests and then a transition back to reactive protests. At the same time, the substantive difference in strategies and identities between Chinese and European protest can be explained by the difference between the persistent hegemony of Confucianist filiality in China and the emergent ideology of popular sovereignty in Europe.

The second part of chapter 6 traces the continuities and ruptures between mid-Qing protests and modern protests in the early twentieth century based on the rich secondary literature. It suggests that China's late nineteenth- and early twentieth-century reactive violence, which had been regarded by Eurocentric views as the starting point of departure from a stagnant antiquity, was in fact the end point of a century-long transformation from proactive to reactive protests in China since the mid-eighteenth century. Despite this transformation, mid-Qing protest repertoires, together with the underlying Confucianist conception of authority, continued to be part of the "symbolic reservoir" among protesters and dissenters throughout the early twentieth century, occasionally reviving in popular protests and sometimes repressed by Westernized revolutionaries. In the epilogue, I extend the analysis in the second part of chapter 6 by reexamining China's contemporary protests, with a focus on the revival of traditionalist repertoires in light of the insights generated by this study.

1

MARKET EXPANSION, STATE CENTRALIZATION, AND NEO-CONFUCIANISM IN QING CHINA

The stereotypical image of imperial China, as theorized by Marx, Weber, and Wittfogel, is of a stagnant agrarian empire governed by an inward-looking, despotic regime. This conception has long been rejected. Mark Elvin and others found that in the twelfth and thirteenth centuries, China experienced a golden age of vital commercial expansion and growth of maritime trade (Abu-Lughod 1989, 316–340; Braudel 1992, 32; Elvin 1973; Ma 1971; Shiba 1970, 1983). These trends abruptly stopped in the early fifteenth century, when the Zheng He expeditions ended and the capital city of the Ming empire (1368–1644) moved from Nanjing, in the southern coastal area, north to Beijing. After this inward turn, according to this literature, China became isolated from the world and was caught in a "high-level equilibrium trap" not broken until the nineteenth century (Elvin 1973; Wallerstein 1974, 53–63). This revisionist image of China does not stray much from the traditional view as far as the four centuries between Ming's retreat from the sea and the Opium War (1839–1842) are concerned. It does not dispute the idea that late imperial China (c. 1600–1911) was a backward, agrarian empire. Nor does it reject the idea that China differed fundamentally from the commercializing and rationalizing early modern Europe until the nineteenth-century "impact of the West," which injected a new dynamism into China from without.

A wave of more recent research challenges this view, showing that after c. 1600, China witnessed a renaissance of maritime trade and internal commerce. During this period, China's level of commerce was at least as high as Europe's. China also experienced an impressive and continuous increase in agricultural productivity, per capita caloric intake, and life expectancy (Flynn and Giraldez 1995; Frank 1998; Goldstone 2000, 2002; Hung 2008; Lavely and Wong 1998; Lee and Wang 1999; Pomeranz 2000; Wong 1997). During the same period, China witnessed a rationalization and centralization of the state not unlike many contemporaneous European states (Faure 2007; Huang 1996; Marsh 2000; Rawski 2004).

The parallel commercialization and state centralization in China and Europe is not surprising, as they both resulted from the surge in the world's silver supply following the European discovery of the Americas. The silver that the European traders brought back to Europe fueled an inflationary commercial expansion in the sixteenth century and formed the revenue foundation for state builders to construct centralized administrative apparatuses. European traders also brought silver to other parts of Eurasia in exchange for large quantities of textiles, spices, tea, ceramics, and other goods. This generated the same thrust of commercialization and state centralization in many Asian societies. Some even estimate that the quantity of American silver that ended up in China was in fact larger than the amount ending up in Europe throughout early modern times (Frank 1998, 131–164).

MARKET EXPANSION IN THE "LONG EIGHTEENTH CENTURY"

The massive flow of silver into China began in the mid-sixteenth century and generated pockets of prosperous markets and handicraft production centers in the eastern and southeastern coastal areas. The political chaos of the closing decades of the Ming dynasty and the turbulent dynastic transition of the mid-seventeenth century, however, constricted the expansion of commercial prosperity to other parts of China. A thriving empirewide market economy did not come into being until the eighteenth century, when the new rulers of the Qing reestablished the empire's stability and unity.

After c. 1500, the Ming's regime capacity decayed rapidly as government corruption grew, intraelite struggles intensified, and budget deficits mounted. Demographic pressure, hyperinflation of the paper currency issued by the state, and the growing power of the local tax-farmer-landlord-moneylender class pushed the peasants to the brink of bankruptcy and starvation. In the meantime, the balance of power between the Ming and neighboring seminomadic tribes to the north was disrupted by the expansion of the Jurchens, who turned to agriculture, incorporated other tribes, and transformed a tribal confederation into an empire of Manchus. On the southeastern coast of China, illicit trade conducted by armed Chinese and Japanese traders flourished, challenging the government sea ban (Goldstone 1991, chap. 4; Huang 1969, 105–123; Tong 1991, 115–129; Wakeman 1985, chap. 1; Wills 1979, 210–211).

The state's continuous attempts to solve the fiscal crisis by increasing land taxation only worsened the situation. It added to the peasants' burden and in the late sixteenth century led to an explosive growth of social disturbances in the form of rampant banditry and tax revolts. Confronted with increasing unrest, the Ming government decided to reform state finance by exploiting the booming private trade. In the 1560s, it abandoned the crippled paper-currency system and shifted to a silver standard—which was possible only after the massive silver influx from overseas trade with Japan and Europe. Peasants' corvée labor, one of the major causes of peasant hardship and unrest, was replaced by a standard silver tax. This reform put China onto a bimetallic monetary system. Small and daily transactions were conducted in copper cash, which was mostly produced in Chinese state-run mines, while bulk transactions and taxation were measured in silver. This monetary system remained intact until the late nineteenth century. Concurrent with this fiscal and monetary reform, the Ming state also lessened its restrictions on maritime trade and taxed licensed seafaring merchants (Atwell 1986, 1998; Flynn and Giraldez 1995; Huang 1969, 105–123; Quan 1996a; Wills 1979, 211). These policies immediately improved the state's fiscal strength, and by the late sixteenth century, the empirewide turmoil had been substantially curbed.

This containment of the chaos, however, broke down at the turn of the seventeenth century. Financial difficulties incurred by the costly Sino-Japanese War in Korea in the 1590s, the outbreak of full-fledged warfare with the Manchus in the 1610s, rampant government corruption, the eruption of large-scale peasant wars in the northwestern and southwestern interior, and the interruption of silver inflow caused by the European "seventeenth-century crisis" and Japanese seclusion policy all caused a return of empirewide turmoil, which eventually led to the collapse of the Ming regime in 1644.

The Manchus shrewdly used this chaos to expand into China proper through military conquest. Within a decade after they took Beijing, in 1644, the Manchus had established control over most of China except part of Fujian province and Taiwan, which became the last bastion of Ming loyalists. The turbulent Ming-Qing transition interrupted China's foreign trade and, thus, silver inflow, as the Manchu state evacuated all the coastal populations in the 1660s and 1670s in a desperate measure to isolate the remaining Taiwan-based Ming loyalists. The termination of silver inflow caused a deflationary economic crisis, known as the "Kangxi Depression," during the first two decades of the Kangxi reign (1662–1722), rolling back the late Ming expansion of the market economy (Kishimoto-Nakayama 1984).

Following the collapse of the Ming loyalist regime in Taiwan, in 1683, as well as the lifting of the maritime-trade ban and the revocation of the coastal-evacuation policy, Chinese-European trade resumed. During the eighteenth century, the mounting European demand for Chinese products and the subsequent influx of American silver into China fuelled the commercialization of the Chinese economy far more ferociously than it had been during the late Ming period (Atwell 1986, 1998; Frank 1998, 108–111, 160–161; Hung 2001, 473–497; Quan 1996a; Naquin and Rawski 1987, 104; Rowe 1998, 177).

Contrary to the traditional "oriental despotism" thesis (Wittfogel 1957), which suggested that the imperial state in China was constantly hostile to private commerce, the Qing state was in fact very active in facilitating commercial growth. The Chinese state's procommercial stance emerged in the late Ming period, as the growing commercial economy began to be recognized as an unalterable reality. Beginning in the late sixteenth century, the traditional Confucianist hostility toward silver, internal commerce, foreign trade, and merchants lost ground to the school of thought emphasizing the "natural law" of the market economy. This thinking proposed that the market economy would flourish under appropriate nurturing, not government control. This pragmatic attitude toward commerce continued to grow in the Qing bureaucracy and had become a mainstream position by the eighteenth century (Chao 1993, 40; Chen 1991b; Gao 2001; Lin 1991, 9, 13–17; Rowe 2001; von Glahn 1996, 215–216; Zheng 1994, 133–150). For example, the Qing government keenly promoted commerce by developing the empire's commercial-transportation infrastructure and stimulating new production and marketing sectors by offering incentive packages and low-interest loans for entrepreneurs in targeted areas (Rowe 1998, 184–185).

Accompanying the commercial expansion was long-term inflation starting in the 1680s, in which average grain prices increased three- or fourfold during the following century (Guo 1996; Quan 1996b, 1996c; Wang 1980, 1992). The inflation was generated by population expansion and continuous silver inflow.

This inflationary pressure during the eighteenth century was not distributed evenly, as it hit economically advanced regions the most. Comparing the price of rice in various regions across the empire in 1723–1735, Quan Hansheng (1996d) finds that the price level was highest in the Lower Yangzi Valley and the southeastern coast and lowest in the southwest, with the Mid-Yangzi region in between. The interregional price difference could be as much as 200 to 300 percent. This touched off extensive regional specialization

FIGURE 1.1 GRAIN PRICES IN THE LOWER YANGZI DELTA, 1650–1900 (*TAELS* PER *SHI*, TWENTY-FIVE-YEAR MOVING AVERAGE) (*SOURCE*: WANG 1992, 40–47)

and economic growth driven by Smithian dynamics.[1] While the high-cost areas in the Lower Yangzi region (e.g., Jiangsu province) and on the southern/southeastern coast (e.g., Fujian and Guangdong provinces) witnessed rapid development of high-value-added production including nonfood cash-crop agriculture (mulberry trees for silkworm raising, cotton, and tea, for example) and handicraft manufacturing (such as ceramics and textiles), areas with lower inflationary pressure such as the Upper Yangzi region (e.g., Sichuan province), Mid-Yangzi region (e.g., Hunan province), and the empire's southwest (e.g., Guangxi province) were transformed into peripheral zones that exported foodstuffs and other raw materials such as timber and fertilizer to more advanced regions.[2]

Speaking of the formation of an integrated national market in eighteenth-century China, Li Bozhong remarks that "China had developed into three major economic zones before the nineteenth century: the advanced zone in eastern China, the developing zone in Central China and the underdeveloped zone in the West," with "the Yangzi Delta as the core and with the other two zones as the hinterlands" (Li 1999, 14).[3] The dynamics of the differentiation of China into economic zones with different levels of development is similar to the differentiation of the European economy into core, semiperipheral, and peripheral zones after the long sixteenth century, a consequence of the uneven distribution of inflationary pressures following the massive inflow of American bullion (Wallerstein 1974, 66–131).

The inflationary market expansion, however, came to a halt in the 1820s, when the skyrocketing opium trade initiated by the British, in conjunction with a reduction in the global silver supply, caused a hemorrhage of silver and a deflationary depression in the early part of the Daoguang reign (1820–1850), known as the "Daoguang Depression" (Kishimoto-Nakayanma 1984; Lin 1991, 2006). The massive contraction of silver supply in the Chinese economy brought about huge increases in the price of silver measured in copper, the supply of which remained more or less constant. The depression hit peasant taxpayers hard, as they found it increasingly difficult to convert their copper cash, earned in daily sales of their goods, into silver *taels* for taxation. In the meantime, the value of land and other property, usually measured in silver, dropped precipitously. The Kangxi Depression and Daoguang Depression therefore marked the beginning and the end of the commercial prosperity of what is known as China's "long eighteenth century," between the 1680s and the 1820s (see Mann 1997).

CLASS AND STATE FORMATIONS

Besides commercial expansion, eighteenth-century China also witnessed mounting ecological pressure. Thanks to political and social stability after the late seventeenth century and the popularization of such New World crops as sweet potato and maize, which turned unproductive highlands into productive areas, the population of China tripled between the mid-seventeenth and mid-nineteenth centuries. The total acreage of cultivable land, however, only doubled during the same period (Ho 1959; Huang 2002; Naquin and Rawski 1987, 24–26; Wang 1973, 7). By the turn of the nineteenth century, the diminishing ecological resources vis-à-vis the expanding population had turned into a looming ecological crisis (Elvin 1998; Marks 1996, 1998).

The eighteenth-century expansion of commerce and population brought forth drastic social change. The predominantly manorial order gave way to a peasant economy in the countryside. Although this transition had already begun in the Ming dynasty (Elvin 1973, 235–267), a substantial portion of the agrarian economy was still dominated by large estates in early Qing, especially in North China, where large amounts of land had been confiscated by Manchu bannermen and noblemen as estates (Myers and Wang 2002, 612). When the population of indentured laborers, such as tenant-serfs (*dianpu*) and bondservants (*nupu*), expanded alongside the rest of the population, estate owners began to eliminate the increasing burden of feeding their workers by partitioning their estates into small lots and selling or renting them out. In the expanding peasant economy, landowners came to rely on themselves, tenants, or hired laborers to work their land. Commercialization of land ownership polarized the peasantry into labor-employing rich peasants and labor-selling poor peasants (Huang 1985, 85–96; Rowe 2002, 493–502). The noblemen–indentured laborer stratification grounded on hereditary status was henceforth replaced by a landlord–tenant–hired laborer stratification based on contractual relations and alienable ownership of land and labor. The trend was exacerbated by the deliberate efforts of the Qing government to emancipate indentured labor in the 1720s and 1730s. This transition was reflected in the revised Qing legal code and changing legal practices in the late eighteenth century, when landlords, tenants, and agrarian laborers began to be treated as commoners with equal status (Buoye 2000; Huang 1985, 97–105; Rowe 2002, 493–502).

While hereditary hierarchy was in decline, the somewhat meritocratic gentry elite remained a dominant sociopolitical force. In Qing China, as in previous dynasties, the imperial examination offered a way for the offspring of many wealthy landowning families, who could afford expensive education, to attain imperial degrees, which gave them gentry or literati status. The gentry class was internally stratified according to the level of degree, with the holder of the metropolitan degree (who passed the capital examination) at the top of the hierarchy and the licentiate (who passed the regular county examination that qualified them for higher-level examinations) and disqualified licentiate (licentiates who failed to renew their status through the county examination) at the bottom.

While some gentry elite succeeded in higher-level examinations and entered the bureaucracy to serve as scholar-officials at different administrative levels, the majority of lower degree holders stayed in their home areas and served as informal leaders, helping local governments explain and enforce their policies and local residents articulate their demands and grievances to the government (Brook 1990; Chang 1959, 1962; Elman 2002, 424; Jing 1982,

163–164; Rowe 1990, 1992; Rawski 1979, 54–80). With the intensive commercialization of the economy, mercantile activities became another legitimate and popular means for commoners to earn their initial wealth, which in turn enabled them to invest in their offspring's education, in the pursuit of gentry status (Chang 1959; Hung 2008; Rowe 1992).

The standardized curriculum for the imperial examination, strictly controlled by the state, created a gentry class with a uniform ideological outlook. Participation in prefecture, provincial, and capital examinations also allowed the gentry elite to develop social networks extending beyond their hometowns and sometimes covering the whole empire (Elman 2000, 2002; Man-Cheong 2004). The gentry status, grounded on educational credentials, together with lineage ties became the glue that bound the mercantile, landlord, and state elites into intermeshing social networks.

At the lower end of society, a large portion of the peasantry experienced downward mobility as a result of commercialization and population expansion. As the per capita acreage of cultivable land decreased, poor peasants working on small plots of land were increasingly exposed to the risk of bankruptcy during bad harvests, forcing them to sell their land for food. In the early eighteenth century, the growing population of landless peasants was effectively absorbed by such agrarian frontiers as Sichuan and Taiwan (Entenmann 1982; Shepherd 1993). However, by the mid-eighteenth century, most of the fertile lands of the frontier had filled up. The landless migrants were left with the choice of settling in the infertile highlands or participating in nonagrarian sectors as peddlers, miners, or boatmen on commercial ships. Some became vagrants, moving from place to place to beg for food and jobs. Others became outlaws, who made a living through illegal activities such as smuggling, private coinage, and banditry (Jones and Kuhn 1978; Kuhn 1970, 39; Leong 1997; Rowe 2002, 493–494). This marginal population was vulnerable to the vicissitudes of nature and market and to abuses by local officials. They were excluded from the safety net of lineage organizations and were beyond the reach of the imperial public order grounded on *baojia*, the village-based mutual monitoring system.

Synchronic with the rise of absolutist states in northwestern Europe in the late seventeenth and early eighteenth centuries (see Anderson 1979; Bonney 1999; Tilly 1990), the Qing regime during the same period underwent rapid centralization and rationalization. Upon their conquest of China proper, and coinciding with the advice of Chinese literati defectors, the Manchus turned their original political system, which was grounded on a confederation of noblemen, into a centralized Confucianist bureaucracy in the occupied areas (Gao 2002). By the turn of the eighteenth century, the Manchu monarch had leveled the powers of local warlords and Manchu noblemen (Wakeman 1985). Then, through successive empirewide land surveys and a "rationalizing fiscal reform" implemented by the Yongzheng emperor in the 1720s and 1730s, the Manchu rulers successfully stamped out the bureaucratic corruption and tax evasion of local elites (Zelin 1984). In the mid-eighteenth century, the fiscal power of the Qing state was at its peak. It is estimated that the monetary tax revenue of the Qing state had remained stable since the mid-eighteenth century and stood at about 8 percent of total GDP of the Qing empire (Deng 1999, 164, appendix G; 2003; Feuerwerker 1984). The fiscal capacity of the eighteenth-century Qing state was comparable to, or even higher than, eighteenth-century European states such as the French state, which commanded monetary tax revenue amounting to 6.87 percent of total GDP in 1751 and 8 percent in 1789 (Goldstone 1991, 204). This echoed the assessment of many mid-eighteenth-century French Enlightenment philosophers, above all Voltaire and the Physiocrats, who claimed that China's level of state centralization, in addition to its level of commercialization, was higher than that of France, and that the latter should emulate and catch up with the former (Hung 2003).

New institutions and techniques of centralized governance, such as the Grand Council and the secret palace memorial system, were created in the 1720s and 1730s (Bartlett 1991). While the Grand Council system allowed the emperor and his closest advisors to surpass bureaucratic routines and handle the most urgent matters of all corners of the empire directly, efficiently, and clandestinely, the secret palace memorial system, which established direct and secretive communication between the Grand Council and local officials at the provincial level, was designed to enhance the emperor's access to information about local affairs and his control of local officials.

As Peter C. Perdue (2005) argues, these institutional innovations of the Qing state in the early to mid-eighteenth century were not unrelated to the Qing military expansion into Central Asia at the time. The expansionism of Qing emperors was intended to show the greatness and might of the Qing empire and to eliminate the centuries-long security threats at China's northwestern frontiers once and for all. The novel centralized institutions were instrumental to maintaining security in the empire's core area as well as to guaranteeing the state's capability in mobilizing vast resources from that core to provision the army fighting at the frontier. In other words, state centralization of eighteenth-century China was a function of its military expansion just as state making and war making were intertwined in Europe's early modern state system. As it turned out, the thrust of political centralization did boost the state's military prowess and accounted for its successful incorporation of a Muslim region in Central Asia into the empire (today's Xinjiang) and its subjugation of ethnic Tibetan areas in the Sichuan province by 1760.

Concomitant with its centralization of resources and power, the Qing state also was active in securing the welfare of its subjects. The Manchu rulers' cognizance of the significance of enhancing people's well being was largely related to their status as alien rulers, whose rule could easily be viewed by the majority Han Chinese population as illegitimate. The Manchu rulers' commitment to enhancing their subjects' well being was first reflected in their reluctance to increase peasants' tax burdens. Throughout its centralization process, the state increased its revenue through combating tax evasion, curbing officials' embezzlement of state income, and other means that increased the efficiency of the taxation process instead of increasing the tax rate. During times of regional famine, the central government never hesitated to grant tax breaks to the affected areas. More important, in 1713, the Kangxi emperor promised that the government would never increase its subjects' burden by permanently fixing the land-tax quotas, even though at that time the Qing state was still suffering from fiscal stringency. This promise was kept by his successors (Guo 1996, 13–14; see also Gao 1995; Zelin 1984).

Another illustration of the Qing state's commitment to popular welfare was the variegated institutions and practices used to stabilize local grain prices. Though the Qing government relied primarily on the commercial circulation of grains to feed the expanding population, it also established a large-scale public granary system, which in the mid-eighteenth century developed into its full-fledged form as a regulatory apparatus to protect its subjects from the vicissitudes of the grain market. Under this system, public "ever-normal granaries" (*changping cang*) were built all over the empire. Local governments purchased grains from the market to stock the granaries when grain prices were low, and they sold the grains back to the market at submarket rates or disbursed the grains as a relief measure when prices were unusually high. If the stock in local granaries was not sufficient to bring down rice prices, higher-level officials would mobilize stocks in other areas (Dunstan 2006; Rowe 2001, 155–185; Will and Wong 1991; Will 1990). If the official granary system was truly unable to handle a subsistence crisis, local officials would resort to persuading or squeezing local gentry and merchants to help. In the 1740s, the Qianlong emperor repeatedly reminded the bureaucracy that local food crises were often exacerbated and sometimes even caused by "wicked merchants" (*jianshang*) or those "rich but not benevolent" (*weifu buren*) gentry who hoarded grains and pushed up prices. Thus one of the best ways to cope with a food crisis was to urge local merchants and gentry to sell their stocks at submarket prices (QSL-QL 193, 13–14, 273, 26–28; see also Dunstan 2006, 15–146; Rowe 2001, 180–181).

After the mid-eighteenth century, these forms of state activism began to fade. Following the success of the Qing's military campaign of 1755–1760 in Central Asia, the impetus for military mobilization was gone, the thrust for institutional innovation and centralization dissipated, and the conservative notion of "sustaining the prosperity and preserving the peace" (*chiying baotai*) became the regime's central goal. Perdue remarks that following the Qing's successful campaign in securing its northwestern border, "much dynamism [ebbed] out of the bureaucracy . . . [as its] incentive to reform itself declined, and the will to control abuses slackened" (Perdue 2005, 549; cf. Kuhn 1990).

The regime's growing conservatism and declining administrative rigor helped precipitate a fiscal crisis. With the tax quota frozen at the 1713 level, the real income of the government dropped when inflation increased during the eighteenth century. When government spending on payroll and public projects shrank in real terms, underpaid officials resorted to bribery and embezzlement to maintain their luxurious way of life, and local governments on the brink of bankruptcy were urged to appropriate unsanctioned surtaxes to make ends meet (Guo 1996, 14–15; Jones and Kuhn 1978, 119–130; Zelin 1984). Local tax bullies reemerged, and the competition for resources between local governments and grassroots communities intensified. From the 1770s onward, the government's capacity to regulate the grain market via the granary system, maintain hydraulic works, and deliver famine relief decreased steeply (Jones and Kuhn 1978; Perdue 1987; Will 1990, 289–301; Will and Wong 1991, 75–92). The decline in the ability of the Qing state to govern, let alone "nourish," society was aggravated by the ever-expanding size and complexity of the population. Figure 1.2, which shows declining governmental activism in offering famine relief starting in the 1770s, illustrates this ailing state capacity.

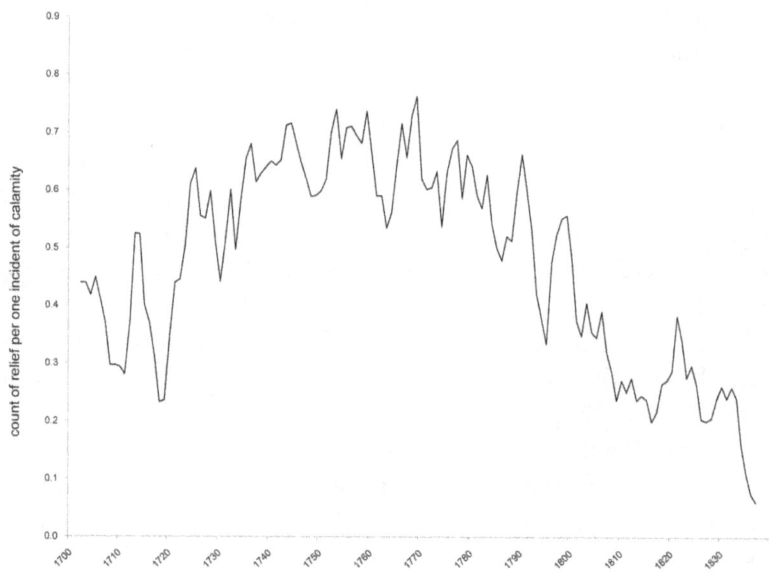

FIGURE 1.2 Ratio of Official Relief to Calamity, 1700–1839 (five-year moving average) (*source*: Li 1995, appendix)

By the end of the eighteenth century, the Qing state had become much more insolvent, corrupt, and inefficient than it was during the peak years of the mid-eighteenth century. It could no longer provide as many public services, such as famine relief and the effective regulation of hydraulic infrastructure, as it had previously, despite increasing tax levies. The fiscal and administrative decay of the state continued to worsen amid the Daoguang Depression of the early nineteenth century.

THE NEO-CONFUCIANIST FOUNDATION OF THE QING STATE

Concurrent with administrative-fiscal centralization and the rejuvenation of a booming market economy at the turn of the eighteenth century, the Manchu ruling elite aggressively established political legitimacy by positing itself as an irreplaceable moralizing agent that promoted virtuous behaviors and sanctioned malicious ones among its agents and subjects (Thornton 2007). The recent literature of New Qing History, which emphasizes the multiethnic nature of the Qing empire, revealed that the Manchu rulers adopted variegated ideological persuasions to justify their rule in relation to the different ethnic-religious groups of the empire, such as Tibetans, Mongolians, and the Manchus themselves (Crossley 1999). In the empire's Han Chinese core, on which this study is focused, the Manchu rulers' effort to establish moral legitimacy was predominated by their conviction to restore the cultural orthodoxy of the Cheng-Zhu School of neo-Confucianism. This was the dominant political ideology in China from the twelfth to the sixteenth centuries, before it was overshadowed by a more liberal version of neo-Confucianism, namely, the Wang Yangming School.

The crux of classical Confucianist thought is the principles of filial loyalty (*zhongxiao*) and benevolence (*ren'ai*). These principles dictate that all familial and extrafamilial social relations must be regulated by a rigid hierarchy based on seniority. Within the family, the imperative of the juniors is to be docile to the seniors, and the seniors must "nourish" (*yang*) the juniors with great care. Applied to the political relations between officials and their subjects, this philosophy holds that subjects must be absolutely respectful and obedient, while officials are obliged to offer paternalist care and fatherly discipline. The same logic applies to the emperor and to officials at all levels. Relations among the emperor, his officials, and his subjects were therefore conceptualized as relations among grandparents, parents, and children (Hamilton 1990; Rozman 2003).

Classical Confucianism was constituted mainly by no more than an array of moral dictums. Facing strong competition from Buddhism after the eighth century, Confucianist philosophers were anxious to devise a metaphysical foundation for these dictums. From the twelfth century on, the Cheng-Zhu School of neo-Confucianism, or the "philosophy of principle" (*lixue*), became the dominant form of Confucianism under state sponsorship. This official neo-Confucianist orthodoxy emphasized that the moral principle (*li*) of filial piety, among others, was inscribed in the natural world, waiting to be discovered by the educated elite through rational learning. The elite were then obliged to inculcate these absolute principles upon others via authoritative institutions such as state academies. The state's educational endeavors were perennial, as eradicating all individual desires incompatible with the *li* was a constant war to secure harmony and prosperity (Liu 1973; de Bary 1981). State elites were also obliged to promote the construction of lineage organizations in grassroots societies, as such organizations could be an ideal crucible for transmitting the Confucianist morality of filial piety to youngsters through practicing those principles (Chow 1994; Ebrey and Watson 1986; Faure 2007).

The Cheng-Zhu orthodoxy remained dominant until the late sixteenth and early seventeenth centuries, when resourceful private academies, which were freed from state control and supported by the mercantile wealth of the southern coastal cities of the Ming empire, became learning institutions where literati were free to contemplate new philosophical tenets outside the Cheng-Zhu orthodoxy. The Wang Yangming School of neo-Confucianism, or the philosophy of the mind (*xinxue*), rapidly became popular among independent-minded intellectuals. Heavily influenced by the Buddhist concept of self-meditation and enlightenment, as well as expressing populist and liberal tendencies, this new philosophy asserted that the *li* was not inscribed in the natural world but was embedded in the human mind. It need not be discovered and imposed by the state elites but could be approached by subjective self-learning and open discussion among free individuals, regardless of their class, ethnicity, gender, and level of education. Everyone was equally poised to be enlightened to the *li*, and hence, "the streets are full of sages" (*man jie shi sheng ren*). It followed that the state's monopoly of philosophical interpretation was illegitimate and that individuals should have the right to pursue and debate these principles freely (Wakeman 1972, 1998; Yu 2004; Zhao 2010, chap. 9).

This school of neo-Confucianism also espoused the horizontal relations of "friendship" (*peng*) among literati as an alternative to the vertical hierarchy based on filial loyalty under the Cheng-Zhu orthodoxy. It promulgated that peer alliance among scholar-officials was politically virtuous, as it helped check monarchial power. Armed with this liberal, populist, and anti-authoritarian ideology, late-Ming literati in southern metropolises coalesced around the private academies not only as public spheres but also as quasi-political associations. The allegedly repressive, corrupt, and predatory regime of the time, grounded on an alliance of the emperor and inner-court eunuchs, became a target of virulent attacks from these academies, which advocated a more decentralized political system based on a federation of self-governing regions. This liberal philosophy helped fuel an array of urban revolts against the central government in the closing decades of the Ming empire (Elman 1989; Masatoshi 1984; von Glahn 1991; Wakeman 1972, 1998; Wu 1996).

Following the collapse of the Ming dynasty and the founding of the Qing in the midst of urban uprisings, peasant rebellion, bureaucratic in-fighting, and Manchu invasion, Chinese literati who defected to the Manchu conquerors blamed the Wang Yangming School for the moral laxity, political chaos, and dynastic breakdown of the late Ming period and called for a conservative restoration of the Cheng-Zhu orthodoxy. The new Manchu rulers of China, anxious to win the support of Chinese literati and portray themselves as Confucianist sages inheriting the Mandate of Heaven from the Ming, were happy to follow the defectors' advice (Elman 1989; Gao 2002; Goldstone 1991; Wakeman 1998; Zhao 2010, chap. 9).

It is in this context that the Manchu emperors aggressively resuscitated the Cheng-Zhu School as the sole legitimate system of knowledge and morality through state-sanctioned curriculums and state-sponsored academies in the late seventeenth and early eighteenth centuries. Independent private academies were closed, and the Wang Yangming School of neo-Confucianism was denounced as a heresy to be excluded from the curriculum of imperial examination (Chow 1994; Elman 2000; Wakeman 1998; Woodside 1990, 2006). As it turns out, what the Qing state achieved was more than a simple restoration of orthodoxy. With its unprecedented capacity to regulate and intervene in society, the Qing state managed to mold social and state-society relations after the neo-Confucianist principle of filiality to an extent unseen in previous dynasties.

Adopting "governing the heaven and earth through the principle of filial piety" (*yi xiao zhi tianxia*) as their governing motto (Ye 2002, 74–75), the Manchu rulers aggressively reinstated the principle that emperor-officials and officials-subjects relations were an extension of father-son relations. Under this filial ideology, the emperor's control of his officials and subjects, as well as government provision of welfare to the subjects, were framed as exercises of paternalist discipline and benevolent care. During the initial phase of state centralization in the late seventeenth century, the *Book of Filial Piety* (*Xiaojing*), which stated in the opening paragraph that "the gentleman's service of his parents with filial piety produces a loyalty that can be transferred to the ruler," was the most frequently reprinted Confucianist treatise by the state printing house (Ye 2002, 74–75; Kutcher 1999, 13). In 1670, the Kangxi emperor issued the *Sacred Edict* (*Shengyu*), which was composed of sixteen "politico-moral maxims" aimed to "indoctrinate the masses with the official ideology" (Chang 1959, 65). The top maxim was to "esteem most highly filial piety and brotherly submission in order to give due importance to all social relations" (translation adopted from Mair 1985, 325). The imperial state reproduced a large number of copies of the *Sacred Edict* to be disseminated to all local governments. County magistrates were required to organize semimonthly lectures to explain the *Edict* to local populaces and interpret current affairs in terms of its creeds. County magistrates also assigned local magnates to replicate this lecture in the villages (Chu 1962, chap. 9.6; Mair 1985; Zhou 2006). This practice was not unlike weekly mass in European churches. It was quite successful until after 1850, and "the remarkably prolonged stability of the eighteenth-century reigns may, in some measure, be attributed to the effectiveness of formal lectures and informal homilies on the *Sacred Edict* in propagating a uniform ideology" (Mair 1985, 337).

To exterminate any remaining influence of the Wang Yangming philosophy that espoused friendship among peer scholar-officials as an alternative to filial loyalty to the emperor-patriarch, in 1725 the Yongzheng emperor authored *The Imperial Discourse on Friends and Parties* (*Yuzhi pengdang lun*) and assigned it as a must-read title among all educated subjects. In the book, the emperor promulgated that parties or cliques among literati could be no more than platforms to advance one's selfish interests. A gentleman who placed the common good of the empire above his self-interest should "only have the emperor in his heart," and he should "attune his judgments to the emperor's judgment, not his friends." The book also justified the absolute primacy of one's loyalty to the emperor by claiming that once a gentleman became an official, he "gives his body to the throne, and can no longer consider the body as belonging to his [biological] father and mother, let alone his friends" (YZPDL).

The emperor relied heavily on routine rites and means of communication with his officials and subjects to constantly refresh his own image as the grand patriarch of the empire. The imperial edicts (*shangyu*) were one such means. They were drafted by the emperor's closest aides in his name and publicized to officials and subjects throughout the empire via the network of county governments. These edicts contained the emperor's dictation of policy guidelines (such as what officials should do to stabilize local grain prices), disciplinary admonitions to his agents and subjects (such as a reminder that local officials should restrain their greed and that commoners should respect local officials), and an expression of the emperor's feeling toward the state of the empire (such as his jubilation for a good harvest or his sympathy for the victims of a famine). Often emotionally charged and filled with moralistic persuasion, these edicts resembled family letters written by a patriarch to his sons and grandsons.[4] In the emperor's utterance, many state institutions and practices were imbued with idioms about parental obligations. One example was the frequent use of the phrase "nourishing the people" (*yangmin*) in reference to the function of the granary systems and other welfare institutions. "Nourish" (*yang*) was the precise word that many Confucianist writings used to summarize parents' responsibility for their children.

In main content of many of the edicts is the emperor's disciplinary admonitions to his officials. The following is a typical example:

> Our state divulges the responsibility of shepherding (*mu*) and nourishing (*yang*) the subjects to local officials. The purpose is that officials could secure the livelihoods of their subjects just like how they secure their families' livelihoods. With the sufficiency in their living, the subjects would love themselves, practice proper rites and virtues, and know of shame. But if provincial officials did not cherish the property and livelihood of the subjects and malicious county magistrates follow suit . . . to exact excessive tax on the subjects, to let government clerks and runners extort the subjects, and to become corrupt, how could the people live in peace? [What follows is a detailed description and criticism of a specific case of tax abuse.] Provincial officials and other high-rank officials should behave by keeping themselves clean, refraining from luxurious life, valuing people's property highly, and cutting back on all excessive taxes. In so doing, the people will live in prosperity, peace, and simplicity. I have high expectation of you.
>
> (DQSCSX JIAQING, 1238 [SEPTEMBER 1814]; MY TRANSLATION)

To be read not only by government officials but also by other literate subjects, these admonitions were as much a reminder to the officials as a proclamation to the subjects that their emperor-patriarch was not responsible for whatever wrongdoings local officials committed and that he was working hard to eliminate such wrongdoings. As we see in chapter 5, this rhetorical strategy helped prevent the fire of resistance against local officials from spreading to the imperial center at critical junctures of regime survival.

Besides promoting the subjects' filial loyalty toward the throne, the Qing state also continued the Ming drive to actively strengthen lineage organizations and regulate real intrafamilial relations at the grassroots level. These efforts were grounded on the Confucianist conviction that stable families were the most effective bulwark against any immoral and unlawful behaviors, as well as the belief that once people had internalized the filial disposition regarding real familial relationships, they would be automatically attuned to the standard of proper behavior toward officials and the emperor as their imagined fathers and grandfather (Chow 1994; Faure 2007; Furth 1990; Ocko 1990; Rowe 2002, 529–537). In the *Great Qing Legal Code* (*Daqing lüli*), extensive sections were devoted to laws that sanctioned against behavior deemed destabilizing to orthodox familial relations, such as extramarital affairs, incest, and homosexuality (see Shen 2007; Somers 2000).

The filial loyalty to the throne and loyalty to local lineage and other pseudokinship organizations (such as native-place associations) constituted two coexisting components within the same orthodoxy of neo-Confucianism. Gilbert Rozman (1991) characterizes these two components as "imperial Confucianism," which centers "on the ideology and rituals supportive of the emperor's rights and the delegated authority of those who exercised power on his behalf" (161), and "mass Confucianism," which was "reflected in lineage organizations at the community level and also by pseudo-kinship or common-local-origin ties" (163). These two components were symbiotic but not totally harmonious with each other. The state elites did value the social-control function of local corporate bodies. But they also constantly kept an eye on the development of such bodies and saw them as potential challengers to the authorities. Whenever these communities became too strong and too large in a given area (such as lineages that monopolized local markets and cultivable land or recurrently resisted government demands), the local government did not hesitate to check their growth through administrative means (Rowe 2002, 535–536).

Other cultural traditions that developed outside the orbit of Confucianism, such as lay Buddhism, grew in tandem with the expansion in population and commerce in grassroots societies. Some studies do point out that the grip of Confucianist orthodoxy loosened gradually during the eighteenth century, when worsening social malaises prompted the literati to focus more on finding practical solutions to those problems than on purifying society with rigid orthodoxy (e.g., Chow 1994; Elman 2001; Furth 1990). But the orthodoxy's dominance was still intact during the mid-Qing period, in comparison with the turbulent ideological crises of the early seventeenth century and late nineteenth century, let alone the radical cultural transformation in early modern Europe. Under the domination of neo-Confucianist orthodoxy, the state carefully scrutinized other cultural schemas such as Buddhism, and some Buddhist groups were persecuted rigorously for allegedly trespassing the moral boundary defined by the orthodoxy. In fact, as we will see in chapter 3, throughout the eighteenth century the Qing state was increasingly active in investigating the doctrines and practices of Buddhist groups and distinguishing the heterodox ones from the nonheterodox, though it often wavered as to where to draw the line between the two. The state was always proactive in rooting out heterodox groups once they were identified. We will also see in chapter 4 that in certain extraordinary times, when the moral legitimacy of the imperial center was in crisis, heterodox Buddhist groups, becoming more capable of recruiting aggrieved commoners, grew unchecked and became galvanizing points of open rebellion.

THE CHANGING MORAL LEGITIMACY OF THE IMPERIAL CENTER

While the Manchu rulers were the key agents to restore the Confucianist orthodoxy, they became captives of it, as government officials and the emperors were subject to the same rigid moral standards derived from the orthodoxy. The enthusiasm of Qing emperors to promote, enforce, and abide by these moral standards varied over time. The moral legitimacy of the imperial center as perceived by its subjects, therefore, was in flux despite the unchanging dominance of the orthodoxy.

This variation is best illustrated by the changing image of the Qianlong emperor over the course of his reign, from 1736 to 1795. In the early years, he was as much a moral activist as his father, the Yongzheng emperor. Under Qianlong, the censorship against writings that allegedly promoted heretical moral values was as draconian as possible. Qianlong was also tireless in issuing extra edicts to ban any "sinful" behaviors that were not yet sanctioned by existing legal codes. For example, having good-looking male actors play female roles had been a time-honored practice in local opera performances. Although it had never caused unease to preceding emperors, this practice was suddenly viewed with great suspicion by the homophobic Qianlong. Seeing it as a grave threat to the Confucianist imperative of maintaining distinct gender roles and behaviors, Qianlong issued an order banning the practice. This act earned him the reputation of being a "micro-managing fundamentalist" in the eyes of Qing historians (Woodside 2002, 248).

Qianlong's credibility as a Confucianist moral crusader, however, began to crumble after the 1760s. This was not only because of the administrative-fiscal decay of the Qing state and growth of corruption in the bureaucracy, which we discussed earlier. It had more to do with the growth of Qianlong's apparent laxity in managing state affairs. Starting in the 1770s,

Qianlong took a backseat in many important decisions and divested much of his responsibility as emperor to Heshen, his personal favorite, who suddenly and mysteriously ascended to become the most powerful figure in the Qing court. Heshen's status and authority were so high that his contemporaries dubbed him the "second emperor."

Heshen was an ethnic Manchu from a bannerman family. He first encountered Qianlong in 1775, when he was twenty-five years old and serving as a palace guardsman. For some unclear reason, Heshen earned the aging emperor's trust and accumulated a spate of the most important posts in the central government between 1775 and 1780, including grand councilor, commandant of the Beijing police, minister of revenue, high official at the four treasuries office, and lieutenant general of a Manchu banner army. In 1786, he even became the grand secretary, the highest civil post in the bureaucracy. He staffed the bureaucracy at all levels with his relatives and protégés (Woodside 2002, 302).

With such greatly inflated power, Heshen became the head of a clique of corrupt officials who profited from embezzlement of public funds. To be sure, Heshen was not the only major official who was corrupt, and his was not the only clique of dishonest officials, though it might have been the biggest and most influential one. However, his dramatic climb to the apex of bureaucratic power at lightning speed, despite his modest background and lack of imperial degree, made him the symbol of the deterioration, corruption, and declining efficacy of the late Qianlong state (Kahn 1971; McMahon 2008; Park 1997; Woodside 2002, 301–305).

By the time of Heshen's rise, the reputation of the Qianlong emperor already had been tarnished by a number of wild rumors involving his appetite for sex and his subsequent neglect of state affairs and his own health. The rumors had spread to grassroots societies in the farthest corners of the empire. In 1765, in the city of Hangzhou, in the middle of Qianlong's southern tour, the emperor mysteriously expelled the empress Ula Nara from his procession and sent her back to Beijing, where she died in 1766. After her death, she was stripped of any posthumous honors and ritual status that were normally assigned to a deceased empress. In the decade following this unusual incident, popular tales about what happened to Ula Nara spread through the empire like wildfire. According to the rumor, the empress, disgusted by Qianlong's all-night-long orgies held during the southern tour with captured local women, requested to leave the imperial family and become a Buddhist nun. When her request was denied, she sheared off her hair with scissors in protest. As cutting one's hair violated Manchu custom and was codified as an act of rejection of the ruling Manchu dynasty, Qianlong was enraged. This story explained the empress's odd and sudden expulsion from the imperial procession in Hangzhou (Chang 2007, 380–387).

In 1776, a former low-rank government clerk in Beijing sent a petition to a central-government organ to ask for the restoration of empress Ula Nara's good name. Shocked by the petition of such "lowly and disloyal subject" and his attempt to interfere with supposedly secretive court affairs, the government arrested and interrogated the clerk. His confession shows how far the rumor about the emperor's profligacy had spread in the empire:

> In 1765 His Majesty was traveling through Jiangnan on a southern tour and sent the empress back to the capital ahead of time. At that time I was in my native district in Shanxi province and heard about this incident. Everybody said that His Majesty wanted to take a consort in Jiangnan and that Empress Ula Nara objected. Because of this conflict she proceeded to cut her hair. Many people spoke of this.
>
> (CITED IN CHANG 2007, 389)

This rumor, which coincided with the worsening corruption and incompetence of the imperial bureaucracy, was only one of many stories about the emperor's immorality. But none was as devastating as the rumor about Heshen's homosexual relationship with the Qianlong emperor.

Following Heshen's rise to the pinnacle of power, imaginative tales about Heshen and Qianlong spread among both the educated elite and laymen. According to the version included in the *Spectacle of Qing Unofficial History* (*Qingchao yeshi daguan*, or QCYSDG), a documentation of popular "unofficial histories" of the Qing circulating among the literati and grassroots storytellers published in 1916, Heshen was actually the reincarnation of Qianlong's secret first lover, an ill-fated concubine of Qianlong's father, Yongzheng. The teenage Qianlong fell in love with her at first sight, but his mother discovered the affair and immediately executed the concubine. Out of sorrow and regret, Qianlong, as the story goes, secretly marked the neck of her corpse with red ink and promised to continue their romance when she was reincarnated. When the aging Qianlong emperor encountered Heshen, he found that he looked like that pitiful woman—and there was a red birthmark on Heshen's neck. Taking into consideration that Heshen was born after the concubine died, Qianlong decided that Heshen was a male reincarnation of his lost lover and entered into an affair with him (QCYSDG 1:45–46; Woodside 2002, 301–305).

This story, believed to have originated in the last decade of Qianlong rule, was probably fabricated by Heshen's enemies, who dared not confront him directly. The tale was subversive in the sense that it suggested that the emperor had violated two of the most serious taboos under the Confucianist orthodoxy he himself had imposed: an incestuous affair with his father's concubine and homosexuality. By extending Qianlong's "sinful" record from the present (the 1770s) back to his youth, the story suggested that he had been morally corrupt from the beginning. This was a death blow to the moral legitimacy of the emperor. Between the mid-eighteenth century and the late eighteenth century, the image of the Qianlong emperor deteriorated from a fundamentalist moral warrior who rigidly defended the neo-Confucianist morality to a hypocritical, sinful soul who defied such morality throughout his personal life.

As a student of late Qianlong rumors noted, these incredible imbroglios about the emperor made "Qianlong's various professions of ethno-dynastic virtue appeared little more than ideological conceits . . . [as they] belied Qianlong's explicit and repeated disavowals of pleasure in favor of the virtues of filial piety, diligence, and benevolence" (Chang 2007, 380). In addition to the rise of Heshen and rumors about the throne's immorality, another contributor to the perception of the throne's declining moral legitimacy was the open dissipation of Qianlong's energy in disciplining his officials. Disciplinary admonition directed at local officials in imperial edicts was a key performative act used by the emperor to ensure his subjects of his diligence and righteousness. But a survey of the *Sacred Directives of the Ten Reigns of the Great Qing* (*Daqing shichao shengxun*, or DQSCSX), a cataloged collection of all edicts issued by each emperor, shows that the number of such disciplinary admonitions, which was high in the early Qianlong reign, drastically dropped in the 1770s and the remainder of the reign, as shown in figure 1.3 below.[5]

With this deteriorating image of the throne, covert comments that corruption and abuse in local governments originated not from individual officials but from a putatively rotten imperial center abounded among the scholar-official class. For example, Wang Huizu, a highly respected scholar-official in the Qianlong reign, lamented openly in 1793 that within the bureaucracy, "not even two or three out of ten behaved uprightly" and that malicious officials had "picked up their evil ways from their mentors." Another prominent scholar, Zhuang Cunyu, lamented in the 1780s in his widely circulated

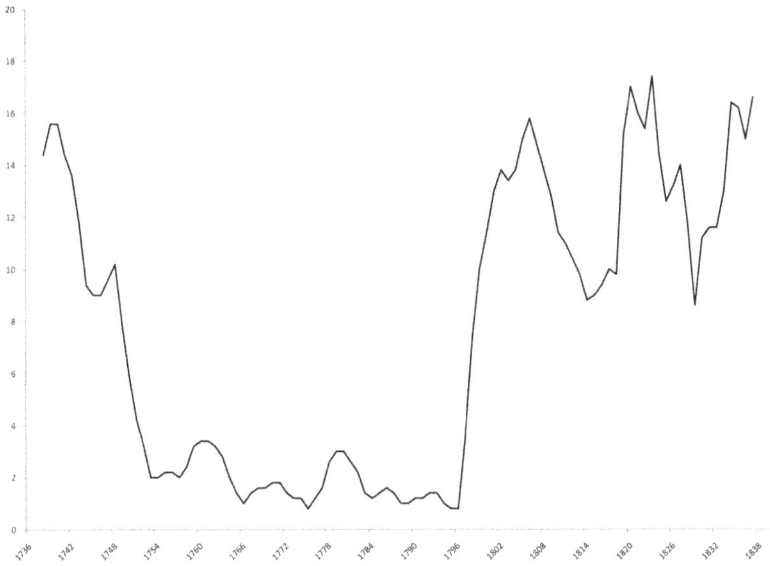

FIGURE 1.3 Number of Disciplinary Admonitions Against Officials in Imperial Edicts, 1736–1839 (five-year moving average) *(source*: DQSCSX)

book, *Gongyang Commentary*, that dynastic decline in the past was always linked to the arrogance and greed of false rulers at the top, implicitly expressing his judgment that that Qing dynasty was in decline and the throne itself was responsible for the social and political ills of the times (cited in McMahon 2008, 237; see also McMahon 2005). Literati factionalism, which had been denounced and rooted out by the Yongzheng emperor by the 1730s, revived within the bureaucracy with the formation of an anti-Heshen coalition. The literati's clandestine attribution of bureaucratic decay to the highest echelon of the state seemed to have filtered into the popular conception. Many late eighteenth-century peasant proverbs, documented by Jesuit missionaries of the time, deviated from the typical perception that lower-ranking officials were more abusive and corrupt while higher-level ones were more righteous and benevolent. Intriguingly, many of these proverbs indicate that "in the eyes of the populace, officials were as greedy for grain as their assistants and that official avarice was even more pronounced at higher levels of the bureaucracy than it was at lower levels" (Park 1997, 990). Viewed in light of all these elite and popular perceptions, it was not a coincidence that since the 1770s a plurality of subversive poems and treatises overtly or covertly questioning the legitimacy of Manchu rule and asking for a restoration of the Ming dynasty had been published and circulated in literati circles (Chang 2007, 394–402).

In 1796, the ailing Qianlong handed his throne to his son Jiaqing. But with Qianlong still alive, Heshen continued to control the bureaucracy, and the new emperor was no more than a figurehead. This situation changed drastically in 1799, when Qianlong died. Seizing the moment, the Jiaqing emperor mobilized the support of scholar-officials who were tacitly resistant to Heshen's domination and worried about the decay of the Qing state by pledging to reform the corrupt bureaucracy and uproot the Heshen clique. The emperor's urge for rectification, as well as the threat to the dynasty's survival posed by the White Lotus Rebellion (1796–1805), unleashed a great discussion within the bureaucracy about how to reenergize the decaying state institutions. Heshen was attacked openly by his many enemies and portrayed as the culprit of all the menaces that the Manchu state was facing at the time. In the end, the Jiaqing emperor ordered the arrest and then the execution of Heshen, as well as the confiscation of all his property. As another gesture to reestablish the righteous image of the imperial center, in the first few decades of the nineteenth century the level of disciplinary admonitions against the bureaucracy, as articulated in the imperial edicts, surged back to the level of the early Qianlong reign, as shown in figure 1.3.

Jiaqing's resolution to reform the Qing state by reverting the ills of the late Qianlong reign was a deliberate effort to revive the throne's moral legitimacy by co-opting the literati opposition to Heshen, and it received popular support. In 1799, Hong Liangji, a member of the Hanlin Academy in the central government, openly criticized Jiaqing's soft approach in dealing with Heshen in the early years of his reign. Jiaqing initially ordered Hong to be executed. But Hong's wide support among the literati made Jiaqing swiftly change his mind. In 1800, he pardoned Hong. The emperor publicly blamed himself for punishing a loyal and remonstrating official in an official declaration. It immediately began raining, according to the official record, and the emperor went on to compose a poem to commemorate the occasion. The emperor even mentioned that he always kept Hong's letter to him under his pillow, a reminder of his obligations as the empire's grand patriarch (Elman 1990, 284–290). Jiaqing's endorsement of scholar-officials resentful of Heshen and his public display of tolerance and righteousness to critical officials revived the literati's trust and faith in the throne. The purge of Heshen was hailed with an outpouring of gratitude among the literati class across the empire.

However, the momentum of the fiscal-administrative decay of the Qing state was too large to be reversed by the reform-minded Jiaqing. Many of Heshen's protégés were so powerful that they reemerged in important positions or retired with their titles intact a few years after they were purged. Though Jiaqing did make some progress in cleaning up the bureaucracy and staffing important posts in provincial governments with more righteous scholar-officials, many reform proposals made at the imperial center invoked endless and fruitless debate, and very few of them were ever implemented (Jones and Kuhn 1978, 116–132; Polachek 1992). The execution of Heshen turned out to be more of a symbolic gesture than a real cure. Jiaqing's reform simply "would not heal the deep-seated malaise in the nineteenth-century bureaucracy" (Jones and Kuhn 1978, 116). Corruption continued to grow throughout the early nineteenth century and beyond. If the laxity of Qianlong and rise of Heshen shattered the moral legitimacy of the imperial center and made the empire's subjects see it as the ultimate source of corruption and abuse of local governments, then the elimination of Heshen and the reformist rhetoric of the imperial center in the Jiaqing reign—though it failed to arrest the decay of the state—at least refreshed the image of the imperial center as a righteous grand patriarch sympathetic with his subjects and disdainful of his predatory local agents. As a student of the Jiaqing period remarked, the representation of Heshen as a symbol of evil and his purge by Jiaqing "became a cultural act demonstrating the throne's commitment to eradicating government evil, averting decline, and restoring the health of the realm" (McMahon 2008, 244).

After the Jiaqing emperor died, in 1819, his successor, the Daoguang emperor, continued Jiaqing's reformist rhetoric and his routine attacks on predatory local officials in his edicts (Jones and Kuhn 1978; Kuhn 2002). Daoguang's symbolic attack on corrupt officials likewise failed to actually arrest the fiscal and administrative decline of the state. Consequently, "the pervasive atmosphere of the 1820s and 1830s was one of corruption in officialdom, nourished and sustained by an elaborate patronage system" (Jones and Kuhn 1978, 116, 144; see also Kuhn 2002). In other words, although the imperial center managed to refresh its moral legitimacy in c. 1800–1839, the fiscal-administrative decline of the Qing state that started in the 1770s continued well into the nineteenth century.

Taking into account the trajectories of commercial expansion, state centralization, and changing moral legitimacy of the imperial center, we can readily partition the mid-Qing period of 1740–1839 into three subperiods: the mid-eighteenth century, when the market economy was booming and both centralized state power and the moral legitimacy of the imperial center were at their peaks; the late eighteenth century, when the market economy continued to boom and both centralized state power and the moral legitimacy of the imperial center were in decline; and the early nineteenth century, when both the commercial economy and state power were in decline but the moral legitimacy of the imperial center revived. Before delving into how the different political, economic, and cultural contours of the three subperiods shape the pattern of popular protest, in the next chapter I will develop an array of conceptual tools to classify and analyze different types of mid-Qing protests. I also outline the general composition and temporal distribution of protest events in 1740–1839.

2

DOCUMENTING THE THREE WAVES OF MID-QING PROTEST

The focus of this study is popular protest occurring between 1740 and 1839 within the eighteen predominantly Han Chinese inner provinces of the Qing empire. I define an event of popular protest as collective, noninstitutionalized, and contentious action initiated by nonelite groups and directed at the policies or incumbents of the state and its agents. An episode of protest can be a single act or a series of acts with consistent actors and demands. For example, a case in which a group of protesters launched a demonstration to call for famine relief on one day and stormed the local government office to call for the same thing another day is counted as one protest event instead of two. Protest differs from a social movement in that the latter constitutes a series of protests under consistent leadership and organization. Revolt or rebellion is a particular form of social movement characterized by its militarized means and its radical goal of toppling an existing ruler. Protests also differ from conflicts among social groups such as classes (in the case of landlord-tenant conflicts) and lineages (in the case of interlineage feuds). Although this study covers cases of rebellion and social conflict, they are not the primary focus.

The mid-Qing period, which is the center of this study, differs from the late Ming and early Qing periods in the seventeenth century and the late Qing period in the mid- and late nineteenth century in several ways. First, eighteenth- and early nineteenth-century China was characterized by the relative rarity of large-scale rebellions that openly challenged Qing rule. The few instances of revolt represent more the exception than the rule of unrest in mid-Qing China and deserve separate treatment.[1] In this study, my analysis is concentrated on protests that concerned particular issues or officials. But I also discuss a few cases of large-scale rebellion within the period by looking at how ordinary protests were related to these rebellions.

Regarding intergroup conflicts such as class antagonism and feuds, previous studies do find that they were abundant in the mid-Qing period (e.g., Buoye 2000; Ownby 1990; Wong 1982). At times, these conflicts became so disruptive and extensive that local governments stepped in to pacify the warring parties, usually with the consequence of turning government agents into targets of resistance from both sides of the conflict, who accused the government of siding with their foes. In other cases, either side of the social conflicts sought the sympathy and support of the government and persuaded it to sanction its antinomies. These intergroup-conflicts-turned-protests are covered in this study. To be sure, there were many cases in which the local government stayed aloof and let the conflict run its course, for fear that state intervention would incite an antigovernment protest. Most of these cases were skipped in official reports and are not covered in this study.

This systematic underreporting of social conflicts not involving the state is not a liability of this study, which centers on how Qing subjects made claims directed at the state rather than on conflicts in general. In addition, some existing studies show that similar situations that could have created class conflict in early modern Europe often caused protests targeted at governments in Qing China. Taking food riots as an example, Bin Wong and Lucien Bianco both reckoned that the hegemony of the Qing Confucianist state, which took the subsistence of its subjects seriously and maintained an empirewide granary system to serve this end, made popular responses to subsistence crises in China very different from those in Europe. While lower classes in Europe were more prone to loot grain from merchants or landlords during a subsistence crisis, their counterparts in Qing China were more inclined to urge the state either to offer famine relief or to pressure merchants to lower grain prices as a fulfillment of its paternalist obligations (Bianco 2001, 158–161; Wong 1997, 222–229; 2006, 541–544). The same can be said regarding conflicts between workers and workshop owners and between tenants and landlords. These class conflicts were regulated more heavily in China by the paternalist state, to the benefit of the subordinated classes, who often sought help from the state to redress injustice through petition or protest (Brenner and Isett 2002; Chiu 2002; Hung 2008).

The reasons for establishing 1740 and 1839 as the temporal boundaries of the study are twofold. First, Qing China during this period was at its height of early modernity. Its levels of centralized state power and commercialized economy were comparable to eighteenth-century Europe. In particular, the 1740s was the decade when the Qianlong emperor inherited and aggressively expanded the centralized state apparatus consolidated by his father, the Yongzheng emperor. Although the centralized power of the state had declined by the early nineteenth century, it remained intact until the Opium War of 1839–1842 threw the Qing empire into disarray. As for economic development, the empirewide commercial economy had fully recovered from the turbulent Ming-Qing transition and reached new heights by 1740. It kept expanding until the early nineteenth century. Despite the Daoguang Depression, which began in the 1820s, the foundations of the empire's economy remained stable until the Opium War.

Second, studies that deal with unrest in the late Ming–early Qing period (from the late seventeenth to the early eighteenth century) and the late Qing period (from the end of the first Opium War, in 1842, to the collapse of the Qing empire in 1911) are relatively abundant (e.g., Bernhardt 1992; Fuma 1993; Marks 1984; Masatoshi 1988; Parsons 1970; Perry 1980; Tong 1991; Von Glahn 1991; Wakeman 1998, 1966; Wu 1996, 142–145, 240–244; Yang 1975; Yuan 1979). In these periods, the legitimacy of the ruling dynasty dissolved, and unrest manifested frequently in the form of armed uprisings that directly and openly challenged the imperial center. In contrast, the century between 1740 and 1839 is often assumed to have been tranquil and receives much less attention from students of unrest. But a limited number of studies, as well as select published sources, suggest that the century in fact witnessed a plurality of new types of conflicts, which rarely challenged the legitimacy of Qing rule, though more systematic knowledge about the general pattern of unrest in the period is lacking (e.g., Bouye 2000; Quan 1996c; Rosner 1987; Wong 1982; Wu 1996; cf. Ownby 1996; Naquin 1976, 1981; KYQ). By filling this gap in our knowledge of protest in 1740–1839 and drawing on existing knowledge about unrest in sixteenth- and late nineteenth- to early twentieth-century China, we can readily reconstruct the long-term trajectory of China's changing protest patterns from early modern to modern times. Comparing protests under the hegemony of the ruling dynasty and unrest occurring when such hegemony unraveled will help us develop a more comprehensive understanding of state-society relations in China.

Geographically, I limit the scope of my investigation to the eighteen inner provinces categorized as "directly administered provinces" (*zhisheng*) in the Qing administrative systems. They include Zhili, Henan, Shandong, Shanxi, Shaanxi, Gansu, Hubei, Hunan, Jiangxi, Anhui, Jiangsu, Zhejiang, Fujian, Guangdong, Guangxi, Yunnan, Guizhou, and Sichuan. These provinces, located in the inner portion of the Qing empire, were where the vast

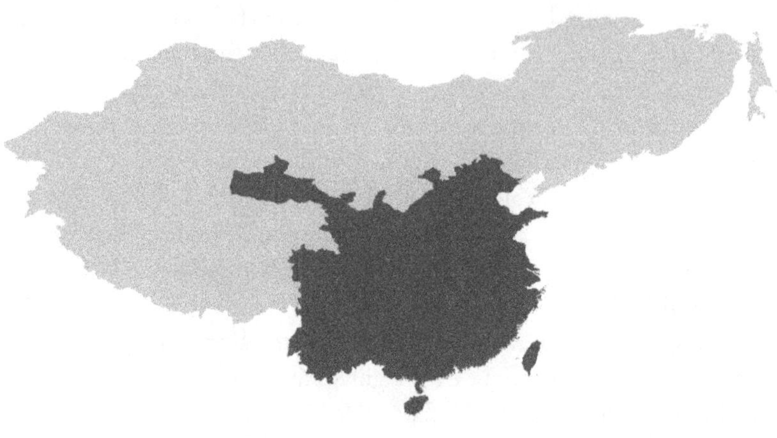

FIGURE 2.1 BOUNDARIES OF THE EIGHTEEN INNER PROVINCES (SHADED AREA) (BACKGROUND MAP: CHGIS)

majority of the empire's population lived and were inhabited mainly by Han Chinese. They were administered by the overlapping networks of provincial governors (*xunfu*; each province was governed by one provincial governor) and governor-generals (*zongdu*; every two provinces were governed by one governor-general).

In contrast, the frontier regions of the Qing empire, such as Tibet and Xinjiang, were inhabited mostly by non-Han ethnic-religious groups (such as Muslims in the Xinjiang region). They were sparsely populated and were administered under different systems of semiautonomous self-governance. The social customs, political structures, and cultural features of these regions were so different that the dynamic of protest there departs significantly from that in the rest of the empire. For example, the centrality of tension between native ethnic groups and Han Chinese migrants that underlines most conflicts in Xinjiang is nowhere to be seen in the eighteen inner provinces.[2] In addition, recent studies by Pamela Crossly (1999) and others find that the Qing emperors resorted to vastly different discourses of legitimation in non-Han areas. For example, the Qing emperors, while presenting themselves as Confucianist patriarchs of all Han subjects in the inner provinces, instead presented themselves as patrons of Buddhism, or even as Bodhisattva, to legitimize their authority in Tibet. The state-society relation in the empire's outer regions was therefore vastly different from that in the eighteen provinces.

DOCUMENTING MID-QING PROTEST

Two key components of this research are to compile a catalog of numerous protest events for 1740–1839 and to construct thick descriptions of select events. The major source for the catalog is *Veritable Records of the Qing* (*Qing shilu*, hereafter QSL). The QSL is a collection of précis of the emperor's edicts and of officials' memorials on a wide range of significant affairs at the national and local levels for the reference of future high-rank officials and emperors. The QSL of a specific reign was compiled by scholar-officials in the succeeding reign by summarizing the totality of palace documents that accumulated throughout the reign. A large portion of the documents were secret reports on local affairs drafted by local officials and sent directly to the emperor, known fully as "secret palace memorials with emperor's inscriptions in red ink" (*zhupi zouzhe*, or ZPZZ).

The secret palace memorials system of the Qing was fully instituted under the Yongzheng emperor. It was meant to guarantee the monarch's access to information on local affairs and to strengthen his control of the bureaucracy in all provinces (Bartlett 1991). Issues reported in the memorials included local weather and harvest conditions, indictments of officials, and investigations of local crimes. On top of these mundane affairs, the memorials also were to be "presented to keep the emperor informed of any local events indicative of a possible local disturbance or insurrection or indication of a lessening of local tension" (Wu 1967, 35). After reading each memorial, the emperor, in consultation with the Grand Council, comprising his most trusted aides, usually inscribed on it his comments and instructions in red ink. The inscribed memorial would then be sent back to the original drafter, who read the memorial and returned it to the central government for archiving.

Inevitably, some local officials would try to hide occurrences of unrest from the emperor for fear that he would accuse them of failing to prevent the outbreak. But intentional underreporting was likely not common for two reasons. First, the emperor severely punished officials who were found to deliberately cover up local unrest. In many cases, deceptive officials were demoted or even executed. Second, the reliability of the secret memorials system was ensured by its own design. The system itself encouraged mutual monitoring among officials. In a given locality, a handful of officials occupying different top civil and military posts were granted the same privilege of memorializing local affairs to the emperor. The contents of each memorial were strictly kept to the eyes of the emperor and the grand councilors. As a result, not including a significant local event in the memorial was risky, as the drafter could never know whether his colleagues had reported the event (see Kuhn 1990, 123, 221; Wu 1967, 36–38).

Information that is covered in secret memorials but omitted in the QSL should not be abundant. The QSL was designated to be a daily, comprehensive documentation of the memorials and the emperor's edicts. As the Manchus were particularly anxious to secure their rule over Chinese society, reports of unrest and conspiracies were one of the major emphases of the QSL's records. Last but not least, the reliability of the QSL (or the *Mingshilu*, for the Ming dynasty) as a source for unrest events has been verified by the reliability test conducted in other quantitative analyses of collective action in other periods of late imperial China (e.g., Yang 1975; Tong 1991).[3] I further confirm the QSL's reliability by comparing the catalog constructed for this research with the corresponding portions of other compiled catalogs derived from different primary sources, as shown in table 2.1 below. One of the years witnessing a particularly high intensity of protest, 1741, is used as a sample year. I find that most events included in other catalogs, though they may be documented in greater detail, are included in the QSL, whereas many events included in the QSL are not necessarily included in others. Similar comparisons are done for other years and they yield the same conclusion: the QSL is the most comprehensive source available.

Despite the tested reliability of the QSL, we still need to assume that some smaller events might have been missed in the documentation. This bias based on scale does not matter, as what we are interested in is the temporal variation of the prevalence of different types, not scales, of protests. In fact, most macroanalyses of unrest that construct samples of unrest events from national news reports and other comparable sources unanimously show that what matters is not the exhaustiveness of the source but its uniformity and systematicity. This uniformity and systematicity ensure that the *sample* of events well reflects the characteristics and pattern of the underlying *total population* of events. We can estimate the validity of such a sample by ruling out as many sources of systematic bias of the sample as possible (e.g., Earl et al. 2004; Markoff 1996; Olzak 1989; Silver 2003).

Other than the bias based on scale of protest events, the two other plausible biases of the sample of events derived from QSL as a source are that the QSL might document more events in the politically and economically

TABLE 2.1 Comparison of Different Sources on Protest Events, 1741

Events	LFZZ-NMYD[a]	KYQ[b]	Wu (1996)[c]	QSL-QL[d]
Petition in Tongzhou	9706–021 9706–014	Nil	Nil	141, 15
Aborigines' petition in Chengdu	Nil	Nil	Nil	141, 22
Market strike in Chaozhou	0333–019 0333–020 9702–061 9704–063 9704–068	571–572 587–589	255	145, 28
Tax resistance in Fuzhou	Nil	Nil	Nil	146, 7
Tax resistance in Xinghua	Nil	Nil	Nil	146, 7
Attacking gov't clerk in Yongchun	Nil	Nil	Nil	146, 7
State factory strike in Beijing	Nil	520–524	255	148, 15
Market strike in Taicang	1376–027 1376–033	Nil	Nil	151, 20
Market strike in Changzhou	Nil	563	254	151, 20
Petition in Zhenjiang	Nil	Nil	255	157, 26
Protest for demoted officials in Hangzhou	Nil	Nil	255	155, 24
Market strike in Yangzhou	8916–032 9703–066 9703–067	Nil	255	157, 26

(Continued)

TABLE 2.1

Events	LFZZ-NMYD[a]	KYQ[b]	Wu (1996)[c]	QSL-QL[d]
Petition against relief reduction in Fengyang	Nil	Nil	Nil	154, 21
Attacking gov't clerk in Tingzhou	Nil	594–595	255	Nil

[a] Archive index number in the LFZZ-NMYD archive catalog, in China's First Historical Archive, Beijing.

[b] KYQ page number.

[c] Page number in Wu's (1996) catalog of collective actions.

[d] Volume and page numbers of the QSL for the Qianlong reign

core areas (such as the Lower Yangzi region) and that the comprehensiveness of the documentation might decline from 1740 to 1839, when the state's falling administrative capacity might have lowered its effectiveness in gathering intelligence across the empire. The actual pattern of protest as shown in my catalog rules out these possibilities. If the QSL's documentation truly varies with the relative political and economic significance of different places and with the administrative capacity of the Qing state at different times, then events in poor, less accessible inland regions should be largely neglected in comparison with events in core regions such as Jiangsu and Zhejiang provinces. This bias also should be more obvious at times when the administrative capacity of the Qing state was low. What I find, on the contrary, is that more protest events from peripheral areas were documented at the turn of the nineteenth century, when state capacity had declined substantially, than were documented in the mid-eighteenth century, when state capacity was high. This spatial-temporal pattern of documented events is clearly more a reflection of reality than a result of any source's bias.

Altogether, segments of the QSL corresponding to the period 1740–1839 consist of 2,096 volumes. Each volume is composed of around thirty pages. On average, one page contains at least two items of information—usually a précis of one discrete official's memorial or of a discrete emperor's edict. Therefore, about 2,096 × 30 × 2 = 125,760 items of information are surveyed in this research. Among these 125,760 items, I document 514 events of popular protest that fit the definition discussed above (excluding all rebellions, class antagonism, and other conflicts) and 450 events of upward appeal including capital appeal, that is, petitions to the imperial center against local injustices, which I discuss in chapter 5. Most records of protest events contain basic information—the location and timing, claims of protesters, whether violence was involved, etc.—sufficient for mapping the events' general pattern.

While the QSL is a reliable source for the survey of protest events, it is not an ideal source for deciphering the details of each event, as most of the QSL's items are nothing more than highly condensed versions of the original memorials. To give a detailed delineation of the dynamics and participants of selected cases of protest, I analyze other archival materials, principally the original secret memorials, copies of secret memorials at the Grand Council (*Junji chu lufu zouzhe*, or LFZZ), copies or excerpts of secret memorials at the Grand Secretariat, the emperor's edicts addressing individual protests, local gazetteers, and, in a few cases, literati memoirs. Generally, what I select for in-depth case description are cases that represent claims or repertoires that are common in the subperiods under scrutiny; represent different geographical areas as much as possible, except for types of events that were heavily concentrated in certain regions; and happen to be documented in more detail in different sources.

The original secret memorials are kept mainly at the ZPZZ archive at the First Historical Archive of China, located at the western gate of the Forbidden City of Beijing. The ZPZZ archive contains original copies of secret memorials, which are the most original reports of local affairs for the emperor. The archive has been categorized. The ZPZZs concerning protest actions are usually indexed under the "category of peasant movements, entries on anti-Qing struggles" (*nongmin yundong lei fan qing douzheng xiang*; Mingqing dangan tongnan bianweihui 2000; Zhongguo diyi lishi danganguan 1985), even though many of these protests actually occurred in cities and involved urban dwellers. Pertinent memorials sometimes can be found under the "category of law" (*falü lei*), as well. The latter are usually about cases that invoked extensive investigation and trials.

Part of the ZPZZ archive was transferred to Taiwan by the Guomindang government when it retreated from mainland China in 1949. That portion is now housed in the Palace Archive (*Gongzhong dang*, or GZD) in the National Palace Museum in Taipei, and the items are categorized by date.

The ZPZZs housed in Taiwan (which I designate as ZPZZ-GZD) appear to contain more materials for the late Qianlong and Jiaqing periods, whereas the ZPZZs in Beijing carry more abundant information on the early and mid-Qianlong reign, at least as far as documentation of protest events is concerned. Given the apparently different time focuses of the materials in Beijing and Taiwan, I have to rely on archives in both places equally.

The only problem with the ZPZZ archive is that some of the memorials might have been lost over time or mixed up with other documents and submerged in the sea of unsorted archives. In this regard, the LFZZ archive, also housed in the First Historical Archive of China at Beijing, is a useful complement. Under the secret memorial system in the Qing dynasty, each secret memorial sent to, read by, and inscribed by the emperor was hand copied by staff in the Grand Council as backup documentation. The contents of LFZZ are identical to the original ZPZZ, and this archive is more complete and more systematically stored than the ZPZZ archive. The index categories used for the LFZZ archive are identical to those used for the ZPZZ in the First Historical Archive. The only disadvantage of the LFZZ is that the drafters usually used a cursive cartographical style that sometimes rendered the contents difficult to read. It is more time consuming to read through the documents in this archive. In addition, selected memorials were copied and transferred to the Grand Secretariat (*Neige*) if the emperor or the Grand Council decided that the content required the attention of and handling by certain ministers in the secretariat. As a result, the Grand Secretariat archive (*Neige daku*, or NGDK), housed at the Academia Sinica in Taipei, also contained valuable information for this study. The archive of imperial edicts (*Shangyu dang*, or SYD), which documents emperors' instructions of various kinds and was published, is also a useful source. Many of these instructions are about how to handle particular protest events.

Another source of information on protest events is local gazetteers, which are documentations of local histories compiled by local literati in a given county or prefecture. Local gazetteers in different localities were created by different authors and at different times, though their formats were more or less standardized. Each gazetteer usually consisted of a chronology section that documented the most significant events, including local unrest, having occurred in the regions from the dawn of time to the time of compilation. The documentations of more recent events were usually more detailed. Local gazetteers have been disseminated among different collectors and have never been centrally archived and indexed. Gazetteers that were not printed in large numbers (particularly county gazetteers) are difficult to find. However, most prefecture gazetteers usually can be found in libraries with good Chinese collections. In this research, I rely mainly on the gazetteers housed at the Chinese University of Hong Kong as well as at Hong Kong University. Both have good collections of gazetteers republished in both mainland China and Taiwan.

My detailed case analysis, surely, is not spared from a problem that plagues the documentation of unrest in most other studies, namely, the heavy reliance on descriptions of the events by subordinating groups, such as government officials. This bias is inevitable, as subordinated groups protesting in early modern China and elsewhere were usually incapable of documenting their own accounts of the event in ways that could be preserved through the ages. My remedy to this problem is to juxtapose as many elite accounts of the same protest event as possible and to verify the accounts with one another. As discussed earlier, the Qing emperor prevented cover-ups of significant local events or issues by granting a plurality of officials in one area the right to submit secret memorials to the Grand Council. As we shall see in the case analyses, descriptions of the same protests by different ZPZZ drafters may differ from one another, as the drafters may emphasize different aspects of the same event. This sometimes stems from different judgments about the event's nature (e.g., whether it is a direct challenge to the authorities or a legitimate and humble appeal) or from attempts to interpret the event in ways that exonerate the reporters (e.g., emphasizing the role of wicked elements in society in stirring up people's anger and downplaying the contribution of government malpractice as a trigger of protest). At times, the emperor, upon finding discrepancies in the reports, sought the truth rigorously by urging more officials from the locality concerned to offer accounts of the event or to initiate follow-up investigations. In some cases, internal bureaucratic communications regarding one event could go on for months before the emperor finished deliberating on the nature of the protest and dictating the appropriate penalty as well as preventive measures in the future.

This multiple reporting on protests left rich and diverse elite accounts of the same events. By comparing these accounts, and with the aid of our preexisting understanding of Qing society and culture, I can construct a reasonably accurate narrative about each event. It resembles how a detective gets to the truth about a murder by juxtaposing the testimonies of all suspects and witnesses, as well as other circumstantial evidence available, even though he or she can never access the victim's account. In some cases, the accuracy of my account can be further enhanced by nonofficial literati descriptions of the event found in local gazetteers or memoirs, which were many times compiled years after the event. These private accounts can be powerful verifiers of the official accounts.

CLASSIFYING PROTEST EVENTS

In this study, I classify the documented protest events into different types according to their claims and repertoires. A protest's claim is a set of articulated demands advanced by the participants. The repertoire of a protest is the set of learned or invented acts that the protesters performed to attract the attention of potential participants and the authorities, as well as to persuade or force the authorities to meet their demands (cf. Tilly 1993, 264).

One way to classify protest claims is the classical reactive-proactive typology devised by Charles Tilly (1978).[4] Reactive protests are defensive and backward looking, aimed at protecting the preexisting rights of protesters. They are usually actions that a social group undertakes to resist the actions of another powerful group. In the literature, reactive protests that drew the most attention included tax riots, in which grassroots communities resisted new claims on their resources by the state, villagers' protection of their customary ownership of local natural resources against appropriation by outside merchants or the state, and food riots, in which grassroots communities forcefully interrupted merchants' purchase of local grains for sale.

Proactive protests are forward-looking actions that call for new rights or the extension of existing rights. Protesters ask a dominant group to advance their interests, such as a demonstration to demand more popular participation in the government decision-making process, protests that seek wider and prompter provision of welfare from the state, and strikes in which workers collectively request a pay increase.

This reactive-proactive classification is useful, but it cannot be directly applied to this study. While Tilly's original study includes not only protests directed at the state but also collective actions that targeted other elite groups such as landlords and capitalists, my study focuses primarily on protests aimed at the state. I therefore modify Tilly's classification slightly to typologize documented protests as *state engaging* and *state resisting*. State-engaging protesters aim to request new rights or the extension of existing rights through influencing state policies and actions or seizing state functions and power. State-resisting protests aim to stop the state from infringing on protesters' rights over particular resources or activities by thwarting certain actions of the state. Under this modified classification, some types of conflicts that are covered in Tilly's study and other historical studies of Chinese contentions, such as food riots, labor strikes, and feuds (see Hung 2008, 578–582; Perdue 1986; Wong 1982; Wu 1996, chap. 4), are included in this study only when these conflicts developed into protests directed at the government. Cases in which the conflicting parties fought off government agents attempting to suppress the conflicts are classified as state-resisting protests, while those in which either of the parties sought government intervention in the conflict to their benefit are classified as state engaging.

Regarding protest repertoires, I categorize protests that involve physical assault of human subjects or property on the part of protesters as violent ones and those that do not involve any such assault as nonviolent. Protest events that involve both violent and nonviolent acts simultaneously are classified as violent. For example, a protest that started as a peaceful petition but ended with protestors' violence against government agents dispatched to quell the event is classified as violent. Only events without any violent acts throughout are classified as nonviolent. As the use of violence was an indicator of the protest participants' disposition toward the state and was a key determinant of punishment, description of violent acts usually was an important component of the government's report and would not be missed.

In creating the catalog of protest events from the QSL, I looked for the following information: (1) what the protesters demanded, (2) what actions were involved in the course of the event, and (3) in what locality and in what year the event occurred. All three types of information are available for most of the documented events, and the information is often unambiguous for coding purposes. But there are a few cases with partially missing or ambiguous information. Those cases are excluded from certain parts of the analysis but not others, depending on which types of information are missing.

The following are examples of how I coded documented events based on QSL passages with full and missing/ambiguous information.

Example 1: "In Yangqu county of Shanxi, peasant Zhao Jinyi complained about heavy taxation and gathered several hundred people to attack the provincial government building with catapults and throw their farming tools at it" (QSL-DG 213, 26–27; my translation). This entry, though brief, conveys all the information I need to know in an unambiguous way. It is a state-resisting and violent protest occurring in Yangqu county in Taiyuan prefecture in Shanxi in 1832.

Example 2: "Fujianese are known for their propensity to protest. For example, during the drought in the province last year, many local residents rallied to perform religious rituals and pray. Many of them took off their hat, held ropes in their hand, marched and chanted slogans along the street. When the local government eventually opened its granary to offer discounted grain sale, they competed with one another to purchase the grains in a disorderly manner" (QSL-QL 162, 12; my translation). In this case, we do not know in which prefecture of Fujian the event occurred, so I cannot include it when mapping the geographical distribution of protest. I can, nonetheless, still include this case in delineating the temporal trajectory of protest by treating it as an incident of state-engaging, nonviolent protest in the year 1742. In the description above, no act of physical violence is mentioned. However, the entry does not clearly say what the participants in the slogan-chanting march and the religious rituals were asking for. Since the incident occurred in the context of a drought and an eventual sale of official grains is mentioned, I infer that this is a protest requesting government relief. This inference is also supported by our established knowledge (from the literature and from other cases) that religious rituals were often used in relief-seeking protest to put pressure on local government (see the next chapter).

Example 3: "Regarding the case of crowd disturbance at the government office of the Xuancheng county of Anhui, an edict has been issued to urge for serious investigation" (QSL-QL 238, 7; my translation). In this case, we know that a protest occurred in Xuancheng county of Ningguo prefecture of Anhui around April 1745, the date corresponding to the documentation (all dates and months mentioned in this study are based on the lunar calendar). I can therefore include this case in mapping the geographical and temporal distribution of the total number of protest events. But there is no hint of what the protest was about and what particular actions were involved (crowd disturbance at the government office, or *juzhong hongtang*, is too general a term to suggest anything). This case is therefore excluded from the analysis of the distribution of claims and repertoires of protest events.

Equipped with the above schema of classification, I outline below the changing macropattern of mid-Qing protest documented in this study, starting with an overview of late Ming and early Qing protests based on previous studies.

FROM LATE MING TO MID-QING PROTEST

Though the late Ming state was dysfunctional in the late sixteenth and early seventeenth centuries because of factional struggles and external war, it heralded centralizing reforms such as simplification of the taxation system into a silver standard, tax increases aimed at enlarging the share of state revenue in the commercializing economy, and tightening control over the private academies thriving in southern metropolises. Plentiful works about social unrest in the late Ming period show that besides banditry and peasant uprisings, reactive violence such as communal tax riots and resistance against corrupt and tyrannical officials proliferated. Many of these resistances were invoked by the centralizing thrust of the state, which increased the government's direct intrusion into local societies. State centralization and the corresponding reactive protests persisted into the early part of the Qing dynasty. Resistance against tax levies, corrupt officials, and the expanding government regulation of local life (such as the imposed adoption of the Manchu hairstyle) continued to be salient themes of protest in the late seventeenth and early eighteenth centuries. Some of these protests, influenced by the oppositional ideologies of the time (resentment against the eunuch influence in the imperial court in the late Ming period and anti-Manchuism in the early years of Qing rule), developed into armed uprisings against the ruling dynasty (Rowe 2007, part 1; von Glahn 1991; Wakeman 1988; Wu 1996; Yuan 1979).

According to a quantitative survey of urban unrest covering the late Ming and early Qing periods, popular protests directed at the state were predominantly reactive, or state resisting, during the seventeenth and early eighteenth centuries. They mainly consisted of resistance against taxes, specific government officials (who embezzled public funds or cracked down on literati activities, for example), and unpopular government policies (such as a new rule restricting private business). Proactive or state-engaging protests, in which protesters asked for government actions such as famine relief, constituted only a slim portion of all documented events. Although that survey does not provide sufficient information about how many of these state-resisting protests were violent, detailed case investigations in it do show that violence against agents of the state was routine (Wu 1996, 142–145, 240–244; see also Tong 1991; Yuan 1979).

Despite the prevalence of state-resisting, violent, urban protest throughout the seventeenth and early eighteenth centuries, as documented in the

TABLE 2.2 Composition of Major Urban Protests in Late Ming and Early Qing China, 1600–1739

	1600–1644 (%)	1645–1699 (%)	1700–1739 (%)
State resisting	**94.6**	**78.5**	**63.6**
Tax resistance	59.5	21.4	19.2
Resistance against officials or policies	35.1	57.1	44.4
State engaging	**5.4**	**21.4**	**36.4**
Workers in state mill requesting wage increase	2.7	7.1	3.0
Requesting retention of dismissed local officials	2.7	7.1	15.2
Asking for famine relief	0	7.1	9.1
Asking for policy implementation	0	0	9.1

Note: Total number of documented events: 187 (Wu 1996, appendix 2).

above table, we can observe a gradual decline in state-resisting protests and an increase in state-engaging ones during this period, concomitant with the growing physical and ideological domination of the Qing state.[5] This trend coincides with the transition from predominantly reactive to predominantly proactive protests in seventeenth- and eighteenth-century Europe, whence centralized state power was continuously rising.

As such, the starting point of this research—the 1740s—is near the peak of centralizing state power and state-engaging protest in the Qing dynasty. We saw in the previous chapter that the centralized power of the Qing state declined in the late eighteenth and early nineteenth centuries. One wonders whether the rise of proactive or state-engaging protest is irreversible despite declining state power, as the unilinear overtones of the theory of protest development seem to suggest, or whether it will change with the reversal of centralized state power. I answer this question by systematically surveying and analyzing all documented protest events in my catalog.

A brief overview of all documented events for 1740–1839 shows that certain claims of protests prevailed. The most common claims found in state-engaging protest include (1) a request for state famine relief amid a subsistence crisis, or a request of increased speed and scope of already pledged relief; (2) a request for popular participation in governmental decisions such as the demotion or promotion of officials, strategies for managing the local dike system, and the planning of the construction of public facilities; and (3) a request for state intervention in social conflicts revolving around such issues as the distribution of local grain supplies. The most common claims among state-resisting protest include (1) retribution against particularly abusive or corrupt officials and against implementation of unpopular policies; (2) tax resistance; (3) resistance to regulation of or crackdown on illicit activities such as an unsanctioned opera show, production of private salt, and banditry; and (4) resistance to government intervention in local social conflicts such as feuds and class warfare.

Likewise, a limited range of repertoires prevailed throughout mid-Qing China and transgressed regional boundaries. Common nonviolent actions include (1) rallies and demonstrations in front of a government office, (2) petitions to higher-level authorities by visiting higher-level government offices or intercepting officials on tour, and (3) market strikes, in which local merchants shut down their businesses simultaneously in protest. Common violent tactics include (1) ransacking a government building or official's residence, (2) collective attacks on or murder of officials perceived as the source of local injustices, and (3) armed blockades of local communities against intrusion by government agents. While each protest event usually corresponds to only one type of claim, it was commonplace for protesters to employ combinations of several repertoires in a single protest event.

Table 2.3 shows that there were more state-resisting protests than state-engaging ones in the whole mid-Qing period, from 1740 to 1839.

To analyze the documented events further, I trace the temporal distribution of all protests and find that they are not distributed evenly over the period but are clustered into three waves, the first wave in c. 1740–1759, the second in c. 1776–1795, and the last in c. 1820–1839 (see fig. 2.2).

This temporal clustering is not likely to be a result of the bias of the source. As discussed earlier, the most plausible bias of the documentation of protest is that local officials might report protests to the center more thoroughly when the imperial center was more activist and more demanding of local officials, and they might be more prone to underreporting protests at times of low political energy at the center. This bias is implausible. If it were the case, then we should not have seen a peak of documented protest in the

TABLE 2.3 Composition of Documented Protests with Known Claims, 1740–1839

Claims	Percentage	Claims	Percentage
State engaging	**35.3**	**State resisting**	**64.7**
Seeking famine relief	14.0	Retributions against policies or officials	11.2
Seeking participation in state decision-making process	15.3	Resisting crackdown on illicit activities	28.9
Seeking state intervention in social conflicts	2.7	Resisting tax levy	16.1
Seizing state functions	3.3	Resisting state intervention into social conflicts	8.5

Note: Events with known claims: 484; events with unknown claims: 30.

late Qianlong reign in the 1780s, and the level of documented protests should have been higher during the Jiaqing reign, from 1796 to 1820.

These three waves neatly match the three subperiods of mid-Qing China that I demarcated in the last chapter. The first wave was in the mid-eighteenth century, when centralized state power was at its peak, the commercial economy thrived, and the state's moral legitimacy was high. The second wave corresponds to the late eighteenth century, when centralized state power was declining, the commercial economy continued to thrive, and the moral legitimacy of the state had crumbled. The third wave corresponds to the early nineteenth-century conjuncture, when state power continued to slide, the commercial economy started to contract, but the state's moral legitimacy was restored.

Figure 2.3 shows how the general forms and contents of protest changed during the mid-Qing period. In this figure, the 1740–1759 wave stands out as the only one in which state-engaging, nonviolent protests prevailed over state-resisting violence. In the other two waves, as well as the in-between periods, state-resisting violence prevailed.

To take a closer look, I adopt the classification of different state-engaging and state-resisting claims as used in table 2.3 to compare the three waves of protests. Figure 2.4 shows that a large percentage of protests in the first wave involved requests for the fulfillment or enlargement of the state's paternalist obligations during subsistence crises and the arbitration of social conflicts by the state. In the second wave, resistance against government repression of illicit economic activities in local communities, together with tax resistance, prevailed. In the third wave, state-resisting protests continued to be dominant, and resistance against state repression of illicit activities slightly declined in salience, whereas tax resistance and retributive actions against officials grew.

Combining the above observation with the established knowledge about changing protest patterns in the late Ming and early Qing periods as outlined earlier, and juxtaposing the characteristics of different waves of protest with the changing political, economic, and cultural constellations of the Qing times, we can readily infer that the rising salience of state-engaging,

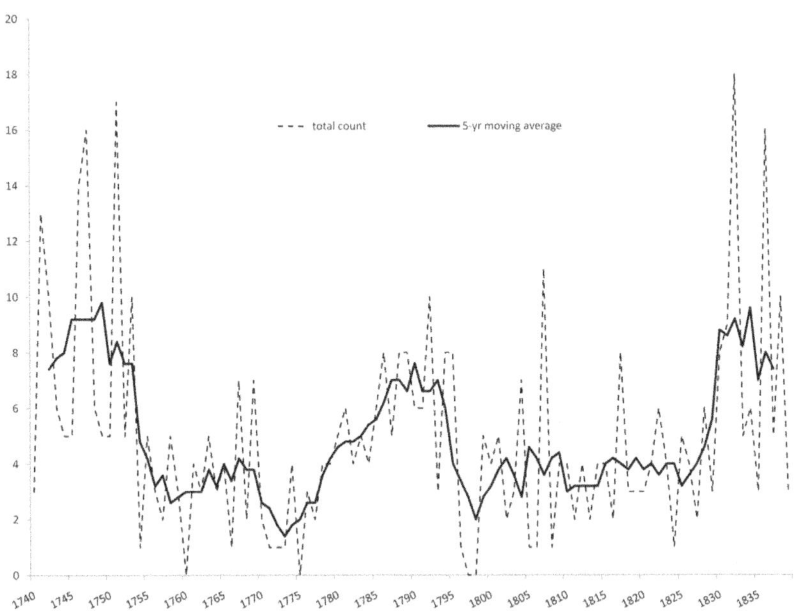

FIGURE 2.2 Temporal Distribution of Documented Protests, 1740–1839

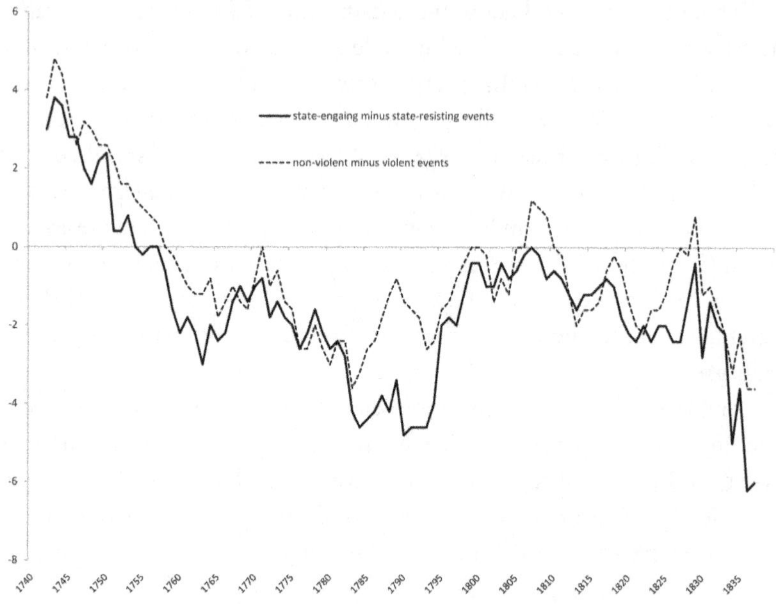

FIGURE 2.3 State-Engaging/Nonviolent Protests in Excess of State-Resisting/Violent Protests (five-year moving average)

nonviolent protests from the late seventeenth to the mid-eighteenth century was a response to the increasing capacity and consolidating Confucianist hegemony of the state. The state's capacity to provide, under the rubric of paternalist care, social and economic support to its subjects increased. Likewise, the subjects' expectation of such care mounted. This salience is reversible. In the late eighteenth and early nineteenth centuries, the predominance of nonviolent, state-engaging protests declined, and violent resistance surged as a reaction to the coercive appropriation by the state and its falling hegemonic persuasion as well as declining capacity to provide public goods. In this period, the state desperately competed with local communities for local resources in the context of population explosion and, in the case of the early nineteenth century, depression of the commercial economy.

The above observation is, of course, little more than a rough sketch of the changing protest patterns in mid-Qing China. It is too broad to shed light on how exactly the changing political, economic, and cultural contexts shaped protest claims and repertoires. To address this issue, we need to delve into the details of representative events in each of the three waves of protests. The questions that we must ask are as follows: What specific demands were the protesters making in the three waves of protest? What particular strategies did they employ, and what identities did they present in their interaction with the state? How exactly did the changing political economy of the empire and moral legitimacy of the state shape the strategic choices and identities of the protesters? How did the protests in the three waves relate to other types of unrest or more institutionalized practices, such as class conflicts, rebellions, and capital appeals?

These are the questions that guide my investigation in the next three chapters, in which I complement the macroanalysis of the documented events with thick descriptions of thirty-two cases of protest covering the three waves.

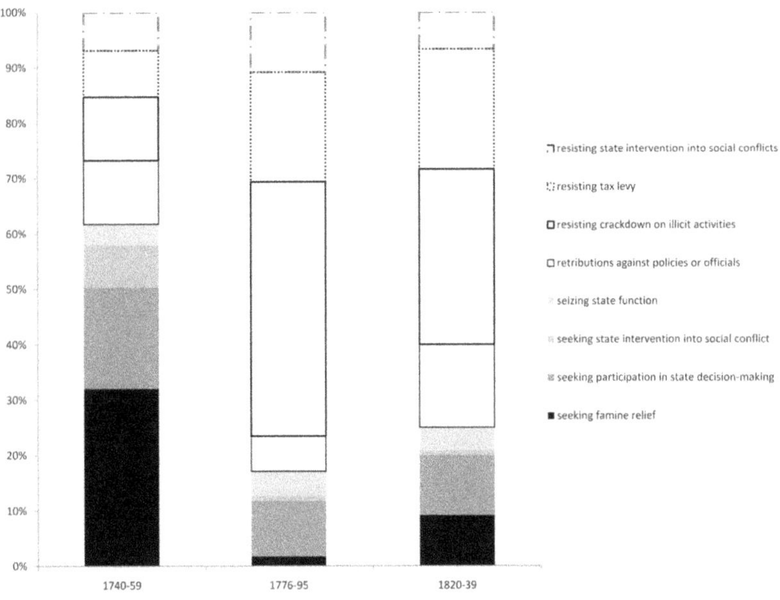

FIGURE 2.4 CHANGING COMPOSITION OF DOCUMENTED PROTESTS WITH KNOWN CLAIMS, 1740–1839 (SHADED BLOCKS: STATE-ENGAGING PROTEST; UNSHADED BLOCKS: STATE-RESISTING PROTEST)

3

FILIAL-LOYAL DEMONSTRATIONS, 1740–1759

The early Qianlong reign, in the mid-eighteenth century, saw the continuation of the thrust of political centralization, which was partly attributable to the empire's war-making activities against ethnic Tibetans in its southwestern frontiers in Sichuan and against the Muslims along its northwestern frontier. Centralized state power was at its apogee by the end of the 1750s, at the moment when the Qing state pacified its northwestern and southwestern frontiers. Commercial expansion in the wake of economic liberalization and reform in the early eighteenth century also continued into the 1740s and 1750s. At the same time, the young Qianlong emperor was at least as rigorous as his father in consolidating the hegemony of the neo-Confucianist orthodoxy and advancing the moral legitimacy of the imperial center.

In this context of centralizing state power, thriving commerce, and the high moral legitimacy of the state, protesters in 1740–1759 shifted from state-resisting violence, which prevailed in the seventeenth and early eighteenth centuries, to state-engaging protests. They either requested action of the state, which appeared to be irrevocably expanding and capable of offering public goods, or attempted to shape state action in their favor. Table 3.1 shows that state-engaging protests constituted 61.4 percent of all documented events in the period, a big surge from the 36.4 percent in 1700–1739 and 21.4 percent in 1645–1699. These state-engaging protests consisted mainly of (1) protests that sought paternalist care from the state, such as famine relief amid a local subsistence crisis; (2) protests that sought to influence specific government policies or decisions, such as asking local government to retain a beloved official or sack a hated one; and (3) protests that solicited state support to resolve ongoing or potential social conflicts, such as tenant cultivators asking the local government to impose rent reduction on their landowners. While the last category of protest was only a small percentage, it was much higher in this period than in any other waves of pro-

TABLE 3.1 Composition of Documented Protests with Known Claims, 1700–1739 and 1740–1759

Claim	1645–1699 (%)	1700–1739 (%)	1740–1759 (%)
State engaging	**21.4**	**36.4**	**61.4**
Seeking famine relief			31.8
Seeking participation in state decision-making process			18.2
Seeking state intervention into social conflict			7.6
Seizing state functions			3.8
State resisting	**78.5**	**63.6**	**38.7**
Redistributions against policies or officials			11.4
Resisting crackdown on illicit activities			11.4
Resisting tax levy			9.1
Resisting state intervention into social conflict			6.8
Total	**100**	**100**	**100**

Note: Events for 1740–1759 with known claims: 132; events with unknown claims: 14; events for 1645–1699 and 1700–1739 based on table 2.2.

test, as we see in the coming two chapters. There were also a small number of events with protesters seizing state functions, for example, famine victims taking control of public granaries and disbursing the grain themselves.

Most state-resisting protests in this period involved tax resistance or retribution against particular policies or officials. There were cases in which practitioners of illicit activities, such as private minters of copper cash, resisted governmental crackdowns, as well as incidents in which participants in social conflicts such as feuds, fought off agents of the state dispatched to halt the mayhem. These state-resisting protests, however, were less prominent in this period than in other periods.

TABLE 3.2 List of Cases Included for Thick Description, 1740–1759

Issue	Province	Type	Page
1. Mobilizing women to request famine relief	Jiangsu	state engaging	72
2. Cross-regional relief-seeking mobilization employing city gods	Jiangsu	state engaging	74
3. Petitioning the touring emperor for famine relief	Henan	state engaging	76
4. Literati mobilizing workers and retailers for relief	Jiangsu	state engaging	78
5. Rallying for rerouting of canal water	Jiangsu	state engaging	80
6. Demonstration for monastery refurbishment	Jiangsu	state engaging	82
7. Coordinated petition to save a Buddhist sect leader	Jiangsu	state engaging	83
8. Mobilization to protect a popular official from dismissal	Zhejiang	state engaging	85
9. Rallying for and against governmental price control	Jiangsu	state engaging	87
10. Seeking government-imposed rent reduction	Jiangsu	state engaging	90
11. Fighting state repression of rent resistance	Fujian	state resisting	93
12. Tax resistance	Shanxi	state resisting	95

Regarding protest repertoires, only 34.2 percent of all known cases involved violence against governmental agents or property. In all other cases, protesters employed peaceful means exclusively, many times to plead for the attention and benevolence of the authorities. One of the most common acts was a popular rally in front of a government office, with representatives (usually local literati) presenting written petitions to local magistrates. Protesters also frequently devised innovative means to attract support from bystanders or to impress on the authorities their filial loyalty to the state. One example is public and symbolic displays of misery through self-inflicted injuries. Another common repertoire, *guixiang*, involved kneeling and holding glowing incense in front of the magistrate's office, just as believers did in a temple when begging for the mercy of a local god. More disruptive actions were not unheard of. One example is a market strike, a novel and popular tactic in the mid-Qing period, one rarely found in earlier times (Rosner 1987). In a market strike, local retailers stalled the local economy by shutting down their businesses in concert to ensure that the authorities would pay attention to their demands.

In what follows, I delve into the strategies, ideologies, and collective identities underlying the wave of protest in 1740–1759 by examining the details of select episodes of each of the three common types of state-engaging protests—protests seeking paternalist care from the state, attempting to shape governmental decisions, and requesting governmental intervention in social conflicts—as well as two cases of state-resisting protest (see table 3.2).

I select cases that are typical rather than exceptional and that are well documented in the archival materials. Most of the selected cases are from Jiangsu province, which is a reflection of the geographical distribution of all documented protests for the period, as we will see later in this chapter.

SEEKING PATERNALIST CARE FROM THE STATE

With the state's acclaimed paternalist obligation to its subjects and its elevated fiscal capacity in the wake of the centralizing reforms of the 1720s and 1730s, its subjects naturally expected that the state *should* and *could* come to their rescue when they were devastated by a subsistence crisis caused either by natural calamity or by a steep rise in food prices. The salience of popular protests that sought state intervention for food relief in the mid-eighteenth century is not surprising.

The following cases show that repertoires employed by relief-seeking protesters across the empire were largely similar. This similarity is, in part, a result of the heavy involvement of local literati elites as key organizers in many of these events. As we have seen in chapter 1, local literati in Qing times were cosmopolitan elites whose long-term participation in the imperial examination system cultivated cross-regional intellectual affinity, cultural assimilation, and social connections among themselves. In many cases, protest participants mobilized by the literati elite came from diverse socioeconomic backgrounds, presenting themselves as universal imperial subjects equally entitled to the same paternalist care from the state. Though there were occasional cases in which protesters resorted to antagonistic or even violent action to put pressure on local authorities, protesters in most cases deliberately manifested their filial loyalty toward the government. By performing symbolic acts to express how pitiful and nonthreatening they were, the protesters projected themselves as loyal, docile subjects of the imperial state, their benevolent patriarch.

One common strategy to display the protesters' docility was to mobilize female participants, as they were often regarded as weaker and less aggressive subjects and motivated by desires to ensure their families' survival rather than by any malicious ambitions. The following incident is a case in point.

MOBILIZING WOMEN TO REQUEST FAMINE RELIEF[1]

In the fall of 1755, a large area of the Lower Yangzi Region was flooded. Local governments sent investigators to assess the damage and disburse famine relief accordingly. But for inhabitants in areas deemed unaffected by the calamity and hence ineligible for relief, life became difficult as well. Although their regions had not been directly flooded, grain shortages in adjacent flooded areas sent local grain prices to sky-high levels.

Finding local grain unaffordable, a large group of women from Jinshachang, in Tongzhou of Jiangsu province, gathered in front of the county office. They knelt on both knees and pleaded for disbursal of governmental relief. They claimed that their families were on the brink of starvation because of the escalating grain prices, even though their homes and fields had not been flooded. Getting no response from the government, the women entered the lobby of the building. To prevent any confrontation or violence, government runners swiftly arrested six women who had led the others through the entrance. The rest of the women fled immediately. After a lengthy interrogation, the magistrate found that the women should not be held responsible for their actions, as they were just "ignorant wives" manipulated by their husbands, who had organized the petition from behind the scenes. The women were pardoned and released, but men identified as the petition's initiators were arrested and subjected to corporal punishment. After the report of this incident reached the provincial government, the governor accused the local magistrate of aloofness to the petitioners' legitimate demands. Claiming that the local government could have handled the event better had it conceded to the petitioning women, the governor dismissed the magistrate from his office.

In many other documented petitions in which women were mobilized to seek famine relief, the government did yield to popular demand or was at least reluctant to respond in repressive ways. For example, in 1746, the Huai'an and Xuzhou areas of northern Jiangsu were flooded.[2] The local government offered food relief to affected poor households, and it adopted a ten-grade system to determine the amount of relief for which each household was eligible. Under this system, households with tenth-grade poverty could obtain the largest amount of relief; those with first-grade poverty could obtain the least. In the fall, women from ninth-grade poor households in many places petitioned simultaneously in front of their respective local government offices, in some cases blocking the entrances, to complain about the relief's inadequacy and to ask for more. A high-rank Manchu official of Jiangsu province, Gu Cong (who had been the provincial governor and became the hydraulic director of Jiangnan region that year), sympathized with the petitioners and drafted a memorial to the emperor to ask for permission to meet their demands. He reasoned that the living conditions of ninth-grade and tenth-grade households were very similar, yet the difference in relief quantities for the two was huge, amounting to one full month of grain consumption for an average household. He suggested that the ninth-graders should receive extra relief amounting to a half-month of grain consumption per household. The Qianlong emperor replied that giving in to petitioners' demands might encourage others to protest but that the petitioning women also seemed to have a legitimate case. Qianlong therefore instructed Gu, in collaboration with other high-rank officials in the province, to investigate the cause of their complaints and to see whether local officials were embezzling relief. Qianlong also authorized these provincial-level officials to adjust the relief amount according to the result of their investigation.

There were also cases in which local governments dispersed women petitioners by simply offering what they demanded without even asking for permission from higher-level officials or the emperor.[3] Though the emperor usually blamed local officials for being too soft on the petitioning subjects, he seldom mentioned the need to resort to repression in dealing with women petitioners. This is in contrast to many male-dominated cases of protest and petitions, which provoked a tougher response from the state, as we will see.

In the above events, women petitioners were mostly from lower strata of the local society. In the next case, the initiators of the protest belonged to a nationally renowned scholarly family with members serving in the most senior bureaucratic posts. They were so well connected and resourceful that they managed to organize concerted demonstrations at different urban centers across a large area by attracting residents from all walks of life, rich and poor alike.

CROSS-REGIONAL RELIEF-SEEKING MOBILIZATION EMPLOYING CITY GODS[4]

In the summer of 1742, continuous rain overflowed many local lakes, rivers, and canals in the highly urbanized and commercialized Yangzhou region. Vast paddy fields were flooded. The Gaoyou and Baoying counties of Yangzhou prefecture and Huai'an prefecture, in northern Jiangsu, were the most severely affected. In response, local governments conducted careful surveys to estimate the extent of devastation in different areas and deliberated on famine-relief and flood-diversion plans.

The government's actions were too slow for the anxious and agitated local population. Local elites, identified by the government as "capable families in the cities" (*zaicheng jumin, youli zhi jia*) and "literati and wealthy families" (*shenjin zhi jia*), organized a wave of concurrent demonstrations at the Gaoyou and Baoying county seats and at the prefecture's capital, Huai'an. It was found that protests in the Gaoyou county seat were initiated by a few licentiates, while those of the Baoying county seat were organized by fellow clansmen of Liu Shishu, a grand secretariat academician of the central government at the time. Protest leaders in the Huai'an city, though not clearly identified in government documents, were also "beyond the rank of common residents" (*bujin shi baixing*). Participants included all types of residents in the area. They requested the termination of the overly slow government survey and the immediate beginning of "universal relief" (*puzhen*), which would disburse official grain to all local residents in all areas, regardless of how much their homes were affected by the flood. Market strikes and rallies in front of government offices were staged.

Accompanying these confrontational acts targeted at local officials were performances through which protesters symbolically invoked higher authorities to put pressure on the local government. Protesters took the statue of a local city god from the temple and conducted religious rites at the rallies. In Qing times, local city gods occupied a special place in the symbolic universe of the political hierarchy. These gods were all sanctioned by the emperor, and they were symbols of the highest imperial authorities in the local area. Local officials routinely led residents in paying tribute to the city god during different festivals throughout the year. As a gesture to assure that their governance abided by the Mandate of Heaven, local magistrates even arbitrated the most serious criminal cases, announced important policy, or held consultative meetings with local literati in the city god's temple, under the gaze of the god's statue (Duara 1988; Wu 2000; Zito 1987). Viewed in this light, invoking the city god in a protest was tantamount to invoking the imperial center. The use of local-god statues and religious rites in protest was so common that the Qianlong emperor once anxiously suggested that local officials should preempt their actions by promptly organizing public prayer at the temple of state-sanctioned local god whenever a subsistence crisis precipitated (QSL-QL 303, 6–7).

In this episode, the emperor stepped in to resolve the conflict in the protesters' favor. In an edict addressing the protests, the Qianlong emperor blamed local officials for their failure in properly educating the local elite. He held these officials accountable for the recalcitrance of the local literati and demoted a number of local officials overseeing education and examination affairs. He also sent a special "consolation and education envoy" (*xuanyu huadao shi*) from Beijing to soothe the protesters. Under pressure from the central government, the local government also declared a universal famine relief. The emperor fretted that "if this kind of action was initiated by common residents, it is understandable, as they can claim that their action is urged by hunger and ignorance, but now it is the wealthy, well-educated literati families with no urgent needs who mobilized malicious commoners to contend. . . . It is definitely unforgivable." But in the end, he recommended no specific penalty for the protest organizers. Liu Shishu, however, was accused of being incapable of restraining his fellow clansmen and was demoted from his post of grand secretariat.

In this case, protesters elicited the symbolic authority of the emperor through the use of the city god's statue to put pressure on local officials. In the next case, protesters attempted to solicit the sympathy of the real emperor by petitioning for famine relief directly in front of the imperial procession.

PETITIONING THE TOURING EMPEROR FOR FAMINE RELIEF[5]

In the spring of 1757, the Qianlong emperor went on an inspection tour in the area at the borders of Shandong, Jiangsu, and Henan Provinces to oversee the river works. As he was about to leave Xuzhou in Jiangsu province, Zhang Qin, a commoner from Xiayi county in Henan, knelt in front of his imperial procession. He explained that his county and three others in the vicinity had been seriously flooded the year before. Despite an earlier imperial edict instructing local governments to waive taxes and deliver famine relief, local officials asserted that these areas were not flooded seriously enough to deserve any government relief. Zhang accused the county magistrate of embezzling the relief fund allocated from higher-level authorities. When the emperor traveled to Zou county in Shandong, he encountered another petitioner from Xiayi county who made the same complaint.

The people in Xiayi must have petitioned the local government for famine relief for months in vain, otherwise they would not have resorted to the risky act of intercepting the imperial procession. Such an attempt could lead to the petitioner's decapitation, as dictated by Qing law. Fortunately, Qianlong was not infuriated by the petition, but neither was he sympathetic to the petitioners. Right after the incident, Qianlong issued an edict to reject the petitioner's request, on April 9:

> County magistrates are the parents of the commoners. [Commoners] complaining about their magistrate is like children pointing fingers at their parents. I therefore cannot respond to their one-sided complaint favorably, otherwise it will set a malign example for them to blackmail local officials. It is just like a grandfather, despite his love of his grandchildren, should not bestow his grandchildren with excessive love and make them disrespect their father. (SYD–QL3, 28–9; my translation)

Qianlong's statement is remarkable, as it explicitly analogizes the relations among the emperor, local officials, and subjects to the relations among grandfather, father, and children. In most other cases, this filial conception of political hierarchy was implicit.

The emperor's rejection of the appeal apparently left his conscience uneasy. On April 18, he issued another edict, admitting that he could not stop thinking of the suffering of the Xiayi people after witnessing the misery of the poor along his inspection tour. He then sent a central-government official in his company to travel clandestinely to Xiayi and investigate what was actually going on there. The special agent shocked the emperor by reporting that the poor residents of Xiayi were hit so hard by the famine that they had started selling their children for as low as four hundred *wen* of copper cash per boy. Deeply disturbed, Qianlong revoked his rejection of the petitioners' appeals and ordered immediate relief for the area. The provincial governor of Henan and the county magistrate of Xiayi, together with another magistrate nearby, were held responsible for the people's plight and stripped of all official titles. The provincial governor was even banished to the empire's western frontier to serve the army indefinitely.

This apparent happy ending, however, was followed by a horrific twist. The sacked provincial governor colluded with his protégés still working in the lower levels of government in the area to arrest two literati from Xiayi who had raised funds for and helped organize the petition. Local government agents conducted a comprehensive search of their homes and claimed to find a military seal from a general who had rebelled against Qing rule in the seventeenth century. The alleged discovery of a stream of anti-Manchu writings in the area soon followed.

The charge that these relief-seeking petitioners were motivated by an anti-Manchu conspiracy sounded absurd. But presented with the evidence prepared (and possibly planted) by the local officials, Qianlong was pressured to prioritize a display of his will to defend Manchu rule over the demonstration of his grandfatherly love for the famine victims. He swiftly restored the titles of the penalized local officials and ordered them to arrest, prosecute, and execute the suspected participants in the putative conspiracy. The network of literati and commoners who participated in the petition to the emperor was persecuted as anti-Manchu rebels.

This case, together with the previous two cases, shows that state-engaging protesters, usually under the leadership of local literati, employed the language and symbols of the Confucianist orthodoxy to articulate their claims as humble requests for the state's fulfillment of its paternalist obligation. They were careful to make their case in a docile manner, just as children pleaded for the loving care of their patriarch. The following case further illustrates how exactly local literati mobilized commoners from diverse socioeconomic backgrounds to seek universal famine relief from the government.

LITERATI MOBILIZING WORKERS AND RETAILERS FOR RELIEF[6]

In the autumn of 1746, prolonged rain led to a considerable increase in the water level in the Shandong section of the Grand Canal. Because of the canal's heavy traffic, dredging work had been unable to keep up with the accumulation of silt, and the rising water level upstream caused extensive flooding downstream, within the Xuzhou and Haizhou areas of northern Jiangsu. The flood in Suqian county, located right at the intersection of the Grand Canal and the Yellow River, was particularly serious. The autumn harvest was devastated, and a hike in grain prices ensued. But there was no sign that the government was about to offer relief.

In the county seat of Suqian, Wang Yuying, a disqualified licentiate, invited a number of his literati friends to draft a petition asking for immediate and universal famine relief. They presented the petition to the county magistrate, only to have their request denied. The magistrate posted a public notice asking his fellow subjects to wait patiently for relief while the government surveyed the impact of the flood on different areas. Infuriated by what was seen as an excuse for not offering relief, Wang drafted three posters calling for a market strike and placed them on three city walls. In the early morning of August 1, just before the time when retailers around the gate opened their booths, Wang went to the city's east gate, where hundreds of jobless vagrants lined up for employment opportunities every dawn, to call for action. The job-seeking workers echoed Wang's call for prompt universal relief, and a rally instantly materialized. They repeatedly yelled "Market strike!" (*bashi*) to ask the incoming retailers to show their support and close their businesses for the day. Some even attempted to forcefully deter the retailers from opening their shops.

Wang was arrested right away. Local officials as well as the governor of Jiangsu thought that his offense was minor. They intended to charge him with "futile initiation of market strike" (*bashi weicheng*) and "blackmailing government officials" (*xiezhi guanli*) and to banish him to the western borderland of the empire as punishment. But the incident captured the attention of Qianglong, who thought that Wang should be charged with "insurrection in action" (*moushi yicheng*) and decapitated immediately. It is not known why Qianlong decided to take such a tough stance on this event, which was not particularly offensive in comparison to the numerous other protests that year. The frequent outbreaks of protest in 1746 might have made the emperor judge this arbitrarily chosen case in the harshest possible manner as a lesson to other potential protesters. The unusual volume of intrabureaucratic communication regarding Wang's penalty and the apparent disagreement between local officials and the emperor suggest that this draconian punishment was more an exception than the norm.

To summarize, all of the above protests (and most other documented episodes that sought the paternalist care of the state) were triggered by the divergence between the authorities' propensity to offer paternalist relief to the neediest—that is, the poorest residents hit hardest by subsistence crises—on the one hand, and protesters' demand for universal relief—that is, relief disbursed to all residents in a large area regardless of their backgrounds and how hard they were hit—on the other. The state's preference for selective relief required it to conduct extensive surveys on the differential impacts of a subsistence crisis across different areas before any relief disbursal. Local authorities always justified this approach by citing limited government resources. On the contrary, the universal relief that protesters sought could be disbursed immediately and could reach everyone. These universal relief–seeking demonstrations, usually attended by residents excluded by the selective relief or those who could not wait for the completion of the time-consuming government survey, are comparable to contemporary social movements in which citizens excluded by a highly selective, means-tested welfare regime struggle for universal, equal-benefits-for-all welfare as their social right.

Protesters often justified their contentious claims by referring to the criteria of loving, capable paternalist officials as repeatedly highlighted by the emperor in his edicts. They attacked local officials for falling short of such criteria. The two most common accusations of local officials were that they were incompetent and slow in disbursing the famine relief authorized by higher-level officials and that they were corrupt and embezzled government relief funds that could otherwise be used for universal relief. These claims were often large enough to intimidate local officials, who were constantly scrutinized and pressured by the emperor from above. It explains why, in many cases, local governments simply accommodated the protesters' demands and did not resort to repression as their first response.

Other common features of relief-seeking protests include the frequent involvement of literati elites as organizers, who mobilized through such communicative means as posters on market walls to encourage more local residents to join. The contingently assembled group of protesters usually manifested the abstract identity of imperial subjects, who were entitled to the universal grace of the emperor and transgressed the everyday identities of the participants, be they retailers, vagrants, workers, or cultivators. This identity of imperial subjects was in line with the protesters' filial-loyal disposition toward the imperial state at large, though their acts toward individual officials might be confrontational. In the next few sections, we will see that these features were not unique to relief-seeking protests but also could be found in protests concerning other issues.

INFLUENCING GOVERNMENTAL DECISIONS

Pleading for relief from the state amid subsistence crises constituted the largest category of protest claims in the mid-eighteenth century. There were also many other protests aimed at shaping governmental actions and policies in other arenas. The first case below concerns how cultivators petitioned the local government and succeeded in making local officials reconsider a plan to reroute local canal water.

RALLYING FOR THE REROUTING OF CANAL WATER[7]

Around the lunar new year of 1741, intensive dredging in the canal networks used for salt transportation in Northern Jiangsu, a national hub of salt production and distribution, was conducted under the auspices of officials from the central government. After February 1741, it rained in areas north of the Yangzi River uninterruptedly, and the water level of the canal network rose so much that the dredging had to be suspended. To keep the work on schedule and to prevent any further disruption of salt transportation, the hydraulic director of Jiangnan, who oversaw water management in all of the Lower Yangzi Delta, suggested draining the excessive canal water into the Yangzi River by opening the Tangjia and Yancang dikes near the city of Tongzhou, which was located at the intersection of the Yangzi River and the canal. In the first few days of March, the weather improved, and local officials were about to open the dikes as planned.

The Tongzhou magistrate Wang Shidan, however, objected to the proposal and submitted an alternative plan in the name of local residents' interests. He argued that it would be dangerous to open the Yancang dike, located immediately west of the Tongzhou city, as the released water could become uncontrollable and threaten the city. He proposed directing all extra water to the city's eastern side and draining the water into the Yangzi River via the Tangjia dike only, which was thirteen miles east of Tongzhou city. To channel all of the water toward the Tangjia dike, Wang planned to construct two temporary dikes west and north of the Tongzhou city and to dig ditches to the city's immediate east. He also suggested that the water level in the canals should not be reduced by more than three feet, so that about five feet of water could be retained in the network and directed to the nearby paddy fields for irrigation.

The drainage was eventually carried out according to Wang's direction. But even though Wang claimed that his plan would benefit the local populace, it still met with opposition. Cultivators from the western suburb of the Tongzhou city complained that the plan would drain all water away from the areas to the east of the city and would lead to a drought in the paddy fields to the city's west during the spring, when irrigation water was desperately needed. The situation was particularly urgent because of the dry weather of the preceding few years. They feared that another drought would harm rice seedlings and threaten the autumn harvest.

On March 12, a large number of peasants from different villages in the western suburb of Tongzhou rallied on the western side of the Tongzhou city. They humbly petitioned for the dike not to be opened (*tongsheng huyu qiumian kaizha*) and for the water not to be drained to the east of the city. An initial report of the incident suggested that some retailers located near the rally echoed the petition and initiated a market strike. This report struck a nerve with higher-level officials, who would define the event as confrontational if a market strike was involved. They ordered a detailed investigation, and to their relief, they found that the retailers had just closed their shops temporarily for fear of violent disturbances during the rally. Reassured that it was no more than a humble petition by some "silly people" (*yumin*), the provincial government ordered the county government to pacify the protesters by promising a serious reconsideration of the plan and taking their demands into account. No arrest or any other suppression was recorded. Higher up in the bureaucracy, the governor-general of Jiangsu and Jiangxi did not blame the petitioners in his report that summarized the event to the emperor. He instead blamed Wang for putting forward his counterproposal in the name of the people without consulting local residents in advance.

In this case, protesters attempted to shape government action through a petition to safeguard their own interests. But material interest was not the only motivation for protesters. In the following case, a group of dedicated Buddhists petitioned for government permission for a fund-raising campaign for the refurbishment of a well-known monastery. They also sought to protect a highly respected monk from interrogation by the authorities.

DEMONSTRATION FOR MONASTERY REFURBISHMENT[8]

In the spring of 1744, Dong Wu, a Buddhist monk in Suzhou, initiated a fund-raising campaign for the refurbishment of the Hanshan monastery, a nationally renowned Buddhist institution located in the Fengqiao town, seven miles west of the city. It had been a historic pilgrimage site for Buddhists from all over the empire since around 510 C.E. The monastery, like all major religious institutions in the empire, was patronized by the Qing government, and any reconstruction project had to be overseen by the local government. Local officials suspected that Dong Wu might be organizing some sort of heterodox sect under the cover of the fund-raising campaign. They refused to endorse the refurbishing project, and they took Dong Wu to the county office on the west side of the Suzhou city for interrogation.

On February 12, when Dong Wu was questioned by the magistrate, two hundred petitioners in support of the refurbishment gathered outside the government building. In addition to dedicated believers, the protesters included local contractors who might benefit financially from the project. The demonstrators, despite their diverse backgrounds, were uniformly docile in their action, employing the *guixiang* repertoire of protest. They knelt and prayed with glowing incense in their hands and bowed in front of the magistrate office, treating him as a god and petitioning him in the way that believers prayed for fulfillment of their wishes in a temple.

The magistrate ignored the demonstration. When he lost his patience and began to torture Dong, the demonstrators foresaw that the government was going to reject the refurbishment proposal again. They dropped their incense and attempted to enter the office to make their case, only to be dispersed by the county clerks. This infuriated the protesters, who escalated their action into a confrontation. Remarkably, they cautiously directed their anger not at the authorities but at a former director of the temple, Jiang. The furious protesters believed that Jiang had used his personal influence to deter the local government from endorsing the refurbishment, because such a project would lead to a prolonged closing of the monastery to visitors and hurt the restaurant and souvenir businesses that he ran outside the monastery.

Blaming all wrongs on Jiang, the protesters marched more than seven miles from the county office to Jiang's residence, in the western suburb near the Hanshan monastery. They smashed the walls and doors of his residential compound. They also stormed the teahouses and restaurants around the monastery and called for a market strike, though their call was not echoed by many. The Suzhou prefecture government at last stepped in and swiftly ended the conflict. It arrested twenty protesters and released them after slight corporal punishment. It also expelled Dong Wu from Suzhou and sent him back to his home town, in the nearby Changzhou prefecture in Jiangsu.

In the above two cases, protesters' attempts to shape state action were directed at the lowest-level authorities. There were also cases in which protesters' claims were directed at the provincial government or even the imperial center. The first example of such a case involves a Buddhist sectarian community that asked the provincial government to lift a ban on their activities and release their leaders.

COORDINATED PETITION TO SAVE A BUDDHIST SECT LEADER[9]

In the autumn of 1746, provincial officials in Jiangsu reported that they had discovered a Buddhist organization named the Burning Lantern sect (*randeng jiao*) active in the prosperous Suzhou, Songjiang, and Changzhou prefectures. This discovery was in the midst of an empirewide search for rebellious sects following an abortive revolt plotted by a heterodox Buddhist sect, the Great Vehicle sect (*Dasheng jiao*), in the southwestern provinces of Sichuan and Yunnan, in the spring of 1746. At first, the government suggested that the Burning Lantern sect was a branch of the Great Vehicle sect and needed to be persecuted. A group of sect leaders from Taicang were arrested. But after initial investigation, they found the sect to be less suspicious than previously thought. Their activities involved no more than incense-burning rites and regular gatherings in which believers confessed their misdeeds. The sacred scrolls found in the sect's gathering halls were simply ethical doctrines urging the sectarians to lead a virtuous life and to avoid evil.

When the news of the arrest of the sect leaders spread around the area, sectarians organized a demonstration. Dozens of representatives from Jiading, Baoshan, Kunshan, and Qingpu counties of Suzhou and Songjiang prefectures formed a delegation and traveled to the Taicang city. They protested at the lobby of the local government, with glowing incense in their hands. They claimed that two of their arrested leaders, Mrs. Wang and her niece Ms. Zhou, were actually reincarnations of Buddha and Bodhisattva, respectively. The protesters requested that the authorities release their leaders immediately so that they could continue to serve and worship them. But the protesters soon learned that the local magistrate was out of town. They left and marched to the Suzhou area to intercept Jiangsu's provincial governor, who was on an agricultural-inspection tour in the city's suburb. The protesters lit their incense and knelt in front of the governor. They said that they had sold all of their property and donated all of their wealth when they joined the sect. Now that their leaders were arrested, they had to see them again. They were prepared to die for them.

This event attracted serious attention from the imperial center, as the speed and extent of the mobilization of sectarians from a vast area into such a coordinated petition surprised many officials. More important, the sectarians' knowledge of the whereabouts of the provincial governor during his inspection trip suggested that some provincial-government insiders must be among the sectarians. A thorough reinvestigation of the sect ensued.

Plausibly out of a fear of the sect's organizational power, the authorities did not yield to the petitioners' demand and redoubled their efforts to suppress the sect. Retracting the favorable conclusion of their previous investigation, official investigators suddenly claimed to find among the sect's sacred scrolls a script written by Zhang Baotai, a leader of an aborted heterodox revolt in Yunnan, who had been executed decades ago. The government also claimed to have discovered that Mrs. Wang's husband was actually a member of the rebellious Great Vehicle sect. Leaders of the Burning Lantern sect were alleged to be communicating frequently with the Great Vehicle sectarians in the western interior. After the discovery (or fabrication) of all this new evidence, the Jiangsu governor decided to take drastic measures to stamp out the sect. The arrested leaders were decapitated right away, and many other sectarian members were imprisoned and tortured.

The above three cases are about government actions or policies that concerned the protesters' own interests (material or spiritual). In the next case, we see how protesters interfered with a factional struggle within the bureaucracy at the national level not for their own interest but to save a beloved official who had fallen victim to intrabureaucratic conflicts.

MOBILIZATION TO PROTECT A POPULAR OFFICIAL FROM DISMISSAL[10]

In the spring of 1741, the provincial governor of Zhejiang, Lu Zhuo, was criticized in a secret memorial drafted by the governor-general of Zhejiang and Fujian. Both the drafter of the memorial and Lu Zhuo were no ordinary officials. The former was a trusted Manchu aide and a relative of the Qianlong emperor. The latter was one of the most respected high-rank officials of Qing times. Lu's career peaked in the Yongzheng reign, when he was in the emperor's inner circle and contributed significantly to the centralizing reforms of the state in the 1730s. He not only served the imperial center well but also earned the reputation of being one of the most benevolent and caring officials in the empire, always putting people's needs before his own career. He took different provincial governorships successively. Wherever he went, according to the praise of local literati, he streamlined and disciplined local governments rigorously, redressed grievances from subjects diligently, and invested time and resources in improving local infrastructure such as dikes and irrigation canals.

Lu was accused in the memorial of taking an astronomical amount of bribes from local elite and building up a clique of corrupt officials at all levels of government in the Zhejiang and Fujian areas. The accuser also criticized that local officials, literati elites, and ordinary people had developed a cult of Lu Zhuo by building monuments and temples in his honor. The memorial suggested that Lu should be purged from the bureaucracy and executed. The emperor endorsed these accusations and dispatched a number of his most trusted agents to Zhejiang to arrest Lu and his protégés. It is not clear whether Lu was corrupt or if the accusation was a result of jealousy of his popularity. In any event, the allegation that a personal cult had developed in the Zhejiang and Fujian provinces must have struck a nerve with the Qianlong emperor, as it could mean that Lu was becoming too popular to be controlled.

Residents of the Hangzhou city, the provincial capital of Zhejiang province, were outraged by the charge against their beloved governor. Local literati made and spread speculations and rumors (*zaozuo fuyan*) about the genuine reason behind Lu's downfall and fomented "boiling public opinion" (*qunyan feiteng*) against his trial. On the day Lu was tried by special agents from Beijing at the office of the deputy admiral of Zhejiang, within the Hangzhou city, hundreds of residents rallied outside the office for his immediate release. Local businesses went on a market strike to support the cause. The protesters were so furious that they smashed the drum pavilion, a structure at the entrance of government buildings used by disgruntled subjects to initiate a complaint by hitting the drum inside. The protesters' actions, though physically confined to the provincial seat of Zhejiang, were in fact directed at the imperial center, as it was known that the decision to purge and try Lu had been made by the emperor himself, and Lu's arrest and trial were conducted by special agents representing the emperor. Though the protesters were challenging the emperor directly, Qianlong decided not to punish them. He reminded local officials not to instigate a witch hunt of the rally's organizers, for fear of triggering even larger-scale disturbances.

Despite its lenience toward the protesters, the government decided to stand firm and refused to release Lu. Nonetheless, the government apparently yielded to the intense popular pressure when making its final verdict on Lu. While a few officials alleged to be members of the Lu Zhuo corruption clique received the death sentence, Lu himself, facing more serious charges, was spared. He was banished to the empire's military frontier. About a decade later, the Qianlong emperor even appointed him to be the governor of Shanxi, but that is another story.

In the above four cases, protesters engaged with the paternalist state to shape state action or policy beyond subsistence issues. Though they were contentious in the sense that their claims contradicted the existing disposition of the state and their actions were mostly noninstitutional, they were simultaneously loyalist, as many of these protests reinforced rather than undermined the legitimacy of the state's paternalist authority through their submissive and filial repertoires of action.

Two of these cases involved Buddhist believers. As we saw in chapter 1, against the backdrop of the continuous hegemony of the Confucianist orthodoxy, religions including Buddhism grew in popularity in mid-Qing China. In most cases, these religions were not in conflict with the Confucianist hegemony but rather subjugated themselves to it. However, the resulting religious networks and identities did occasionally become a rallying point for protests. This automatically invoked the suspicion of the state, which knew very well that many of these religious networks were harmless but also took pains to distinguish the legitimate ones from those with heterodox and rebellious tendencies. This state-protester interaction mediated by popular religions is well illustrated in the sect and monastery cases above. In the next chapter, we will see more closely how some of these religious networks developed into heterodox and rebellious organizations that in the late eighteenth century directly confronted the state through open revolts.

INVITING STATE INTERVENTION IN CLASS CONFLICT

Besides seeking relief from the state and attempting to influence governmental decisions in varying realms of state action, protesters also urged for state intervention to advance their interests against the interests of another class when the two groups came into conflict.

Class conflicts in the mid-eighteenth century were mainly the result of rapid commercialization, which fomented the commodification of essential foodstuffs and contractualization of land tenure. These conflicts included food riots in which hungry commoners looted the grain stock of merchants or wealthy households when food prices soared (Wong 1979). They also included conflicts over rent payment and land rights between landlords and tenants (Bouye 2000). As we discussed in chapter 2, these conflicts were largely underreported in official documents, as local administrators were inclined to let them run their course and turned a blind eye unless the target shifted to the authorities. The following cases were among the few in which the lower classes, instead of taking on their wealthy antinomies directly, collectively asked the authorities to protect or advance their interests at the expense of the upper classes.

The first case concerns a food crisis caused by escalating grain prices in the wealthy city of Suzhou. Instead of directly forcing local merchants to lower their grain prices or looting their grain, as in many food riots elsewhere, protesters in Suzhou organized large-scale rallies to press the provincial government to order grain sellers to lower their prices.

RALLYING FOR AND AGAINST GOVERNMENTAL PRICE CONTROL[11]

In the autumn of 1747, harvest in the Suzhou area was disappointing, and rice prices escalated. In February 1748, paddy fields in the area were flooded by continuous rain. The situation was aggravated by a hail storm that hit large areas of the Jiangsu province on April 5. The resulting widespread decline in grain output led to price jump of 20 to 30 percent. The municipal government of Suzhou set up several grain-distribution stations in the city to deliver famine relief to the urban poor. But the official granaries ran out quickly, and rice prices continued to rise (Wang 1992, 40–47; Wu 2001, 256; see also the primary sources for this case). The rest of the Lower Yangzi area was hit hard as well, and foot riots broke out in numerous places, where hungry residents attacked grain merchants and gentry families and looted their grain stock.

Citizens in Suzhou were calmer and did not resort to class warfare. Instead, they appealed to the local government to act against grain merchants on their behalf. On April 20, Gu Yaonian, a petty peddler in the city market, bound his own arms behind his back and kneeled in front of the Jiangsu provincial governor's office in Suzhou. With a placard hung around his neck that read "No money to buy rice and livelihood of poor people is difficult" (*wuqian maimi qiongmin nanguo*), Gu requested that the government force local merchants to lower grain prices. In another account based on recollections of local literati, the slogan on the placard was "[My protest was] for the state and the people and not for myself" (*weiguo weimin fei weiji*).[12] A large number of local residents gathered at the office in support of Gu. According to the local gazetteer, "People who echoed Gu's call gathered like ants." The governor's office was located in the heart of downtown Suzhou, with the Changzhou county office and Suzhou prefecture office both within walking distance. The street was lined with thriving markets and the fancy mansions of officials and prominent gentry-merchants.

The provincial government was reluctant to deal with this petition, and the Changzhou county office was ordered to dispatch a group of runners to arrest Gu and a handful of other petitioners. They were immediately taken to the county office a few blocks away for interrogation. Other petitioners followed them. Changing their target from the provincial government to the county government, the petitioners became more confrontational. They blocked the office entrance and urged for the release of all arrested petitioners. Jiang Shunjiao, the prefecture magistrate of Suzhou, led a team of guardsmen in a rush to the county office, only to find that the protesters had already smashed into the building and liberated Gu and others.

With the chaos escalating, the prefecture magistrate, Jiang, walked to the provincial governor's office to request reinforcements. But Jiang was followed by the tenacious protesters, including Gu and others who had just been freed. When they arrived at the provincial governor's office after Jiang, a local security force was dispatched from the office compound, and the protesters finally dispersed. Thirty-nine participants, including Gu and a number of major protest leaders, were arrested. All the other participants escaped unscathed.

But the event did not stop there. Once the petition to the provincial government and the violent confrontation with the county government subsided, wealthy local elites, probably out of fear that the authorities would yield to the lower-class protesters or fear of food riots targeted at them, accused the local authorities of causing the grain-price escalation. They openly called for a higher-level official to step in and quell the lower classes.

The elites drafted anonymous pamphlets, which were first found circulating in a popular market on April 28, to publicize their positions. They asserted that the lives of notable gentry and merchants in the city were miserable, because they were bullied constantly by the prefecture magistrate and the stone-hearted provincial governor, An Ning. They also justified their reluctance to lower grain prices by complaining that during the preceding winter, An Ning had already forced local merchants to sell their stocks at ridiculously low prices. Prefecture Magistrate Jiang Shunjiao resorted to terror to implement the governor's will. The pamphlet reported that twenty-one grain merchants who refused to lower their prices were beaten to death by government runners. In a panicked response, most merchants sold all their rice at rock-bottom prices. By the beginning of 1748, the grain stock of most local wealthy families and grain retailers had been depleted, and this was the real underlying cause of the skyrocketing prices in April. In a poem—"If Yin comes, it means the heaven is not blind, if An does not go, the land's topsoil will die"([*Yin*] *jifu rulai tian you yan,* [*An*] *lushan buqu di wu pi*)—the pamphlet requested that An Ning step down as governor and urged Yin Jishan, the governor-general of Jiangsu and Jiangxi and An Ning's superior in the bureaucracy, to resolve the conflict.

The Qianlong emperor at last conceded to this elite demand and sent Yin Jishan to Suzhou to pacify both the contentious poor and the aggrieved notables. In the meantime, Gu and the other two initiators of the original petition were executed, seven others imprisoned, and the rest released after being flogged.

This is an interesting case. Protesters, who tried to bring a reduction in market grain and rice prices, and local gentry and merchants, who resisted such a price reduction, did not confront each other head on. Instead, both appealed to the provincial or higher authorities to intervene on their behalf. The next case shows that a similar dynamic can be found in landlord-tenant conflicts triggered by the tenants' call for a government imposition of rent reduction. But in that case, overt class conflict between tenants and landlords did break out when the local authorities refused to intervene.

SEEKING GOVERNMENT-IMPOSED RENT REDUCTION[13]

In June and July of 1741, frequent, heavy rains flooded many cotton fields in Taicang of Jiangsu province. Tenant cultivators from different counties feared that their diminished output would make them incapable of paying their annual rent in the fall. They petitioned the respective county governments to request that their magistrates impose an across-the-board rent reduction through special decree. In Jingjiang county, the petitioners brought rotten arches of cotton bush to the county office to symbolize their plight. A similar petition was recorded for Chongming county.

The local government in Chongming, nonetheless, decided that the flooding was not bad enough to justify state intervention in rent payment that year. After a purportedly careful assessment of the impact of the flooding, local officials found that the southern highland of the area was unaffected and that the flooding brought at most only a 40 percent reduction of output for the flooded fields in the northern lowland. As rent levels in the area were negotiated between landlords and tenants every August according to the actual harvest of each field, the impact of the flooding would be factored into the rent assessment for the year. Government imposition of rent reduction was therefore unnecessary.

Failing to obtain any help from the government, cotton cultivators in Chongming county decided to take on the issue themselves. On August 12, a day before the annual rent assessment by Huang, one of the largest landowners in the area, a tenant cotton cultivator surnamed Shi'er deliberated over a plan of rent resistance with other tenants of Huang in a market town. They decided to organize a team of resisters to expel Huang's agents and threatened that any tenants who dared to make deals with the landlord privately would have their houses demolished. Because of the threat and the assumption that a successful resistance against Huang could intimidate minor landlords, preventing them also from collecting rent for the year, many local cultivators supported the Shi'er plan, and a rent-resistance team was assembled.

On August 13, a few of Huang's agents arrived in the village to start assessing rents and encountered dozens of tenants armed with farming tools. A fight between the two parties broke out in the rain. Huang's agents, outnumbered by the tenants, were hurt badly and stripped of their account books, cotton overcoats, umbrellas, and bamboo hats. They left the scene, and the contentious tenants won the day.

Huang immediately petitioned, on behalf of himself and other landlords in the region, for help from the county government. The magistrate could not refuse his request for the maintenance of order, and he sent a few runners to the village to arrest two of the rent resisters, including Shi'er's son, on August 15. Reluctant to become too involved in the conflict, the county government did not imprison the arrested tenants but handed them to Li, the head of the local village security squad (*baozhang*, usually a landowner who takes up the post in exchange for a reduction in his tax quota). Li imprisoned the arrested tenants in his own home.

On August 16, Shi'er gathered his rent-resistance team to storm Li's house and liberate his son and the other imprisoned tenant. In revenge for Huang's reporting of their rent resistance to the government, they marched to the shacks that Huang had set up in the village to stock collected rent and burned them to the ground. To further intimidate Huang and prevent him from reporting to the government again, the resisters displayed their wide support in the area by mobilizing a market strike in local market towns on August 17. Personal persuasion, posters in the markets, and the threat of violence against those who failed to join the strike were used in the mobilization process. The strike materialized as planned. On August 18, the resisters burned down Li's residence. Despite the upheaval, there was no documentation of government repression or any other kind of intervention. The local authorities seemingly sat on their hands and waited for the class warfare to run its course.

It is unclear what happened during the rest of August and in September. What is certain is that the warfare had not subsided by October. Early that month, the county government decided to step in to end the chaos and prepared for a mass arrest. The news about this pending repression spread among the contentious tenants. When they learned that one of the rent-resistance leaders had already been captured and detained by the county government, they feared that the mass arrest might have begun. In response, they planned a petition to the county office to plead for amnesty (*shangcheng qiukuan*). On October 7, Shi'er raised a flag in front of the village, and Shi'er's son summoned his fellow villagers by hitting the gong. After assembling more than a hundred petitioners, they marched to the county seat. They were intercepted by local troops near the city wall, and the crowd dispersed, with several leaders being placed under arrest.

The local government was remarkably lenient with the arrested. The county magistrate decided that they had never been confrontational toward the government and that their march to the county seat was nothing more than a petition for the government's forgiveness of their rent-resistance activities. The magistrate emphasized that their actions, including the assault of rent-collection agents, market strikes, and the demolition of others' houses, were not targeted at the government and should therefore be distinguished from a government-oriented protest. He decided that the Qing legal code dictating harsh punishment for anti-government protesters did not apply in this case.

In the above two cases, the lower class, in the midst of sharpened hardship, pleaded for assistance from the paternalist authorities—not for government disbursal of relief, as in the cases discussed earlier, but for government intervention to force the well-to-do to alleviate their plight. And in both cases, the upper class, as the ultimate target of this popular rage, also sought state support in response. In both cases, the lower class's attempts were not successful. But their initial expectation that the authorities would come to their aid was not outlandish. As I showed in chapter 1, given the Confucianist conviction of benevolent governance and the authorities' self-assigned paternalist commitment to protect the weak against exploitation by the strong, the Qing state was often on the side of grain consumers and tenant peasants. Persuading or even forcing landlords and merchants to reduce rent and grain prices was not a rare governmental action (as indicated by the elite complaints in the price-control case, above; see also Gao 2005; Hung 2008, 579–580). Without such a record of governmental sympathy with the weak and bias against the wealthy, grain consumers and tenants would not have thought of asking the government for help in the first place. In the next chapter, which covers the late eighteenth century, when state capacity had significantly declined, we see cases in which conflicting classes or lineages preferred to settle scores among themselves without requesting state assistance at all.

VIOLENT RESISTANCE

To be sure, state-engaging protests, despite their prominence, were not the only kind of protests in 1740–1759. There were also state-resisting protests, which were more common in marginal areas. Two examples are resistance against state intervention during an episode of class warfare deep in the poor inland area of Fujian province and tax resistance in the northwestern province of Shanxi.

FIGHTING STATE REPRESSION OF RENT RESISTANCE[14]

The Tingzhou prefecture was located deep in the mountainous region of Fujian. In Qing times, most tenant cultivators in this infertile region were ethnic Hakka who rented land—mostly on the hill—from local notables, many of whom were absentee landlords residing in the cities. In the summer of 1746, cultivators in most of Fujian were hit by a bad harvest. In response to their difficulties, local governments offered a universal tax reduction for landowners. The governments also suggested that landlords should share 60 percent of the benefits incurred by the tax reduction with their tenant cultivators in the form of rent reduction, meaning that landlords could enjoy only 40 percent of the cut.

But the anticipated rent reduction never materialized in Shanghang county. In mid-July, tenant cultivators demanded an immediate rent reduction, citing the government order that landlords should share the benefit of the tax cut with their tenants. The landlords, nevertheless, declined. Local officials backed the landlords' decision and stipulated that local governments had only *encouraged* landlords to reduce rent; it was not obligatory. With their request rejected, tenants in Shanghang launched a violent rent strike.

Afraid of their contentious tenants, absentee landlords living in the county seat of Shanghang were hesitant to go to the mountain areas, where most of their land was located, to collect rent. They solicited help from the county government. In the end, several government runners were sent on July 23 to accompany the landlords on their rent-collection tour. When they reached the mountain, more than one hundred tenants armed with spears and poles charged down the hill under the leadership of the tenant Luo Riguang. Outnumbered and with a landlord's servant badly injured, the rent-collection team retreated.

It was reported that more than one thousand well-armed tenants organized themselves to prevent a return of the landlords and officials. They set up barricades in the main road leading to the mountain. It was also reported that the armed tenants had started to sabotage and loot traveling merchants of their goods—mostly grain—and cash along the trade routes in the area. Tenant households that were willing to pay their rent were harassed and their houses burned down. There were also rumors that the tenants were planning to seize the county seat.

More government runners and imperial troops were dispatched to quell the recalcitrant tenants, only to retreat again under fierce resistance. When the government force reached the area one more time, tenants threw rocks at them from the top of the mountain. The government force relentlessly charged up the hill and captured a number of resisters. But the arrested were soon liberated by other tenants. After sunset, the government called off the mission and regrouped the security force. The unrest was eventually put down, but only after a series of reinforcements and setbacks.

In this case, a local subsistence crisis prompted the tenant cultivators to demand a rent reduction from their landlords. The tenants launched a rent strike when their demand was not met, and the strike turned into anti-government violence once the local authorities stepped in on the side of the landlords. This case diverges from the previous two cases, in which poor residents in the economically and politically core region of the Lower Yangzi Delta, instead of taking on the wealthy by themselves, demanded that the paternalist local authorities impose a reduction in grain price or rent on their behalf. Despite this difference, the local authorities in Tingzhou did encourage local landlords to alleviate their tenants' hardship by sharing with them the benefits of tax cuts. It was exactly this initial paternalist disposition that induced the tenants, who probably expected that the government would be on their side, to demand rent reduction.

While this case of state-resisting violence was an outgrowth of a class conflict, the following case was triggered directly by the attempt of a corrupt local government to clear tax arrears.

TAX RESISTANCE[15]

Jie zhou was located at the southern tip of the Shanxi province on the Loess Plateau. In the Anyi county of Jie zhou during the early Qianlong reign, the local magistrate was unable to discipline his clerks and runners, who made huge fortunes by extracting unauthorized surtaxes and fees from the peasant households. In 1746, the magistrate was on a duty trip for a year, and the local government fell completely into the hands of his clerks and runners, who redoubled their predatory activities. They let the local government's workshops produce low-quality silver *taels* and forced taxpayers to convert their copper cash earned in daily transactions into this low-grade silver, which had an actual value much lower than the marked value. They also turned the official granary system into their private loanshark business. Hungry households that borrowed five *dou* of rice from the granary had to pay back seven *dou* in a year. In response to this tyranny, many local cultivators simply refused to pay taxes.

In March 1747, these predators in the local government decided to deal with the tax-evasion problem by arresting those who accumulated tax arrears of two *taels* or more. The tax-collection teams also harassed the villages by extorting meals and wine from them. The abuses became so unbearable that organized resistance materialized. On March 13, Zhang Yuan, a well-to-do peasant who had long resented the local government and owed a large amount of tax arrears, ran into his uncle, who lived in another village, on his way home from the county seat. Their conversation reinforced each other's grievances, and more passersby joined the heated discussion. They decided that something had to be done.

The group formed a plan to rescue fellow villagers who had been arrested and imprisoned in the county jail for their tax arrears. Under the coordination of Zhang, some of them drafted pamphlets to mobilize other villagers to join. Some raised funds for the action, and others handled the logistics for the march to the faraway county seat. Several meetings were held over the following few days. On March 15, a large number of pamphlets were distributed to each village in the area. Besides the use of persuasion, the pamphlets also stated that villagers who refused to support the collective action would have their houses burned to the ground. In the meantime, some participants started transporting essential supplies such as food to the county seat to prepare for the protesters' arrival.

On the night of March 19, everything was well in place, and a group of seven hundred to eight hundred villagers were assembled. To prevent local officials from noticing, they disguised their protest as a collective tax-submission trip. They departed in the middle of the night and arrived at the eastern gate of the county seat early the next morning. Upon their arrival, they started to chant slogans and demanding the immediate release of the arrested villagers. Hearing no response from the government, they tore down an ornamental arch from the gate. They dispersed when security forces emerged, only to gather again at the northern gate of the city around noon. By that time, all the city gates had been locked. The demonstrators then set the gate on fire with the tons of dry grass that they had prepared. When the runners opened the gate to extinguish the flame, intense conflict broke out, and three of the demonstrators were arrested. Learning that imperial troops were on their way to the scene, the protesters dispersed. After dark, they again gathered at the northern gate and tried to liberate the three protesters who had been arrested and detained nearby. Their efforts were in vain. The villagers then gave up and escaped home.

Back at the village, residents anticipated mass arrests and even an attack by government forces. They barricaded the village entrances and dug trenches around its perimeter. The event ended in an anticlimax when troops finally entered the village without much resistance, on April 17. The major leaders and identifiable participants of the protest were arrested. The ringleaders were decapitated right away and the other participants punished severely.

Tax resistances of this kind were far from common in the mid-eighteenth century. But during the late eighteenth and early nineteenth centuries, tax resistance proliferated in tandem with the empirewide fiscal crisis and increasing tax levy. The Daoguang Depression, starting in the 1820s, further aggravated the antagonism between taxpayers and local governments. These factors are addressed in detail in the next two chapters.

THE PARADOXICAL DOCILITY OF MID-EIGHTEENTH-CENTURY PROTESTERS

Generally, most documented popular protests in 1740–1759 manifested the following features: First, protesters in most cases accepted the legitimacy of state regulation of a wide range of local affairs, such as alleviating subsistence crises, managing the flow of local rivers and canals, regulating religious activities, and arbitrating conflicts of class interests. Rather than resisting the intrusion of the state into society, as did many violent resisters during the late Ming and early Qing periods in the seventeenth century, different social groups mobilized themselves to engage the state and ensure that its actions would enhance their benefits and rights. Most famine-relief-seeking protests, for example, involved a request for universal relief (*puzhen*) in lieu of the selective, need-based relief preferred by the government. Protesters often referred to the criteria of competent and clean officials, as advocated by the emperor himself, to criticize and put pressure on local governments. In so doing, they were making good use of the emperor's disciplinary scrutiny of local officials. For example, a local official accused by protesters of embezzling resources designated for famine relief would fear that the popular charge of embezzlement could taint the emperor's trust in him, and thus he would be inclined to yield to the protesters' demands. Many other protests involved the protesters' quest for their right to participate in the government's decision-making process. Most of these protests were aimed at the lowest level of government. There were also a few cases in which protesters directly appealed to the provincial governments or even the imperial center. These cases show that the Manchu rulers had successfully warranted the legitimacy of the paternalist and activist state in the wake of centralizing and moralizing reforms in the 1720s and 1730s. The state-engaging protests constituted a majority of all documented cases in the period. Protests resisting the intrusion of the state, such as tax riots, were not nonexistent. Nonetheless, their percentage among all documented protests was the lowest among the three waves of protest.

Second, certain protest tactics became standard repertoires that were repeated in different episodes concerning different issues across the empire. One example is the market strike. Another example is the employment of a statue of the local city god, which symbolized the imperial center, to put pressure on local officials. They also include public displays of the protesters' plight, such as bringing along barren arches of cotton bush and tying one's own hands. It is difficult to establish how widespread each of these repertoires was among all of the documented episodes, as many documentations in the QSL are brief and do not describe all acts employed in each case. But a skimming of the catalog gives the impression that these repertoires were by no means rare. For example, 17 percent of all documented protests involved a market strike. These are only the cases that we can be sure about. The actual figure must be higher, as there are likely other cases in which the employment of a market strike was not documented. *Guixiang*, or kneeling and praying with glowing incense in front of officials, was also common. We will see in later chapters that these repertoires continued to occur well after the collapse of the Qing empire and, in fact, are still seen today.

The spread of standard repertoires is related to the third feature of protest in the period: the heavy involvement of literati elites either as participants or, more frequently, as organizers. The elites in Qing times, as in other times, were national, cosmopolitan people, given their absorption into the unitary cultural orthodoxy through the standardized curriculum of the imperial examination. Despite their orthodox ideology and their dependence on state recognition for the reproduction of their status, this elite group was far from an unambiguous agent of the state. Besides their obligation to aid local officials through explaining government policy to commoners, managing local infrastructure, collecting taxes, and so on, the Confucianist orthodoxy also bestowed on them the responsibility of articulating the grievances and demands of the uneducated people and conveying them to the authorities. It is the latter role that legitimized their involvement in organizing petitions or more confrontational protests directed at the state. Among all documented cases for the period, we are sure that 19 percent involved the leadership of the literati elites. Again, this figure is an underestimation, as we do not know whether literati were involved in cases that include scant information about the organizers' social backgrounds.

Fourth, many protest participants came from diverse socioeconomic backgrounds. Among all documented episodes, 53 percent involved participants with more than one socioeconomic background, whereas others involved only participants from singular communal bodies (e.g., villages, clans, or military garrisons). The collective identities as articulated in protests composed of diverse groups were distant from the parochial identities embedded in the everyday routine of each of the participating groups—or what Charles Tilly called "embedded identities" (Tilly 2002, 62). In many cases, the protesters expressed an identity of universal imperial subjects that transgressed the occupations, lineage membership, and residential locations of individual protesters. For example, a peddler participating in a petition for famine relief did not petition as a peddler but as part of a larger community of imperial subjects residing in the area. This identity, which can be categorized as a "disjoined identity," articulated at the site and moment of protest and detached from individual participants' identities in their everyday life (Tilly 2002, 62), united participants with different backgrounds, such as tenant farmers and shopkeepers. Concomitant with this disjoined identity of imperial subjects was the protesters' subservience to the authorities and their claims of a universal entitlement to the paternalist care of the state. One common example of such claims was the call for "universal relief" from the government, the equal disbursal of relief to everyone under the local government's jurisdiction, regardless of their class backgrounds and areas of residence.

Given these common features, many protests in mid-eighteenth-century China converge with Tilly's characterization of "proactive," "cosmopolitan," and "modular" protests emerging in late eighteenth-century France and England. Tilly explains the rise of such collective actions in terms of the political opportunities created by political centralization and commercialization. The dramatic increase in state intervention in different realms of society led most people to accept, reluctantly or otherwise, the state as an unavoidable part of their lives. It made them protest more proactively to ensure that the state acted in their favor. At the same time, state centralization and commercialization fomented the erosion of localistic corporate identities and the rise of more inclusive and abstract identities such as "citizens." The two processes also gave rise to new means of long-distance communication that facilitated the geographical diffusion of standard repertoires of action. Chapter 1 shows that the level of state centralization and commercialization in mid-eighteenth-century China was as high as many late eighteenth-century European states. It is therefore not at all surprising that the 1740–1759 wave of Chinese protests would be as proactive, cosmopolitan, and modular as the protests of late eighteenth-century Europe.

The association between state-engaging protest and legitimate centralized state power, as well as commerce, in mid-eighteenth-century China is also reflected in the geographical distribution of different types of protests. As figure 3.1 shows, state-engaging protests documented in the QSL for the period were concentrated in areas with higher levels of commerce in eastern China, where the intensity of commercial interaction brought people of different walks of life closer together, making protest mobilization easier. These areas also had a higher concentration of literati elites, who were agile in using the language of the political orthodoxy to assemble protesting identities and claims acceptable to the state (Hung 2009). The relatively high capacity of the state in these wealthy regions made the state more responsive to proactive demands from its subjects, who in turn developed higher expectations of the state.

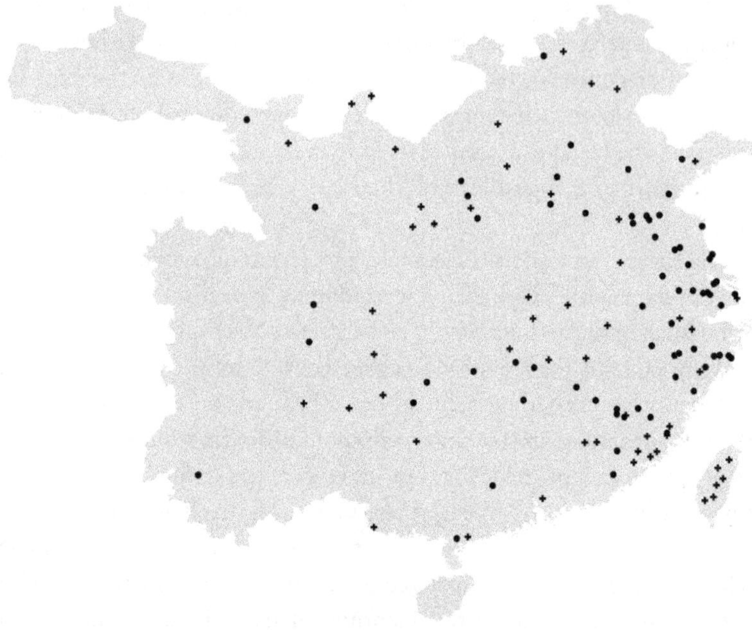

FIGURE 3.1 Geographical Distribution of Documented Protests with Known Claims, 1740–1759 (background map: CHGIS)

Despite the strong parallels between mid-eighteenth-century Chinese and European protests in the similar context of state centralization and market expansion, Chinese protests and their European counterparts diverged radically in the actual languages and identities that the protesters employed to define their relation with the state.

In most of the above cases, proactive protesters were anxious to affirm their filial loyalty toward the paternalist state when seeking to influence its action. Through such subservient acts as kneeling upon both knees, bowing their heads to the ground, and holding glowing incense to pay respect to the magistrate, protesters put themselves in an inferior position to plead for the action of the paternalist authorities, just as children pleaded for the attention and care of the grand patriarch. No matter how confrontational their actions, protesters often confined that confrontation to individual officials and lower levels of government, and they were earnest in reproducing the legitimacy of the existing political order by invoking symbols of higher authorities such as statues of local city gods or by petitioning directly to higher-level officials (or even the emperor). The Qianlong emperor explicitly stated in the edict that we saw in the touring-emperor case that petitioners' complaints to the imperial center against the local authorities were like children's complaints to their grandparents about their parents. In other words, even in cases in which protesters were disrespectful to the local authorities, the ideology invoked in the protest was still likely to be marked by the protesters' filial loyalty to the emperor. The cosmopolitan, universal identity expressed in many Chinese protests is an identity of filial-loyal imperial subjects under the neo-Confucianist orthodoxy.

This was in contrast with the identities expressed in proactive protests in Europe that emerged in similar conditions of state centralization and market expansion after the mid-eighteenth century. Western European protesters of the time were increasingly immersed in the emerging ideology of popular sovereignty and citizenship. Students of early modern European petitions and protest find that underlying the loyalist language and submissive claims of eighteenth-century petitioners was often a transformative appeal that tacitly challenged the core of the old sociopolitical order. Examples include a petition to the French monarch that requested the abolition of seigneurial rights and a demonstration seeking increased representation in the English parliament (Chartier 1991, 141–151; Tilly 1995). I explore this difference between China and Europe in greater detail in chapter 6.

The features of mid-Qing protest as seen in this chapter were not unchanging. In the next two chapters, I decipher how the different political, economic, and cultural contexts in late eighteenth- and early nineteenth-century China fomented shifts in the claims and repertoires, as well as the corresponding ideology and identities, of popular protesters.

4

RIOTS INTO REBELLION, 1776–1795

While the commercial boom underlying the mid-eighteenth-century wave of protest continued through the late eighteenth century, what differentiated the two periods was the state's decaying administrative discipline and capacity. After the end of the frontier wars in 1760, the impetus for institutional innovation and maintenance of administrative rigor dissipated, and the chronic inflation of the economy and growth of the population, coupled with the fixed tax-quota regime instituted in the 1710s, precipitated a fiscal crisis and a drop in the state's capacity. Consequences of this administrative deterioration included declining state activism in social and economic affairs (such as regulation of grain prices via the public-granary system) and increasing illicit surtaxes levied by local governments.

Declining state capacity in providing public goods, soaring tax burdens, and the continuous expansion of population and commerce were the most significant backdrops against which late eighteenth-century protests took shape.

In contrast to the 1740s and 1750s, when villagers and city dwellers alike frequently engaged the paternalist and activist state to request intervention or to influence state action to enhance their interests and rights, state-engaging protests declined in the 1776–1795 period, as shown in table 4.1. A straightforward explanation for this decline is that the popular expectation of what the state could do for society slid with the state's falling capacity. Simultaneous to this decline was the rise of state-resisting violence, which could be broken down into three main categories: tax resistance, resistance to state intervention in social conflicts, and outlaws' resistance against state repression.

Tax resistance constituted 19.8 percent of all documented protests in 1776–1795, up from 9.1 percent in the 1740–1759 wave. This increase is attributable to the surge of illegitimate surtaxes imposed by local governments, which redoubled their appropriation of local surpluses to make ends meet amid the

TABLE 4.1 Composition of Documented Protests with Known Claims, 1740–1759 and 1776–1795

Claims	1740–1759 (%)	1776–1795 (%)
State engaging	**61.4**	**17.1**
Seeking famine relief	31.8	1.8
Seeking participation in state decision-making process	18.2	9.9
Seeking state intervention into social conflict	7.6	0.9
Seizing state functions	3.8	4.5
State resisting	**38.7**	**82.9**
Retributions against policies or officials	11.4	6.3
Resisting crackdown on illicit activities	11.4	45.9
Resisting tax levy	9.1	19.8
Resisting state intervention into social conflicts	6.8	10.8
Total	**100**	**100**

Note: Events for 1776–1795 with known claims: 111; events with unknown claims: 3.

unfolding fiscal crisis. In comparison with the mid-eighteenth century, there was a sharp drop in protests in which conflicting parties in a feud or episode of class warfare requested state intervention in their favor (a drop from 7.6 percent in 1740–1759 to less than 1 percent). Instead, incidents in which participants in social conflicts resisted state intervention mounted (an increase from 6.8 percent in the preceding wave to 10.8 percent). In the late eighteenth century, feuding social groups apparently lost their trust in the state and came to prefer settling their scores by themselves.

Above all, the most salient type of resistance in this period was the conflict between outlaws, such as smugglers and bandits, and agents of the state attempting to curb their illicit activities. This type of resistance, which constituted only about 11.4 percent of all documented cases in 1740–1759, surged to 45.9 percent in 1776–1795. The rise stemmed from the swollen population, which, given the slow increase in the amount of cultivable land available,

TABLE 4.2 List of Cases Included for Thick Description, 1776–1795

Issue	Province	Type	Page
1. Petition seeking government intervention into an episode of class warfare	Hubei	state engaging	105
2. Fighting corvée	Shandong	state resisting	107
3. Tax strike under chaotic tax assessment	Zhejiang	state resisting	110
4. Feuding lineages expel government agents	Fujian	state resisting	113
5. Feuding fishermen resist government troops	Zhejiang	state resisting	115
6. Loggers fight forest rangers	Fujian	state resisting	118
7. Armed salt smugglers battle inspectors	Sichuan	state resisting	119
8. Resistance and organization of the Guolu bandit group	Sichuan	state resisting	120

created an enlarging class of vagrants or cultivators living in ecologically fragile areas. Many of these marginal men survived by living off the commercial wealth along major trade routes via peddling and a range of illegal activities such as salt smuggling (which was a profitable business, given the state monopoly of salt sales), private coinage, and banditry. These predatory activities were common throughout Chinese history as "aggressive survival strategies" when resources were scarce and the state was incapable of safeguarding its subjects' livelihoods (Perry 1980, 58–80). Having grown into a serious threat to law and order (in the case of banditry) or to the state's economic interests (in the case of salt smuggling and private coinage), these activities became a key target of state suppression, which frequently provoked violent resistance of the outlaws, who became increasingly armed and organized. Their militancy and coordination invited fiercer repression, locking the two groups into a vicious circle.

Accompanying the rise of state-resisting protests and the fall of state-engaging ones, violent repertoires of action involving attacks on government agents or public property (constituting 69.5 percent of all protests) prevailed over nonviolent forms of claim making such as market strikes, peaceful rallies, and petitions that used to dominate the mid-eighteenth century. This is understandable, given that the state was no longer seen as a credible and caring protector of the people that the protesters sought to humbly persuade. Instead, the state was viewed as a predatory antinomy of the protesters, who felt they had to fight off the authorities by all means necessary to defend their interests and survival.

In what follows, I detail the genesis and development of select representative cases of late eighteenth-century protest, which were predominantly state resisting. The locations and issues of these cases are summarized in table 4.2.

Following the case studies, I discuss how these late eighteenth-century resistances helped fuel the outbreak of large-scale, sustained armed uprisings, which peaked at the turn of the nineteenth century.

DECLINING STATE-ENGAGING ACTIONS

As we see in table 4.1, state-engaging protests that sought state paternalist care or state intervention in social conflict were not nonexistent in the late eighteenth century, but they were much less salient than they were in the mid-eighteenth century. The connection between falling state-engaging protests and falling popular expectation as well as the capacity of the state is illustrated in the following case, in which a petition for justice after a mass atrocity during an episode of class warfare was ignored by local officials.

PETITION SEEKING GOVERNMENT INTERVENTION INTO AN EPISODE OF CLASS WARFARE[1]

In 1785 and 1786, the Xiaogan area of Hubei was hit by a bad harvest and famine. The central government had channeled a famine-relief fund to local governments to purchase grain to be disbursed to the famine victims. But because of the officials' alleged embezzlement of the fund, the actual relief turned out to be far from sufficient in keeping the victims from desperation.

On February 8, 1786, Liu Jinli, a poor cultivator from the Meijiawan village in the county, met with a few of his fellow clansmen and friends to exchange complaints about the lack of famine relief even after they had consumed all the relief disbursed the previous year. They decided to invite other acquaintances to organize a group of about a dozen men to visit one of the richest landlords in the area, Liu Mianxiao, who also belonged to the Liu clan, to request an emergency food loan. Liu declined their request and angered the loan seekers, who looted his stock of grain and seized clothes that they found in his compound. Emboldened by the success of the loan seeking–turned-looting operation, Liu Jinli gathered an increasingly larger group of famine victims to loot the residences of major landlords one after the other on February 16, 23, 26, 28, 30, and March 8. Their looting was never suppressed, and the local government apparently turned a blind eye to it. The list of looted items expanded from grain and clothes to animals and other valuables.

Local wealthy elites threatened by the looting never sought help from local government, probably because they were well aware of the officials' reluctance to intervene. On February 26, Mei Diaoyuan, the most influential and feared landowner in the area and notorious for his brutality toward his tenants, called a meeting with other major landowners to discuss their collective response to the looters. Mei, who was feared by the looters and was so far unscathed by the unrest, organized a private security force to crack down on the contentious tenants. During the looting operation on March 8, Liu Jinli was killed by the newly assembled security force, while other looters escaped.

But Mei and other landlords were not satisfied with the ringleader's death. The security force stormed Liu Jinli's house, confiscated all putative booty from the looting, and captured four of his family members and friends. The captives were transferred to a local temple, where they were tortured and forced to provide the names of all the other looters. They came up with a list of nineteen people, including innocents who were simply the fathers of alleged looters. The security force acted swiftly to capture everybody on the list and detain them at the temple. With twenty-three associates of Liu Jinli under arrest, the fearsome Mei Diaoyuan decided to bury them alive as a deterrent to further looting. The landlords' private security force then prepared a mass grave on a local mountain. On March 10, when the grave was ready, the twenty-three captives were tied up, transferred to the mountain, and buried alive.

After this incident, the mother of one of the buried victims attempted to seek justice by petitioning the prefecture government, calling for an investigation into the atrocity. Her case was instantly dismissed. Despite Xiaogan's proximity to the provincial capital, not a single official in the county, prefecture, or provincial governments bothered to report the incident to the emperor, pretending to be unaware of the mass killing. This incident was brought to light only after the county magistrate of Xiaogan was toppled in an intrabureaucratic struggle in September of that year. His foes in the government discovered records of the petition when they searched for evidence of his wrongdoings. The provincial government then ordered a recovery of the bodies from the mass grave. A careful forensic examination of the corpses, which had not totally disintegrated, suggested that they had been tortured with their hands tied and that they died of suffocation. This event exasperated the aging Qianlong emperor, who ordered the arrest and execution of those involved in the killings. Mei Diaoyuan was sentenced to death by a thousand cuts, and his associates were decapitated. The members of the private security force were mostly banished to the frontiers or enslaved to Manchu noblemen.

This incident started with a subsistence crisis and the state's failure to offer relief. Unlike many protesters in the mid-eighteenth century, the famine victims in this case did not even consider pressuring the government. Instead, they appropriated grain from local notables by themselves. Those notables, with their property threatened by the hungry peasants, did not seek help from the state either, instead taking the governmental function of arresting and punishing the grain looters through their private security force. When the mother of one of the victims finally petitioned the local government for justice, the magistrate simply refused to handle the case.

The reluctance and incapability of the local government to intervene in food riots and even in the private, mass execution of peasants illustrates why disgruntled subjects in the late eighteenth century were not as enthusiastic as their midcentury predecessors in petitioning the state to fulfill its paternalist obligations. Worse, many local governments of the time were not only ineffective but also insolvent, so much so that they needed to raise taxes. It is this source of the increasing frequency of tax resistance to which I now turn.

TAX RESISTANCE

FIGHTING CORVÉE[2]

Since the Yongzheng tax reform in the 1720s and 1730s, most corvée and other levies by the government on cultivators had been merged into a standard silver land tax, which became the main revenue source that local governments used to pay their staffs, restock local granaries, and cover the expenses of infrastructure projects and other occasional costs. With the fiscal deterioration of the Qing state after the 1750s, corvée increased in different parts of the empire in the name of mobilizing extra manpower for emergency construction work such as levee repair. The emergency project to dredge the section of the Yellow River in Henan province and reinforce the levees along the riverbank in 1781 is a case in point.

In the fall of 1781, the central government and the Henan provincial government decided that the silt in the Yellow River had accumulated so much, and the levee along the riverbanks was so dilapidated, that the upcoming rainy season would cause serious flooding in Henan and Shandong provinces, the latter located downstream of Henan. The authorities therefore proposed a large-scale dredging project of the river's Henan section. Apparently owing to financial stringency, the local government decided not to fund the proposed project out of its coffers but relied instead on an extensive mobilization of unpaid labor through administrative decree in Henan and Shandong.

Altogether, ten thousand men were needed for the project. The corvée was allocated to tax-paying cultivators according to their regular tax dues, with the formula that each thirty *taels* of tax quota inferred the obligation of providing one adult male laborer. For example, a peasant household paying ninety *taels* of tax annually would be required to provide three adult male laborers for the project. Each laborer was responsible for fifty days of work and had to dredge at least twenty-five *fang* of silt out of the riverbed. Peasants owning fewer than three acres of cultivable land were exempted from the corvée. Because of the large number of laborers needed and the benefit that this project would bring to cultivators living downstream, in Shandong, the corvée order was extended to villages in Shandong province, though most of the work would be carried out in Henan.

Yanggu county in Shandong was ordered by higher-level authorities to contribute three hundred men for the project. In ordinary times, county government relied on tax farmers (*dibao*), each of whom oversaw one *li*, a grassroots administrative unit that contained a few dozen villages, for tax collection. But on this occasion, which required urgent labor mobilization, the county magistrate opined that tax farmers would not be expeditious or efficient enough to mobilize the required hands, given the large geographical area that each of them was responsible for. It therefore turned to village heads (*zhuangtou*) to mobilize their fellow villagers. This was a grave mistake. As the village heads identified more with the villagers' interests than with the government's, they were reluctant to help mobilize the villagers for such harsh, unpaid work.

The heads of four villages in the northern part of Yanggu county, led by Wang Wei and Wang Taihe, boycotted the corvée. They complained to the county government that a corvée of such a scale and for a project in another province was unprecedented. The villagers, including the educated literati among them, even speculated that the corvée mobilization was in fact a scheme of corrupt officials to sell the unpaid villagers' labor power for their own financial gain. The county government responded by arresting the two Wangs and others who refused to fill the corvée quota. It detained them in the government compound at the county seat. Learning of their arrest, a local licentiate, Xue Zi, and a commoner, Wang Shikui, planned a rescue action and a coordinated collective resistance to the corvée. They gathered on September 28 in the home of another licentiate, Gu Youcheng, to draft two copies of a handbill. Wang Shikui and Gu Jiejie (probably a member of Gu Youcheng's family) each took a copy and traveled around the county to raise funds for litigating the government agents and to persuade villagers across the area to help liberate the arrested village heads.

On October 4, when the county magistrate had left town for the periodic market in a nearby city, more than twenty furious villagers emerged and attacked the county government compound. They forcefully released the Wangs and other arrested village heads, then moved on to tear down the residence of the county's treasury secretary (*liangfang*), who was allegedly the chief designer of the corvée-mobilization scheme. The resistance shocked the provincial authorities, who mobilized two prefecture governments in the region to hunt down the villagers participating in the attack. All of the twenty-plus attackers were arrested. Popular sympathy for these attackers was high, and a large rally took place outside the county government to ask for their release while they were interrogated inside. But the protesters were dispersed by government runners without much conflict. The local authorities, under the direct instruction of the emperor, ordered the decapitation of nine core resisters, including the two Wangs and those who planned the attack of the county government back in the September meeting.

This resistance of a local community against the state diverged from petitions that sought state assistance, but its mobilization process was reminiscent of many cases of state-engaging protest as discussed in the previous chapter.

Local literati were instrumental in articulating the collective action's claim, and written communications (a handbill, in this case) were employed to persuade others to join. In contrast, the following case of tax resistance shows a different dynamic. It was spontaneous, communal, and was not mediated by the educated elite.

TAX STRIKE UNDER CHAOTIC TAX ASSESSMENT[3]

Starting in the early eighteenth century, marketization of land ownership increased the frequency and volume of land transactions, particularly in the highly commercialized southeastern coastal region. The initial phase of commercialization generated many disputes, sometimes violent ones, over land rights among commoners (Buoye 2000). It also increased the burden of local governments in keeping their roster of land ownership for tax-assessment purposes. The problem appeared even more menacing in the third quarter of the eighteenth century, when the Qing state started to lose its administrative rigor and lag further behind the society's commercialization and demographic expansion. Disputes between taxpayers and local governments regarding the official record of tax-yielding property sometimes developed into violent tax resistance. The tax resistance in Sheng county of Shaoxing prefecture in Zhejiang province is such a case.

Sheng county was highly commercialized and was an important postal and commercial passage through the mountainous areas of Zhejiang province. Land tax in the county was collected by village secretaries (*zhuang shu*), each of whom maintained records of land ownership and transactions in all of the villages under his jurisdiction. At the turn of the new year, when the weather was cold and agricultural work halted for the season, village secretaries brought their land-deed records to the villages to collect land taxes household by household. The secretaries then submitted the collected taxes and returned the record books to the county government.

Wang Kaijing was a peasant living in a village in the fifteenth district of the county. He was well known for his reluctance to pay his yearly taxes on time. In 1778, Wang, together with two of his fellow villagers, Weng Hualong and Dong Kaifu, filed a plaint claiming that their estate secretary had altered the local land registration illegally so that land owned by others was also listed under their names. They charged that it was a common trick on the part of the secretary to double tax some land and pocket the extra levies.

The three aggrieved taxpayers decided not to pay their yearly dues until the issue was settled. On January 6, 1778, when the village secretary Wu Yueqian visited their village, Wang invited him to his home, where Weng and Dong captured him and seized his land records. Wu escaped and reported the incident to the county government. The magistrate then issued a warrant to order Wang, Weng, and Dong to return the land-registration record and report to the county government to facilitate a full-fledged investigation of the case. They never showed up.

After reviewing the land-registration record, Wang, Weng, and Dong told their fellow villagers that many individual land records were chaotic and seemingly fabricated. They declared that a large-scale injustice was involved in the tax assessment and urged other villagers not to pay their dues that year. Most villagers echoed their call. On March 24, a county-government runner named Song Lian visited the village and managed to meet with Wang's father, Wang Qiude. Song urged Wang to persuade his son to clear his tax arrears as soon as possible, and Wang responded that it was still early and that his son would not pay anything until April or May. This infuriated Song, who arrested Wang and took him to the county office. Learning of his father's capture, Wang Kaijing and his friends went after Song and liberated his father. Intimidated, Song had no choice but to report the event to his superior.

Expecting that the government's security force would soon arrive, Wang, Weng, and Dong gathered eleven other villagers at a station on top of a hill overlooking the village entrance. On March 25, when a group of government runners arrived, they bombarded them with stones. Seriously hurt, the runners fled and reported back to the county government. Offended by the villagers' adamant resistance, the county magistrate, Wu Shiying, led an armed squad of twenty men to storm the village and arrest the resisters. In response, Wang and the original resisters redoubled their efforts to urge other villagers to come out and fight, threatening to harvest and sell the crops of those who refused to help in the conflict. In the end, a force of more than fifty men was assembled. When the magistrate's squad arrived in the village, on March 26, the villagers threw rocks and attacked them with farming tools. Most of the government runners were severely injured, and Wu himself suffered injuries to his legs and back. The government force, overwhelmed by the intense attack, retreated in disarray.

In anticipation of retaliation, many villagers involved in the fight fled and hid in the mountains. Wang and his family took refuge deep in the forest but were still caught. The Shaoxing prefecture office mobilized security forces from two neighboring counties and, aided by the security force of the nearby Taizhou prefecture, proceeded to search for the renegade villagers. Fifty-three villagers, including Wang, Weng, and Dong, were arrested. Initiators of the resistance, together with those involved in harming government agents, were all sentenced to immediate decapitation. Other participants who had not harmed anyone received a deferred hanging sentence. Even those who were involuntarily recruited under threat by the resistance organizers were sentenced to one hundred strokes of flogging.

After this heavy-handed crackdown, the provincial government sent the prefecture magistrate of Taizhou to Sheng county to scrutinize all land-registration records and tax quotas. The investigation concluded that although the allegations of Wang, Weng, and Dong were groundless, their grievances were not fabrications, as they were rooted in the local government's inability to keep up with the increasing fluidity of land ownership, given frequent commercial transactions.

Regarding Wang Kaijing's complaint that he was taxed for a tract of land that did not belong to him, the investigation found that the dispute stemmed from a transaction in 1769, when Wang had purchased 1.5 *mu* of land from Chen Faqing. The two parties signed a receipt certifying that the tax quota on the land had been transferred from Chen to Wang. Later, Chen's father-in-law, who was the owner of the land, objected to the transaction, as the land was part of his daughter's dowry. The transaction was therefore interrupted, and Wang never obtained the land he purchased. Only after five years of persuasion did Chen manage to obtain his father-in-law's consent to the sale, and the land finally fell completely into Wang's hands in 1774. The disputed tax due was from the period when Wang had purchased but not yet owned the land. In a similar vein, Dong Kaifu's complaint that he was taxed on a piece of land that he did not own was caused by the complications of two transactions, one in 1752 and the other in 1755. In the first transaction, Dong sold his land to another person. In the second transaction, Dong bought back the land from that person. But the land registration had not changed the name of the land's owner for the years between the two transactions, which caused the dispute. On Weng's complaint, the investigator found that the problem lay with a typo in the land-registration record that inflated the size of his land ten times, from two *fen*, three *li* to two *mu*, three *fen*, and his tax quota was therefore vastly overestimated. Similar mistakes were found in many other entries of the land record.

Resistance against tax and corvée considerably increased from 1740–1759 to 1776–1795. Besides resistance against levies, the expanding commercial economy in the midst of falling state capacity also heightened social conflicts and illicit economic activities, both of which easily developed into state-resisting violence when the authorities attempted to step in and curb such conflicts and activities. The following two cases concern state-resisting violence that began as a local feud.

RESISTING STATE INTERVENTION IN SOCIAL CONFLICTS

FEUDING LINEAGES EXPEL GOVERNMENT AGENTS[4]

Taiwan had been an immigrant society since its incorporation into the Qing empire in the 1680s. Most of its agrarian inhabitants in the fertile lowland were migrants from the Zhangzhou and Quanzhou regions of southern Fujian province, across the Taiwan Strait, who drove the Polynesian aborigines into the mountains. When the swelling local population placed demands on the limited local resources, Zhangzhou and Quanzhou villagers became increasingly militant in securing and expanding their control of such resources. Commercialization of the local economy also increased the wealth of local lineages, which could then maintain larger and more professional armed forces specializing in lineage defense and interlineage fights.

Zhangzhou and Quanzhou migrants usually settled in separate, fortified villages. Organized feuds between the two groups became the most prominent form of social conflict in Taiwan in the eighteenth century (Ownby 1990; cf. Lamley 1977). Feuds in the mid-eighteenth century were more or less contained by the state. Their intensity increased in the late eighteenth century, when the capacity of the local state declined and the population pressure in Taiwan reached crisis proportions. The large-scale Zhangzhou-Quanzhou feud in 1782, which spread to multiple counties and lasted for over a month, well illustrates this trend. The feuding parties not only ignored local officials' warnings and their efforts to impose a truce but also attacked local troops dispatched to contain the violence.

The feud was sparked by a minor dispute. On August 23, Zhangzhou migrants in Zhanghua county hosted a local opera show in the evening and set up a gambling tent to entertain the audiences. Among the gamblers were a group of Quanzhou migrants, who lost money badly to the Zhangzhou host. They paid in allegedly substandard silver *taels*. The quarrel between the Zhangzhou host and Quanzhou gamblers escalated into a brawl, in which Liao, a Quanzhou elder, was killed. Immediately afterward, Quanzhou villagers in the region mobilized for an attack on Zhanghou villages to avenge Liao's death. Expecting this attack, Zhangzhou villagers also mobilized their armed forces. On August 25, an unknown person (plausibly somebody representing the local government or local gentry) tried to mitigate the tension and hosted a negotiation between village leaders from the Quanzhou and Zhangzhou communities, but this yielded no result. On August 26, a feud broke out when some of the Quanzhou and Zhangzhou villages were burned by the other side. All-out protracted warfare ensued.

The fighting was well organized and well financed. Village headmen employed their corn and silver lineage reserves to conscript fighters. To avoid the bloodshed, women and children were to leave Taiwan at the port of Luzaigang and return to their villages of origin in mainland Fujian. Villagers living in small settlements moved to bigger, fortified settlements. On September 2, fighting squads on both sides, heavily armed, met at the agreed-upon site of Fanzaigou in Zhanghua for a battle. Government troops were dispatched from a nearby garrison to stop the fight. The feuding parties dispersed, only to regroup once the government force left. The war lasted for most of the rest of the month. Later investigations found that the fight had been planned by prominent literati in both Zhangzhou and Quanzhou villages, and the troops on both sides were as professional as any standing army's. In the battle, mounted commanders gave detailed orders on the squads' formation and the rhythm of attack. Cannons were used. Some wealthier villages also hired guards to protect their homes while the men were fighting outside. Lineage-ancestry halls were converted into infirmaries and handled burials, which helped cover up the extent of the casualties and fatalities from the local government.

On September 9, the local authorities launched a concerted effort to stop the fight. Superintendent Lin Shen, who had recently assumed duty in Taiwan, led ten other soldiers to a fortified government position to prepare for repressing the feud. When they passed a Quanzhou village, however, they were kidnapped and taken into the village. Lin was held in a private library, and his troops were detained elsewhere. While the Quanzhou village leaders gathered in a local medicine shop to discuss the strategy for defending the village against a rumored Zhangzhou attack, Lin managed to escape. The gathered village leaders grabbed their knives and went after him. They captured and stabbed him to death. Some of the other captured soldiers managed to escape from the village and reported the incident to the government.

The killing of Lin alarmed the higher authorities, who started to suspect that rebellious secret societies might be involved in the conflict (they were not). The provincial government soon mobilized reinforcements from the mainland and transported them to Taiwan. Partly because of heightened government suppression and partly out of an exhaustion with the bloodletting, the feud subsided in the middle of September, and many participants escaped from Taiwan and resettled in their original Zhangzhou or Quanzhou villages in Fujian. But the feud spread to the Bengang region, in another county, just as it declined in Zhanghua. In Bengang, Quanzhou villagers living in the northern part of the region, who resented the bullying by Zhangzhou villagers monopolizing most local markets, organized repeated plunders of Zhangzhou settlements from September 20 to October 15. It was not until the end of October when conflict across the island faded and mass arrests and investigation by the government started.

Government reports in the aftermath of the incidents admitted that the local garrisons and local administrations were so resource poor and disrespected by local populaces that they simply did not have the means or credibility to stop the fight once it broke out. And when the local authorities finally tried to step in, they were simply ignored or fought off by the villagers, as the slaughter of Superintendent Lin illustrates.

Eighteenth-century Taiwan was known for interlineage tension among its restive migrant population. It is therefore not surprising that one of the most deadly feuds, as well as numerous other feuding events that developed into state-resisting violence in the late eighteenth century, occurred there. But it was by no means the only region to experience this trouble. The following is another case of a feud that turned into state-resisting violence in an unlikely place—the water off the coast of Zhejiang province—and among unlikely actors: local fishermen.

FEUDING FISHERMEN RESIST GOVERNMENT TROOPS[5]

In the participants' audacity in expelling state intervention, this case of a fishermen's feud in the offshore fishing fields in Zhejiang was similar to the Taiwan feud, above. In this case, however, some participants not only resisted repression by local troops but also recruited some of the troops to participate in the feud itself.

The coast of Zhejiang province was a bountiful fishery. Unlike cultivable land, which was divided into discrete slots among landowners, the offshore fishing area was seen as a common field exploitable by all commoners having a fisherman status (*yuhu*) granted by the state. The management of the fishing ground was based on a tacit agreement among fishermen households, which roughly demarcated the ground into smaller areas through which individual households could rotate to cast their nets. As the number of fishermen grew along with the general expansion of the population, conflicts over fishing rights in different areas mounted during the latter half of the eighteenth century. Population pressure on cultivable land only made matters worse, as it forced some of the peasants living near the coast to fish occasionally, putting them into competition with the fishermen.

In the spring of 1792, a bitter fight among a group of commoners and fishermen broke out in the sea outside the Dinghai county of Zhejiang. The provincial Green Standard army sent Deputy Commandant Lin Fengming and the deputy brigade commander of the Dinghai garrison Li Tinghan to lead their troops to stop the fight. Upon their intervention, the feuding parties put their conflicts aside, joined forces, and attempted to expel the arbitrating troops as their common enemy. The troops responded by firing thirty shots at the resisters with their rifles, and the conflict seemingly subsided.

Curiously, the county magistrate of Dinghai did not report the conflict to any higher authorities. But when Zhejiang's provincial governor, Fu Song, and its provincial military commander, Chen Jie, looked into the matter themselves, they were surprised to find that the troops' response to the resistance was not impartial: they had selectively fired at one feuding party and spared the others. They also found that this bias was attributable to the bribes that some feud participants had paid to Lin Fengming, who in turn shared an amount of 100,000 *wen* of copper cash with Li Tinghan, to ensure that all of the troops dispatched to the area would act in favor of the feuding party that had paid. Shocked by this revelation, the provincial government of Zhejiang arrested Lin and Li, together with seven feud participants who had allegedly bribed the troops. The country magistrate of Dinghai, Yan Chengxia, who was suspected of collusion because of his reluctance to report this incident of resistance, was also arrested and transferred to Zhejiang's provincial capital at Huangzhou for interrogation. Yan committed suicide on his first night in custody.

After reading the detailed report about the incident from Fu and Chen, the Qianlong emperor judged that this was not an isolated incident and that it must have involved a corrupt ring in which local administrators, the local Green Standard army, and the armed fishermen had colluded. He ordered the provincial government to handle the case quickly and penalize the wrongdoers as harshly as possible. In the end, Lin and Li were decapitated, and their sons were banished to Xinjiang to be enslaved by the frontier troops stationed there. The seven fishermen responsible for the bribery were hanged. The provincial governor, Fu Song, was held responsible for the malfeasance of the lower level of his government and was given a pending disciplinary penalty. The provincial military commander, Chen Jie, who reported to the emperor that the troops only fired blanks at the fishermen, contradicting Fu's account that real bullets were used, was charged with protecting his own subordinates by fabricating details of the case. This allegation, on top of the charge that he had not disciplined his army strongly enough, led to his demotion. He was ordered to continue serving the army on an eight-year probation and at half salary.

The increasing resistance against the state's effort to contain social conflicts is only the tip of the iceberg when discussing the escalating social conflicts of the late eighteenth century. Circumstantial evidence suggests that there were far more instances of violent feud and class conflicts and that these were deliberately ignored by local authorities and not reported in official documents. The escalating social conflicts, as exemplified by the above two cases, were related to the ineffectiveness of local authorities in preventing their outbreak and to the rising demographic pressure across the empire, which intensified competition for natural resources. Another consequence of this mounting demographic pressure was the expanding population of landless vagrants, who were forced to survive by engaging in such illegal activities as appropriating state-protected natural resources, smuggling, and banditry. These activities, whose rates soared in the late eighteenth century, invited frequent state repression, which led to the increasing militancy and organization of the outlaws, thus inducing more violent resistance from the state authorities, creating a downward spiral of intensifying repression and resistance.

OUTLAWS AGAINST THE STATE

LOGGERS FIGHT FOREST RANGERS[6]

Fujian province was a region under extreme ecological pressure, and its marginal population employed a wide range of strategies to exploit its limited local natural resources, including clearing forest to generate saleable timber and new fertile lands. This practice, however, conflicted with the local government's policy to limit public access to forestry resources, which were reserved for a handful of licensed loggers, who made significant contributions to the government coffers. Illegal logging by unlicensed commoners, as a result, became a flashpoint of repression and resistance.

The forest on the mountain of Gu to the east of Fuzhou, the provincial capital of Fujian, was a government preserve. This forest was not only marked by its economic value but also by its strategic, religious, and geomantic value. Gu was Fuzhou's natural shield against pirates or rebels arriving from the sea. The mountain also was the home of the Yongquan monastery, a nationally renowned sacred site and tourist spot. In 1743, the provincial government closed the forest off from public access and granted the Yongquan monastery the exclusive right to exploit its timber resources. The government assigned a superintendent and twenty rangers to enforce this rule.

On January 6, 1783, a ranger, Xue Wei, spotted a group of nine unauthorized commoners logging in the forest. He and two other rangers attempted to capture them. The loggers swiftly dispersed, but one was arrested. The logger attacked Xue with his pole, breaking his finger, then ran away. The furious rangers searched all over the mountain and caught one of the other fleeing loggers, Ni Yuyu. Having tied Ni up, the rangers took him to a nearby garrison for interrogation. Realizing one of their comrades was under arrest, the loggers regrouped and attempted to liberate Ni, for fear that he would disclose their names to the authorities. When the rangers and Ni were passing through the Piqiaodiao area, at the foot of the mountain, the other loggers attacked them. Ni broke away in the chaos and ran back to the forest with his arms still tied. Seeing that Ni had run away, the other loggers fled, and the outnumbered and injured rangers gave up chasing them. The authorities, humiliated by the incident, initiated a full-scale hunt for the loggers. By the end of January, all suspects involved in the logging and the assault on the rangers had been arrested.

Illegal logging was surely a profitable business in late eighteenth-century China, given the diminishing timber resources and the continuously rising demand for paper and building materials across the empire (Myers and Wang 2002). But it was not likely to be as profitable as smuggling salt, a commodity heavily regulated by the state and in great demand. Only a few monopoly business groups, which paid substantial taxes and fees to the government, were allowed to produce and sell it legally. The scant supply and high price of legal salt fostered an expanding black market. Governmental suppression of salt smuggling was a key trigger of many incidents of violent resistance.

ARMED SALT SMUGGLERS BATTLE INSPECTORS[7]

Starting in the late seventeenth and early eighteenth centuries, the Qing government encouraged peasants from overly populated provinces such as Hubei and Hunan to resettle in the Sichuan basin and claim the fertile land there. As a result, the Sichuan lowland became a vibrant immigrant society. Commercial towns along the Sichuan portion of the Yangzi River, such as the city of Chongqing, developed into prosperous markets linking Sichuan to the rest of the empire. By the middle of the eighteenth century, most of the fertile lowland in Sichuan had been claimed, but the influx of migrants continued (Entenmann 1982). The new migrants, who tended to be poor, single males, began to settle in the infertile highlands, where they could grow only marginal crops such as taro and corn. Many of them found it difficult to survive on agriculture, and they alternatively served as day laborers, couriers, or traveling peddlers. Many peddlers smuggled illegal goods alongside legitimate items, with salt being the most profitable—and risky.

On Leap March 26, 1784, five peddlers doing business in Hejuchang of Jinzhou county of Sichuan discussed a joint visit to Wenjiang to purchase bulk linen to sell back in Jinzhou. They also discussed the news that Peng county, which lay between Jinzhou and Wenjiang, was experiencing a hike in salt prices. They decided to purchase salt locally in Jinzhou and sell it in Peng county, so that they could earn sufficient cash to cover their business trip to Wenjiang. Each of them would buy sixty *jin* of salt—the maximum amount an individual was allowed to purchase—from the official salt wholesalers. Two of them did not have enough cash and purchased thirty *jin* each instead. Loaded with 240 *jin* of salt altogether, they set out for Wenjiang, via

Peng county. On the road, they ran into seven other friends, who offered to facilitate the transportation and sale of the salt in exchange for a share of the profits. The original five agreed, and all twelve continued on their way.

They started to look for a salt buyer once they arrived in Peng's county seat, on March 28. Meanwhile, five salt inspectors were patrolling the streets for smugglers. They soon identified the peddlers from Jinzhou and attempted to arrest them. The smugglers attacked the inspectors with their carrying poles and small knives. Some of them even managed to seize the inspectors' swords. Three of the inspectors were killed in the fight, and all twelve peddlers fled. The incident immediately caught the attention of the higher authorities, who mobilized a security force from the prefecture capital to search for the runaway resisters. They were captured one after the other across the province. After extensive interrogation, the authorities cleared the peddlers of affiliation with any secret brotherhood or heterodox organizations—a suspicion that explains the authorities' initial level of anxiety over this incident. Nevertheless, local officials considered their smuggling activities as equivalent to banditry and ordered their immediate execution.

The salt smugglers, similar to the illegal timber loggers in the previous case, were no more than an ad hoc alliance of occasional scofflaws. In many other cases, in contrast, salt smuggling was conducted by professional, long-standing smuggling organizations. These organized smugglers were usually heavily armed, and their acts of resistance to state suppression could be much more lethal.[8] Organized or not, salt smugglers could be regarded as benign outlaws, as they did benefit local society by helping bring down salt prices (although their activities did affect government revenue, in a time of worsening fiscal crisis). In comparison, bandits, who consisted mainly of unemployed vagrants who preyed on local society, were a more pernicious type of outlaw. In the late eighteenth century, most banditry in the empire was conducted by highly organized bandit groups, with the Guolu in Sichuan as the most notorious.

RESISTANCE AND ORGANIZATION OF THE GUOLU BANDIT GROUP[9]

As we saw in the previous case, the large population pressure in Sichuan's highlands as well as its ever-expanding vagrant population accounted for the proliferation of illegal activities such as salt smuggling. Banditry offered another opportunity for marginalized men to survive. With time, disorganized bandits active in Sichuan consolidated into hierarchical bandit groups in the form of secret brotherhood associations. The Guolu society, which was characterized by its fraternal ideology and paramilitary organization, was the most prominent of such groups.

The activities of the Guolu society were first documented by the imperial government in the 1740s (Cai 1984, 486). At first, the society was no more than a nuisance to the authorities. The Guolus usually exacted protection fees from commuting merchants or robbed them at trade-route intersections in gangs of no more than a few dozen people. They played cat and mouse with government inspectors, and state repression rarely triggered open resistance from them. But by the 1770s, the Guolus had grown so powerful that they dared to plunder market towns in broad daylight and wage war on government forces. The society recruited members in blocs and developed elaborate rituals to welcome new brothers. Each new member was granted a machete from his superior, and he was asked to cut his queue and burn it into ashes, which were then mixed with wine and shared by all attending members. This ritual signified the formation of fictive blood ties among the members.

The queue was imposed by the Manchu rulers in the seventeenth century as a symbol of subservience to Manchu rule. Cutting it, therefore, manifested a bold defiance of the authorities. It also facilitated the daily activities of the Guolus, who were divided into brigades (called *peng*) of about ten members each. Each brigade was led by one commander, who followed the orders of a higher commander. When an order to plunder a group of merchants or raid a market town was issued to different brigades, members of these brigades, who had not met one another before, could recognize their queueless brothers instantly when they arrived at the scene and charged in concert. If an individual member was pursued by the authorities, he could identify queueless people on his escape route and entrust them with his loot, which he could recover later after evading the hunt. While the grassroots brigands led a nomadic life and maintained hideouts in caves, remote temples, and mountain shacks, brigand commanders lived like law-abiding commoners and used local teahouses and other unsuspicious sites as nexuses to coordinate with other brigades, gather intelligence, and pass on orders. (Commanders were not required to cut off their queues.)

In April 1781, the Guolus launched large-scale, simultaneous raids on several of the most prosperous market towns in the Sichuan lowland, including

He zhou in Chongqing prefecture and Liangshan county in Zhong zhou. Hundreds of brigands were reportedly involved in each raid. They resisted governmental repression violently and slaughtered a large number of inspectors and local troops dispatched to stop them. The scale of their operations, their defiance toward the authorities, and the skillfulness in battle against government troops caught the attention of the emperor. A coordinated, provincewide hunt for the Guolus was launched. In response, the brigands dispersed and fled in different directions. While some escaped into the mountainous areas of northern Sichuan, others hid on Sichuan's borders with Hunan, Hubei, and Guizhou. The hunt was not very fruitful, given the Guolus' high mobility in inaccessible regions. But by the fall of that year, nevertheless, the government had arrested some brigands and extracted from them lengthy confessions, which offer us a glimpse of the Guolu society's organizational structure, recruitment methods, and members' backgrounds.

One of the arrested brigands was Zhang Laoda, a migrant to Sichuan from Hunan's Wuling county, under Changde prefecture. After resettling in Sichuan's Shehong county, Zhang opened a tofu shop with his wife and children. Later, his business declined, the shop closed, and he was left with no money. His wife left with his children, and he became a beggar, wandering around the region. In August 1780, when he was traveling to Fuzhou, he encountered a young beggar, Pi Xueli, who was an unemployed migrant from Hubei's Lichuan county. He successfully lured Pi into becoming his adopted son and begging companion. During their trip to Fuzhou, Zhang raped Pi, and the two entered into a relationship. In March 1781, the two traveled to Taiping county, where Zhang ran into a number of unemployed old friends. Zhang organized a bandit group with them to plunder passing merchants in the area, and as a symbol of membership they all wore grass hats with a white stripe. While fleeing from the authorities, they encountered a few Guolus also on the run. They merged forces and turned the group into a large Guolu brigade, with Zhang as the commander. They continued their journey to the Guizhou-Sichuan border, plundering whomever they encountered while escaping from government inspectors. In the end, under the intensifying pressure of the authorities, they disbanded, and Zhang escaped back to his hometown in Hubei, where he was arrested.

Another example: Zeng Laoyan and his younger brother Zeng Lao'er were from Hunan's Mayang county. They lived together. The two Zengs traveled to Tongren prefecture in Guizhou, where the junior Zeng married Teng. The party of three then moved, in 1774, to Hubei's Laifeng county. Finding it difficult to make a living as cultivators in Laifeng, they all traveled to Youyang zhou, in Sichuan, on February 2, 1781, to look for jobs. In the hostel where they stayed, they encountered Liu Laosi and his fellow Guolu brigands. Liu invited them to join the Guolus, and they agreed. They were armed with machetes by Commander Liu, and the brigade of ten started looting merchants and retailers in the region. After hearing about the large-scale crackdown on the Guolus in Sichuan, the brigade disbanded, and the Zengs left Sichuan to move back to their hometown, Mayang, where they were identified and arrested on September 26.

In the last example, Wang Sanbao was an orphan from Hunan's Changsha county. He worked as a wage laborer in various places. In 1778, he moved to Shaanxi to work in a salt pan. After a while, he and four coworkers found that their wage was too low to live on. They decided to form a bandit group, and on May 16, 1780, the group went to Ziyang county, bordering Sichuan province, to loot salt couriers passing through the area. They managed to take in 3,600 *wen* in copper in their first attack. A Guolu brigade commander, Hu Fannian, and his followers traveled to Ziyang and were impressed by the skills and courage of Wang's bandit group. Hu invited Wang's group to join them, and the latter agreed. The enlarged Guolu brigade then moved on to Taiping and Kai counties of Sichuan to raid local shops and travelers. In May 1781, learning of the intensifying government campaign against the Guolus, Hu's brigade escaped to the mountains of Taiping county and hid in a cave. In a violent encounter with government troops, the bandits killed a number of soldiers and managed to escape unharmed. Wang fled with three comrades to Guizhou province and looted the local area. After amassing sufficient cash, the four dispersed, and Wang traveled back to his hometown in Hunan's Changsha, on July 21. Wang's suspicious neighbors, curious about his sudden return from Sichuan, reported him to the local authorities. Wang was arrested after local inspectors searched his home and discovered bloodstained machetes and other weapons.

The Guolu example shows that in the late eighteenth century sporadic robberies and state-resisting violence by outlaws were converging into organized predation and resistance undertaken by brotherhood associations. The Guolus were not the only group. The Tiandihui (Heaven and Earth Society) of the southeastern coastal region was another prominent example. We will also see that these brotherhood organizations were the catalysts that helped transform sporadic antistate violence into the building blocks of large-scale rebellion.

FROM RIOTS TO REVOLT

Mounting state-resisting violence in the late eighteenth century troubled the Qing state not only because of the direct threat to law and order in local societies but also because of the propensity of the conflicts to merge, possibly becoming larger revolts that could challenge the Manchu state's Mandate of Heaven. The late eighteenth-century surge in state-resisting violence occurred along with a surge in armed rebellions against the Qing government. The three biggest rebellions against the state during this time were the Tiandihui uprising in Taiwan, in 1785–1788 (unleashed by a brotherhood organization); the White Lotus Rebellion in central and southwestern China, in 1796–1805 (initiated by a heterodox religious sect that we will turn to in a moment); and the Cai Qian rebellion (participated in by pirates and fishermen) along the Fujian and Zhejiang coast, in 1798–1805. Figure 4.1 shows the temporal distribution of (1) state-resisting protests as documented in

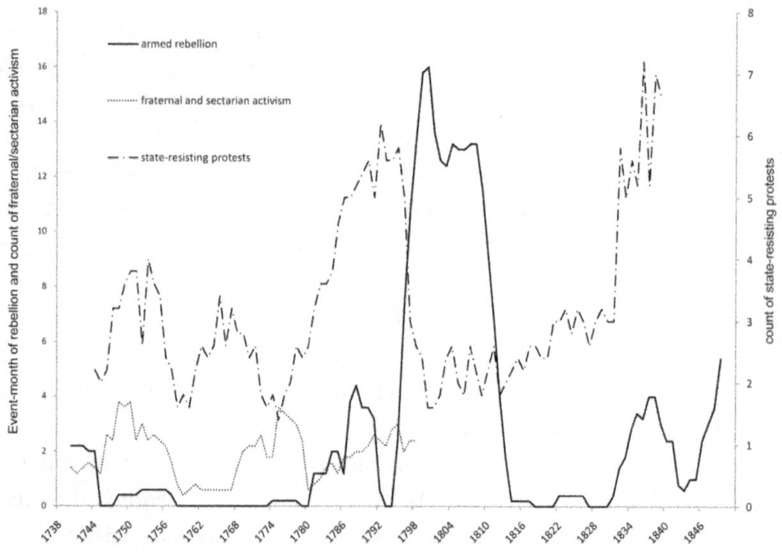

FIGURE 4.1 Event-Month of Armed Rebellions, Reported Cases of Heterodox and Secret-Brotherhood Activism, and State-Resisting Protests, 1736–1849 (five-year moving average) (*source*: QSG; QSL; Zhang 2003, table 2)

this study, (2) the level of fraternal and sectarian religious activism, and (3) the intensity of armed revolt during the eighteenth century. The level of fraternal and sectarian activism is based on a recent survey of all available documentation about government persecution of such organizations during the Qianlong reign (Zhang 2003). The intensity of armed revolt is measured in the event month of armed rebellion against the ruling dynasty for each year based on the documentation in the chronology section of the *Draft History of the Qing* (*Qing shigao*, or QSG).[10]

This figure shows that the surge in armed revolts in the late eighteenth century did not correspond to any surge in secret brotherhood or heterodox religious activism, which remained relatively constant during the eighteenth century. At the same time, the proximity of the crest of state-resisting protests in the late eighteenth century to the crest of armed revolts, with a slight time lag, suggests that the revolts could be the outgrowth of protests. This plausible association between protests and revolts is supported by figure 4.2, which shows that the regions where the three major rebellions unfolded were also hotspots of resistance. Altogether, 41 percent of all documented protests across the empire in 1776–1795 were concentrated in those regions of rebellion.

The connection between resistance and revolt, given the temporal and geographical coincidences between them, can be further verified through an examination of the beginnings of the Tiandihui and White Lotus Rebellions. Some important building blocks of the two revolts, the Zhangzhou-Quanzhou migrant lineages in Taiwan and the Guolus in Sichuan, were exactly the same social groups that accounted for the rise of antistate protests in the two places prior to the revolts, as we saw earlier.

THE TIANDIHUI REBELLION IN TAIWAN

The Tiandihui Rebellion in Taiwan was launched by the Tiandihui, a secret brotherhood association that had been active in the region since the early eighteenth century, if not earlier (Ownby 1996). Its members were mainly poor tenants, petty landowners, peddlers, smugglers, landless vagrants, and other segments of the mobile population. This organization, like other brotherhood organizations in other parts of the empire, engaged in banditry, racketeering, mutual aid among members, and resistance against government levies and abuses (Harrell and Perry 1982; Overmyer 1981; Ownby 1986; Yu 1987a, 1987b).

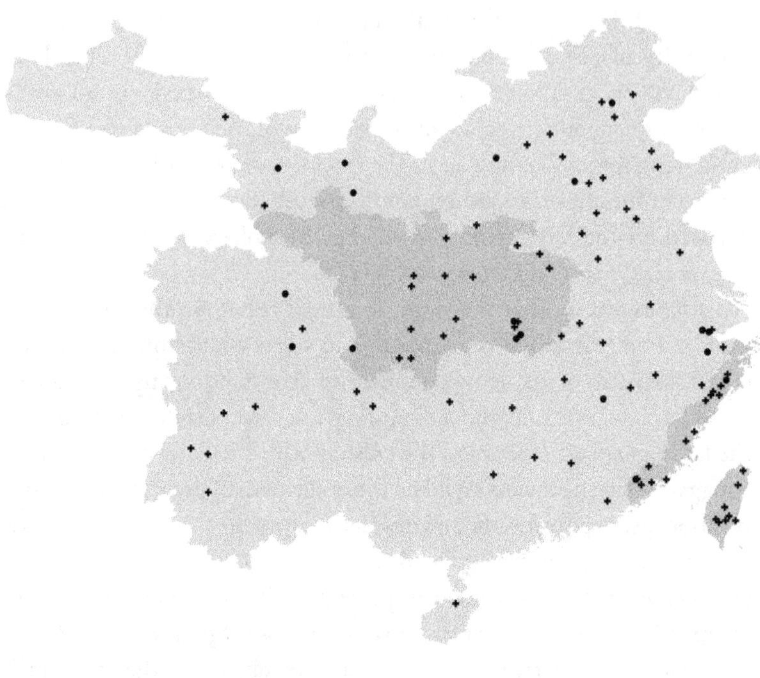

• state engaging protest

✦ state resisting protest

Han areas affected by major revolts

FIGURE 4.2 Documented Protests in 1776–1795 and Locations of the Three Major Revolts of the Late Eighteenth Century (background map: CHGIS)

The immediate trigger of the rebellion was that certain branches of the association were involved in a deadly feud within the Zhangzhou lineage that had been involved in the bloody, large-scale feud that developed into antistate resistance in 1782, as discussed earlier. In the context of escalating social disorder in Taiwan and with memories of the 1782 feud still vivid, the local authorities were determined to curb the feud in its formative stage and repress the Tiandihui, who were fanning the conflict. This crackdown on the association not only threatened its survival but also enabled abusive local officials and government runners to extort extra levies on local residents, who already resented the ordinary levies but were threatened with arrest as Tiandihui suspects if they refused to pay. Lin Shuangwen, a leader of the Tiandihui, declared that he would launch a "rebellion as a response to official repression" (*guanbi minfan*). The rebellion swept the island like wildfire.

Lin's revolt openly rejected the rulership of the Qing government and followed the script of dynastic transition from the start. He titled himself the "Great Alliance Leader Who Complies with the Heavenly Way" (*Shuntian da mengzhu*), formed a government-like structure to administer the territory seized by the rebel army, and assigned official titles to his comrades. He even began issuing quasi-imperial edicts to the people newly under his rule and adopted a new imperial calendar of the reign of *Shuntian* (Complying with the Heavenly Way). Lin's imperial pretensions were fully expressed in his edict to the Taiwanese people that denounced the existing dynasty for its failure to fulfill the Confucianist ideal of paternalist and benevolent rule. He went on to portray himself as a righteous heir of the Mandate of Heaven:

> Only if the officials love the people as their children do they deserve to be called the fathers and mothers of the people. Those on Taiwan today are all corrupt officials and dirty underlings who harm the souls of the people. Your commander could not bear not to extirpate such evil, and in order to save my people, I raised a righteous army, and swore before heaven that the inhumane and the unrighteous would perish under 10,000 swords.
>
> (QUOTED IN OWNBY 1996, 84; SEE ALSO QIN 2004, 549.)

The rebellion's leadership was composed of Tiandihui members who were already persecuted by the authorities. Their participation in the rebellion can be interpreted as a desperate attempt to survive governmental repression. But the sustenance and scope of the revolt, which lasted over two years and put most of Taiwan's fertile lowlands under rebel control, would not have been possible without the enthusiastic participation of non-Tiandihui members. Interrogation reports on captured rebels show that many foot soldiers of the rebel army were not Tiandihui members. They came not only from the mobile, reckless segment of the local population, peddlers, smugglers, seasonal labor, and the like but also from small cultivators hard pressed by mounting tax burdens. This population segment also constituted the driving force of many resistances and banditry activities in the local society preceding the rebellion (Qin 2004; Ownby 1996; cf. Ka 2003).

The many participants of the rebellion who were not Tiandihui members were not subject to the draconian persecution that drove the Tiandihui to revolt. They therefore did have the choice of preserving their ordinary life and not joining the rebellion. One key motivation behind their decision to take the risk and revolt against the incumbent dynasty must be the idea that the Qing's Mandate of Heaven was over and that a new dynasty, plausibly represented by the rebels, was about to come. But why would they be convinced that the Qing's Mandate of Heaven was over? I return to this question after looking at another major rebellion of the time, the White Lotus Rebellion.

THE WHITE LOTUS REBELLION IN THE SOUTHWEST

The dynamics that led to the outbreak of the White Lotus Rebellion, which lasted from 1796 to 1805, were quite similar to the eruption of the Tiandihui Rebellion. The White Lotus sect, a thriving heterodox Buddhist sect in eighteenth-century China, was growing rapidly in the mountainous, forested area in the interprovincial border regions of Sichuan, Hubei, and Shaanxi in the 1780s and 1790s. Their activities, comprising mostly collective worshipping, posed no immediate threat to the authorities. But their potentially subversive millenarian belief unnerved the imperial state, which decided to launch an all-out crackdown on the sect before it grew too large to be contained. Draconian persecution in the mid-1790s caused the desperate sectarians to rise up against the Qing government. Their revolt, which started as a knee-jerk reaction to ferocious repression, developed into the longest rebellion in eighteenth-century China, lasting nearly a decade.

The key difference between the White Lotus sect and Tiandihui lies in the former's millenarian worldview. The White Lotus sect could be characterized as utopian as much as Tiandihui could be characterized as fraternal. The origins of the White Lotus tradition in China could be traced back to circa 1100 C.E. It represented a convergence of the religious traditions of Taoism, Buddhism, and Manichaeanism. The core of the religion was the idea of cyclical kalpas (*jie*), a classical Sanskrit term meaning successive transformations of the world between immensely long periods of time. The religion's followers worshipped the Eternal Venerable Mother (*Wusheng laomu*), the supreme deity controlling the recurrence of kalpas. Each kalpa was governed by a particular Buddha, and the present kalpa was governed by the historical Shakyamuni Buddha. When the current kalpa ended, the material world would be destroyed by horrific famines, diseases, and other catastrophes. The Venerable Mother would then send the Maitreya Buddha (*Mile fo*) to earth and initiate a new kalpa. Followers of the religion were told to practice vegetarianism and to lead an ascetic way of life so that they would attain salvation and be brought back to the womb of the Venerable Mother during the calamitous kalpic transition (Harrell and Perry 1982, 290–291; Overmyer 1976, 1981; Ownby 1999;Yu 1987a).

The White Lotus religion spread throughout China among the lower classes after the twelfth century. Independent and competing White Lotus sects proliferated (Gaustad 2000). Many of these sects were entrepreneurial, and their leaders used sectarian activities for personal gain. They attracted people by demonstrating their magical powers of exorcising and healing. They told followers that their chance of salvation during the kalpic transition increased with their contributions to the sects (Qin and Zhang 1999, 296).

The organization of many of the sects was redistributive and alien to the Confucianist orthodoxy. Within the sect, wealthy members were expected to contribute more, and their donations were used to help poorer members (Entenmann 1982, 192). The guru-disciple hierarchy overturned Confucianist social hierarchies such as those between men and women and the old and young. Young women were frequently found among the prominent leaders in sectarian organizations (Liu 1988, 788–793; 2004; Yu 1987b).

Time and again, the White Lotus religion was appropriated as an ideology to call for rebellious action. In those instances, the content of the religion mutated, with a utopian twist. It prophesized that during the imminent kalpic transition, the Maitreya Buddha would be reincarnated, and his followers should aid his work of cleansing the world of corruption to earn their salvation. The new kalpa would be the dawn of an egalitarian world in which there would be no distinction between men and women, rich and poor, old and young (Harrell and Perry 1982, 290–291; Yu 1987a). The first major outbreak of a large-scale uprising with a White Lotus outlook was in the mid-fourteenth century, when heterodox sects in the south declared in the midst of plagues and famines that the Maitreya Buddha had come and that people in search of salvation should take up their arms and overthrow Mongolian rule. The Red Turban Army, to which Zhu Yuanzhang, the founder of the Ming dynasty, belonged, was one of the militant sects inspired by the White Lotus religion. After the establishment of the Ming dynasty, in 1368, the new emperor persecuted the White Lotus sects aggressively, for he was well aware of the religion's rebellious potential. But toward the mid-seventeenth century, as the imperial government was weakening, White Lotus activism revived and fueled a number of major rebellions contributing to the final collapse of the Ming.

The White Lotus religion was suppressed once again after the consolidation of the Qing dynasty. But the Qing government was never able to root out heterodox sects altogether. During the eighteenth century, White Lotus sects proliferated alongside the growth of mobile, landless vagrants, who found social support and spiritual comfort in sectarian activities (Harrell and Perry 1982, 297–301). Countless semisecret vegetarian halls were established, where believers gathered to have vegetarian meals and perform religious rituals. The mid-Qing period witnessed rapid expansion of many other Buddhist sects as well. The authorities often could not clearly tell whether these sects were connected to the White Lotus tradition and if they had rebellious propensities or not. As we saw in a number of cases in the last chapter, different levels of government could sometimes spend much time deliberating on whether a particular sect threatened the state and whether to persecute them.

There were also unambiguous cases throughout the eighteenth century in which White Lotus sects initiated open revolts, such as the aborted uprising of the Dasheng sect in Sichuan in 1746 (ZPZZ-KYQ 640–647; QSL-QL 242, 30; 245, 10; 249, 31–32; 265, 11–12, 265, 37–38; 267, 31), the vegetarian uprising in Fujian in 1748 (ZPZZ-KYQ 648–734; QSL-QL 316, 4; 317, 29–30; QSL-QL 309, 4–5; 309, 8–9; 309, 38–44; 312, 12–13), and the Clear Water sect revolt in Shandong in 1774 (ZPZZ-KYQ 746–771; Naquin 1981). They were mostly composed of sectarians themselves and never lasted long. For example, the Clear Water sect revolt, initiated by Wang Lun, was put down swiftly because "Ch'ing [Qing] social order was not yet close to a breaking point [as of 1774]. . . . The intensity of class conflict, population pressure, ecological vulnerability, or elite unresponsiveness was not so great as to produce more than a handful who were willing to gamble on Wang Lun" (Naquin 1981, 153).

What was so special about the White Lotus Rebellion of 1796–1805, in contrast to previous short-lived White Lotus revolts, was in how it resembled the Tiandihui Rebellion of 1785, in that the sectarians' initial revolt was echoed enthusiastically by nonsectarian commoners. The confessions of arrested rebels revealed that many of the rebellion participants were propertied cultivators and taxpayers who were outraged by local officials' heavy exaction (Qin 2004, 413–414, 417–418; QZQ 5, 63–64, 79–80). In addition, the rebellion also attracted a large group of marginalized people and social outcasts identified by the Qing authorities as "perverse and lawless people" (*wulai bufazhi tu*) and the "unemployed" (*wuyezhi tu*). They included shack people in the hills (*pengmin*), salt smugglers, counterfeiters, and organized bandit groups, predominantly the Guolu association, which we encountered previously (ZPZZ-KYQ 825). As in the Tiandihui case, these segments of the local population, who became the revolt's foot soldiers, had been actively involved in escalating violent resistance against local authorities in the region prior to the outbreak of the revolt (Jiang 1980, 19–27; Zhang n.d., cited in Feng 1998, 236, 239).

The White Lotus rebels, despite their utopian convictions, adopted the script of dynastic transition upon the revolt's eruption. Leading rebels assumed imperial titles (such as *zhenzhu*—"true sovereign"). They even added a Ming restorationist theme to the movement by spreading the following poem:

> The Qing dynasty is over;
> the four Buddhas are now at the gate;
> after the end of barbarian [i.e., Manchu] rule,
> who is going to assume the throne?
> The Sun and Moon will restore the Ming;
> the *niu* and *ba* will turn out to be the earthly King.
>
> (CITED IN LIU 1988, 780; SEE ALSO MCCAFFREY 2003, 102)

In the poem, the characters for *niu* and *ba* are code words that combine to generate the word *zhu*, the imperial surname of the Ming dynasty preceding Manchu rule.

Just as in the case of the Tiandihui Rebellion, what is left to explain about the scale and duration of the White Lotus Rebellion was why so many men and women who had been resisting local authorities on their own would take the risk to exacerbate their localistic confrontations into a revolt against the dynasty. They had to believe that the Manchus had lost the Mandate of Heaven. This popular belief was surely associated with the falling administrative and fiscal capacity of the state, as well as the rise of tax bullying, corruption, and social disorder in the late Qianlong reign. But perhaps the single most important precondition for such a belief was the perception that administrative decay and corruption were not caused by individual officials but rooted in the irreversible moral degeneration of the throne.

As we saw in chapter 1, the popular and elite conception that Heshen was the ultimate culprit of rampant corruption, the rumor about Heshen's homosexual affair with Qianlong, and all the other popular tales about Qianlong's infidelity propagated across the empire in the late eighteenth century. These rumors severely damaged the moral legitimacy of the imperial center, and the emperor was no longer seen as infallible and morally supreme.

After the White Lotus Rebellion, the Jiaqing emperor, who executed Heshen in 1800 to restore the state's moral legitimacy, openly attributed the revolt to the declining moral authority of the imperial center, brought on by the rise of Heshen to the pinnacle of imperial power:

> The sectarian rebels used opposition to officials' abuse and exaction as an excuse to revolt. . . . If the people expected prosperous times and were content with their works and lives, if they were not absolutely desperate, how would they ignore their own family and property to take such risky action? The rebellion must be rooted at the malaise that the supposedly benevolent officials failed to rule according to the virtuous intention of the dynasty, turned greedy and became exploitative. County officials' exploitation of the people was not totally for the officials' own benefits alone, but also for their tribute to their superiors. Provincial governors' exploitation of the people was not only for themselves, but also for their tribute to Heshen. The layers of exploitation originated at one person—Heshen, and my people had to bear all burdens of the resulting endless exaction.
>
> (ZPZZ-KYQ 834; MY TRANSLATION)

This explicit denunciation of Heshen amounted to an implicit criticism of Jiaqing's father, Qianlong, who was responsible for Heshen's rise and was believed to be in a relationship with him.

As Dingxin Zhao (2009) notes, dynasties in imperial China have grounded their rule on performance legitimacy. Besides their ability to maintain the peace and stability of the empire, another crucial source of this legitimacy was the rulers' performance in setting a moral example to the empire's subjects. If the imperial center failed to live up to the moral standard prescribed by Confucian teachings, then it would be perceived as having lost the Mandate of Heaven and would be vulnerable to revolt. The rise of large-scale revolt in late eighteenth-century China must be attributable to the alleged moral degeneration of the imperial center and rumors about the emperor's promiscuity. This explanation also coincides with studies of the English and French Revolutions that recurrently point out the significance of popular perception about the moral decay of the authorities, usually expressed in widespread rumors about the private lives and sex scandals of the monarch and the ruling elite, in precipitating popular revolts (Chartier 1991, 111–135; Merrick 1990; Stone 1965). The rebellions in the late Qianlong reign, amidst the alleged degeneration of the imperial center and rumors about the emperor's immorality, provide more support to this thesis.

Another example that illustrates the connection between popular perception of a degenerating imperial center and the transformation of apolitical resistances into rebellion against the dynasty is the Nien Rebellion in North China, in the 1850s, as investigated carefully by Elizabeth Perry (1980). The rebellion was launched by Nien bandit groups, which had never challenged the Manchu state directly before the 1850s. Their chieftains had originally adopted apolitical titles such as "Big Cannon Chang," "Water Pipe Wei," "Cat-Eared Golden King of Hell Wang," and the like. But in the aftermath of the Qing defeat in a series of wars with Western imperialist powers and the beginning of the Taiping Revolt in South China (which I address in chapter 6), the Nien chieftains, though seeing no rapid deterioration of their immediate material conditions, began to assume rebellious and politically inflected titles such as "King of the Han," which "indicated not merely imperial pretensions, but a direct attack upon the legitimacy of the Ch'ing [Qing], who were, of course, Manchus and not Han Chinese" (Perry 1980, 121). The rebellion grew when other commoners, tax rioters, and even gentry elites formed militias to seize local governments and cooperate with the Niens, whom they saw as a more promising ally than the Qing state (Perry 1980, 121–127).

To be sure, the perceived moral degeneration of the state alone could not have caused these revolts had it not been for the growing marginal population created by century-long demographic expansion and commercialization, the deepening fiscal crisis that forced local officials to raise taxes, and the drop in the ability of the state to maintain social order in the late eighteenth century (Kuhn 1970). Nonetheless, if these latter factors were sufficient conditions for revolt, then we should have seen a continuous outbreak of rebellions in the early nineteenth century, when all of these problems worsened. On the contrary, as we will see in the next chapter, the wave of violent resistance toward local officials in 1820–1839 was less connected to large-scale revolts than was the late eighteenth-century wave, even though early nineteenth-century China also had its share of persecuted sectarian groups that dared to launch rebellions. The failure of these sectarian rebellions to last for any protracted duration, as well as the reluctance of local resisters to join these rebellions, needs to be understood in the context of the reform efforts of the Jiaqing and Daoguang emperors. Though this reform did not succeed in arresting the actual administrative decay of the state and curbing illegal levies and other abuses of the bureaucracy, it did reestablish the moral legitimacy of the imperial center and distance the throne from the wrongdoings of local governments.

To fully understand what difference the moral legitimacy of the imperial center—or the lack of it—can make to the development of popular resistance, we need to make a more elaborate comparison between the revolt-prone local resistances of the late eighteenth century and the less rebellious resistances of the early nineteenth century. We will turn to this in the next chapter.

ILLUSTRATIONS OF CHINESE PROTEST FROM QING TIMES TO PRESENT

PICTORIAL DEPICTION OF popular protest in the mid-Qing period was rare. But the rise of newspapers and illustrated books on current affairs in the late nineteenth century led to increasing visual documentation of the different repertoires employed in contemporaneous protests, which manifested substantial continuity with repertoires of earlier periods. The following pictures all depict protest events that occurred in the last few decades of the Qing dynasty.

ILLUSTRATION 1 In many protests in Qing times, protesters kneeled and prayed with glowing incense to the authorities, which resembled the action of dedicated worshippers in temple. In this case, former opium sellers requested assistance from the government after opium sales were banned.

SOURCE: *TUHUA XINWEN*, 1909 (COURTESY OF NATIONAL LIBRARY OF CHINA)

ILLUSTRATION 2 Petitioners gathered at the provincial government of Sichuan in 1911. The petitioners, led by local literati and constitutional monarchists, pleaded for the release of a few protesters, arrested a few days ago, who had resisted the appropriation of local private railroad by the national government and foreign powers. Note that the kneeling continued even after the guards had brought out guns and begun shooting. Government brutality against the petitioners helped trigger the Republican Revolution that toppled the Qing dynasty later in the year.

SOURCE: SONGQINGTANG ZHUREN ED. 1915. *XINHAI SICHUAN LUSHI JILUE* (CHRONOLOGY OF PROTECTING RAILROAD MOVEMENT IN SICHUAN). CHENGDU: QIANGFU GONGSHI (COURTESY OF NATIONAL LIBRARY OF CHINA)

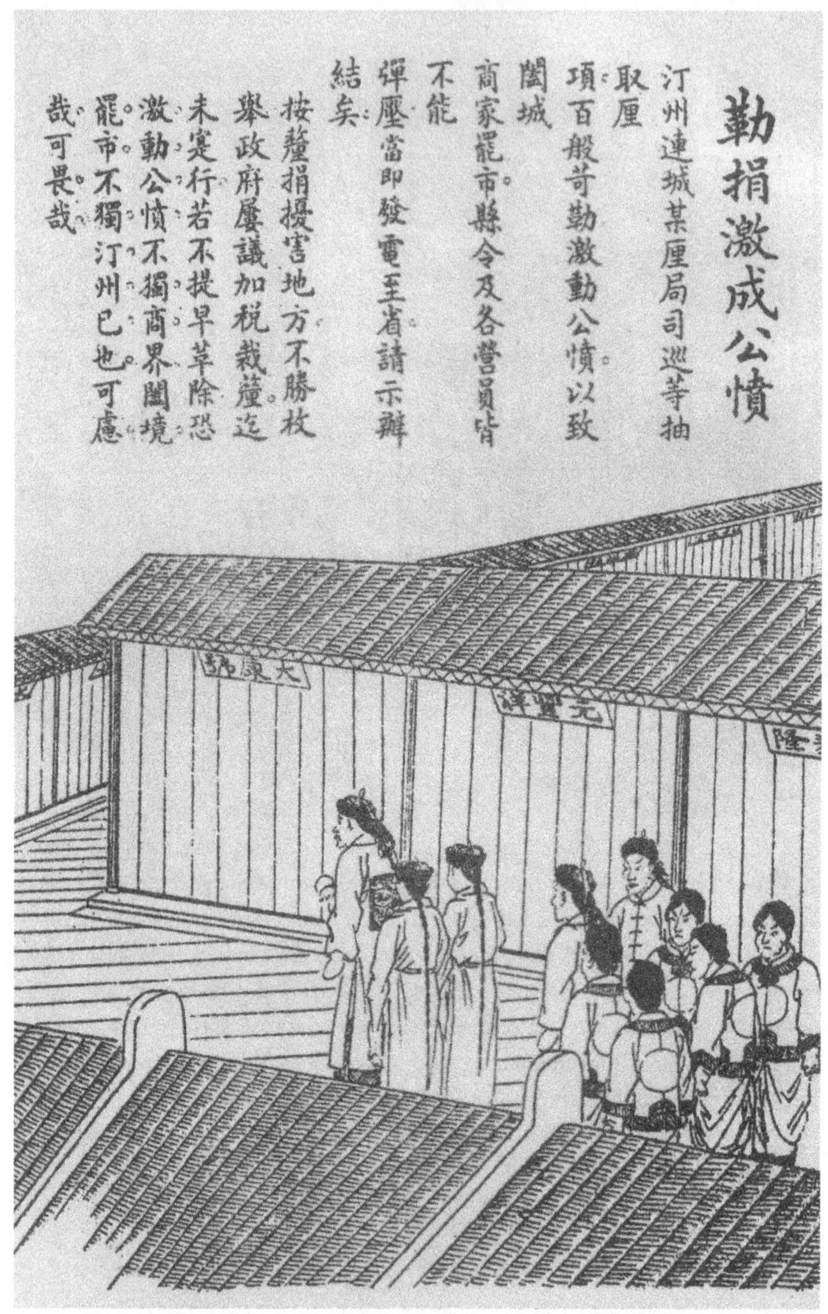

ILLUSTRATION 3 Sometimes merchants shut down their shops in concert to put pressure on the authorities. Amid a market strike against a new tax, the local magistrate, who seemed to be anxious, inspected the empty street and closed-down shops. *SOURCE: TUHUA XINWEN*, 1909 (COURTESY OF NATIONAL LIBRARY OF CHINA)

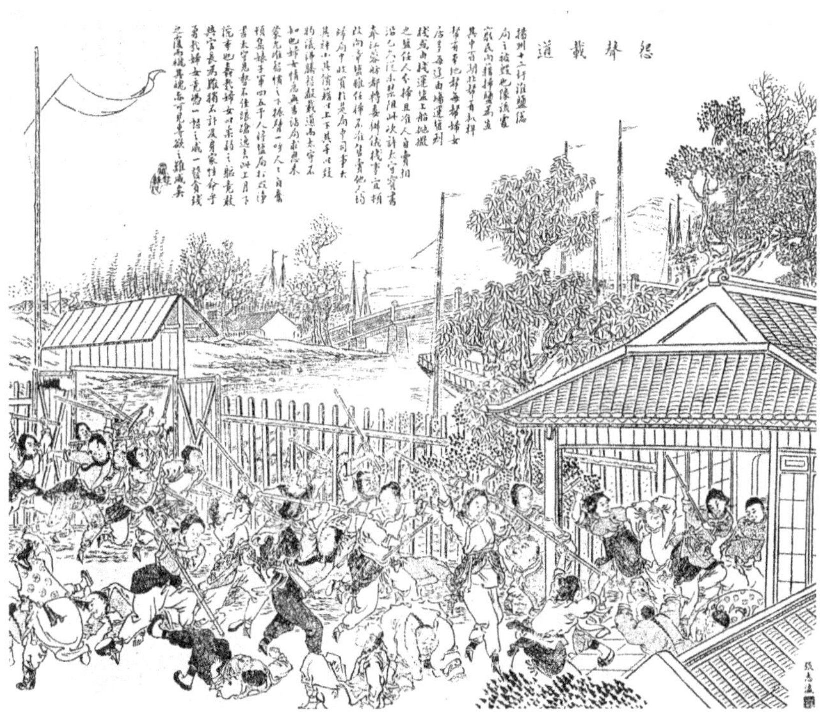

ILLUSTRATION 4 Illegal private salt makers, mostly women, in Yangzhou demolished the official salt-selling station in reaction to the government's intensifying effort to eradicate private salt sales.

SOURCE: *DIANSHIZHAI HUABAO,* 1897 (COURTESY OF NATIONAL LIBRARY OF CHINA)

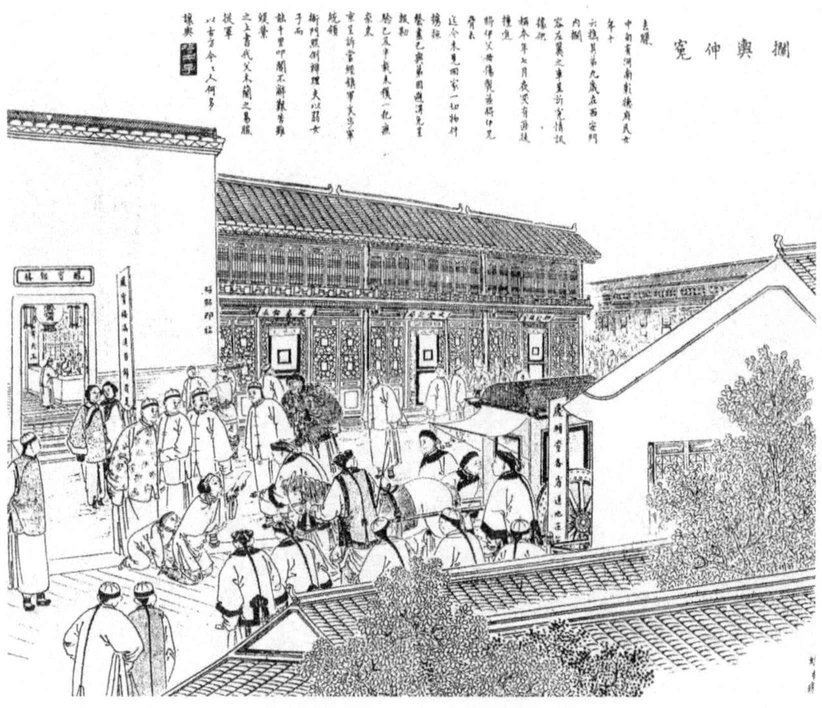

ILLUSTRATION 5 Though protesters could become confrontational toward the local government, they would also respectfully appeal to higher authorities. This scene shows a case of such appeal in which a girl and her younger brother, representing their family, traveled from Henan province to Beijing and intercepted the procession of a high-rank official to lodge a complaint against the local government, which allegedly failed to hunt down the bandits who looted their home, slaughtered their parents, and kidnapped their older brother.

SOURCE: *DIANSHIZAI HUABAO,* 1885 (COURTESY OF NATIONAL LIBRARY OF CHINA)

ILLUSTRATION 6 The tactic of respectfully appealing to higher-level authorities against the acts or decisions of lower-level officials took an intriguing turn in the age of imperialism. In this incident from the 1880s, women from a neighborhood straddling the Chinese and Western territories in semicolonial Shanghai petitioned the authorities in the Western territory, accusing the Chinese authorities of levying an illegitimate property tax on them. This petition manifested a conception of Western powers as being higher authorities than the ailing Qing state.

SOURCE: *DIANSHIZAI HUABAO*, 1887 (COURTESY OF NATIONAL LIBRARY OF CHINA)

ILLUSTRATIONS 7 AND 8 Contemporary protests in China manifest a strong parallelism with Qing protests. In the winter of 2005, villagers from a Guangdong county protested against a land grab without compensation by the local government. The local security force shot dead more than a dozen villagers and seized their bodies. In the aftermath of the killing, villagers kneeled and pleaded with glowing incense, while requesting the security force to let them reclaim the victims' corpses.
SOURCE: (COURTESY OF BOXUN NEWS)

ILLUSTRATION 9 The filial-loyal repertoire of protest toward the authorities is by no means restricted to less educated citizens. In the early phase of the 1989 student movement in Beijing, three student representatives kneeled in front of the Great Hall of People to plead for a dialogue with the highest leaders of the government.

SOURCE: (COURTESY OF 64MEMO)

ILLUSTRATION 10 The continuity of the practice of Qing repertoires of protest up to the present is attributable to the reproduction of historical memory through such cultural vehicles as *Bashan Xiucai* (Scholar from Ba Mountain), a popular classical Sichuan opera. It was created in 1983, won major national awards, and was recreated in 2002 to be toured across the country. It was also performed in Sichuan and Beijing in 2009 as one of the special events celebrating the 60th anniversary of the People's Republic of China. The plot was based on a folk-historical legend from Qing times. Stricken by natural calamity, hungry villagers from Bashan kneel in front of the county office to request famine relief in the opening scene. The county magistrate, who has embezzled the famine-relief fund, refuses to help and orders a bloody crackdown on the petitioners. The villagers then turn to a member of the local literati, who helps them write complaints and appeals to higher authorities. Years of tenacious petition finally touches a conscientious official higher up in the government, and justice is done.

SOURCE: VIDEO SHOW OF THE PERFORMANCE AS PHOTOGRAPHED BY AUTHOR

5

RESISTANCE AND PETITIONS, 1820–1839

In the aftermath of the White Lotus Rebellion, the fiscal and administrative crises that contributed to the wave of violent resistance and revolts in the late eighteenth century continued to deepen. To make matter worse, the Sino-British opium trade and the resulting hemorrhage of silver from China led to an empirewide deflationary economic crisis, the "Daoguang Depression," beginning in c. 1820. The falling price of agricultural products as measured in silver *taels* made it increasingly difficult for peasant cultivators to meet the ever-rising tax and surtax quotas imposed by increasingly extractive local governments. It was in this context that the 1820–1839 wave of protest unfolded.

From table 5.1, we can see that the majority of documented protests in 1820–1839, similar to the wave in 1776–1795, were state resisting. Tax resistance continued to be prominent, and it represents a larger proportion in this wave than in the earlier one. This can be explained by the heightening tax burden on taxpayers as a result of the deepening fiscal crisis of the state and the nascent economic downturn. The second difference between the late eighteenth-century and early nineteenth-century waves is the sharp increase in collective retribution against government agents in the latter period. This type of action includes collective violence against specific officials who were alleged to be corrupt or bullying (such as government agents who ate without paying) as well as violent reactions to unpopular policies that damaged local interests (such as tightening regulations on local businesses), among others. This increase, like the rise in tax resistance, can be seen as the result of a general intensification of competition over diminishing resources between local communities and the increasingly coercive local states amid an economic crisis.

The third difference is the moderate decline in resistance against state crackdowns on illicit activities. One reason for this decline was the state's

TABLE 5.1 Composition of Documented Protests with Known Claims, 1776–1795 and 1820–1839

Claims	1776–1795 (%)	1820–1839 (%)
State engaging	**17.1**	**25.1**
Seeking famine relief	1.8	9.2
Seeking participation in state decision-making process	9.9	10.9
Seeking intervention into social conflict	0.9	0.8
Seizing state functions	4.5	4.2
State resisting	**82.9**	**74.7**
Retributions against policies or officials	6.3	15.1
Resisting crackdown on illicit activities	45.9	31.1
Resisting tax levy	19.8	21.8
Resisting state intervention into social conflicts	10.8	6.7

Note: Events for 1820–1839 with known claims: 119; events with unknown claims: 4

loosening monopoly on salt and, in the early 1830s, the partial legalization of the private salt trade. This reduced salt smuggling and thus salt smugglers' resistance against the state. The other plausible reason for this decline is the Qing state's newfound reliance on local militias in maintaining local social order. These militias, usually mustered by local officials and funded and staffed by local gentry, were the key to the successful pacification of the White Lotus rebels after the Qing government found the imperial troops unreliable. Local militarization persisted in the early nineteenth century, as the local social order continued to deteriorate (Kuhn 1970; Wakeman 1966). During this period, the growing population and the economic crisis pushed increasing numbers of bankrupt cultivators into the rank of landless vagrants, who were susceptible to recruitment by bandit groups. As suggested by several studies, armed banditry did not cease to grow in the early nineteenth century (Antony 2003, 2006; Perry 1980, 2002; Wakeman 1966). But with the transfer of responsibility for bandit suppression from official security forces to militias, banditry became less likely to develop into antistate violence as it had in the late eighteenth century, as outlaws no longer were confronting agents of the state as much as before. There is even evidence showing that in some regions infested by banditry and smuggling, the outlaws were so militant and organized that local governments simply gave up on containing them and let them thrive (Macauley 2009, 19–21).

Protests in 1820–1839 were predominantly violent. Overall, protests involving violent repertoires constituted 65.0 percent of all protests in the period, in contrast to 69.5 percent in 1776–1795 and 34.2 percent in 1740–1759. Remarkably, even state-engaging protests in this period tended to be more violent and confrontational than those in the earlier two waves of protest. Blackmailing government officials with violence, in lieu of offering humble petitions, became a popular way to request local government action such as famine relief. This was rarely seen in the earlier two waves.

The following are detailed studies of several cases of tax riots, retribution against state agents, and other collective violence against the state in 1820–1839, with a focus on retributive violence, as it was more prevalent in this period than in other periods.

We shall see that these protests resembled many of the antistate actions of the late eighteenth century as far as their violence and confrontational stance toward local governments are concerned. But as we will see in the latter half of this chapter, these protests seldom coalesced to become the building blocks of open revolt against the dynasty, as violent resistance in the late eighteenth century did. In contrast, many early nineteenth-century resisters restricted their antagonism to local authorities while maintaining their filial loyalty toward the central government. In particular, the surge of violent resistance in this period was concomitant with the rise of the practice of capital appeal (*jingkong*), in which local communities sent appellants to Beijing to petition representatives of the emperor against corrupt and abusive local officials. I argue that this bifurcated disposition toward local and central authorities among aggrieved subjects—violence against the former and filial loyalty toward the latter—is a consequence of the successful regeneration of the empire's moral legitimacy under the reformist rhetoric of the Jiaqing and Daoguang emperors, even though this rhetoric never succeeded in arresting the worsening malfeasances of the bureaucracy.

TABLE 5.2 List of Cases Included for Thick Description, 1820–1839

Issue	Province	Type	Page
1. Lineage group fights against tax collectors	Fujian	state resisting	139
2. A spontaneous tax riot	Jiangxi	state resisting	141
3. Soldiers' assault on their general	Gansu	state resisting	142
4. A community fights against Manchu bannermen	Fujian	state resisting	144
5. Fighting a nepotistic local magistrate	Hunan	state resisting	145
6. Storming an indifferent government during a subsistence crisis	Fujian	state resisting	146
7. Blackmailing the state for famine relief	Jiangsu	state resisting	149
8. Seizing control of public infrastructure	Jiangsu	state resisting	151
9. Capital appeal as an alternative to a tax riot	Anhui	capital appeal	159
10. Deliberating between appeal and protest against tax abuses	Shandong	capital appeal	161
11. Riot and capital appeal as a two-pronged strategy	Hubei	capital appeal/ state resisting	162
12. Violence and appeal against the appropriation of a local temple	Zhili	capital appeal/ state resisting	164

TAX RESISTANCE

Tax resistance continued to be salient in the early nineteenth century. In the late eighteenth-century cases that we saw in the last chapter, a tax-resistance protest event usually stemmed from the reluctance of some taxpayers to submit their payments. When they were pressed by tax-collection agents, they reacted fiercely by fighting them off, and in many cases they were joined by their fellow clansmen or villagers. This scenario is also common in early nineteenth-century tax resistance, as shown in the following case.

LINEAGE GROUP FIGHTS AGAINST TAX COLLECTORS[1]

The Fujian area is known for the strength of its local lineage organizations and the practice of tax farming. In the mountainous east-central and southeastern provinces, including Fujian, local governments often did not have sufficient manpower to collect taxes and assigned the task to tax farmers, who were usually gentry leaders of local lineages. They collected taxes for the local government in exchange for a fee. As lineage leaders were sometimes too powerful to be adequately controlled by local officials, this custom opened the way for abuses on the part of tax farmers, who might routinely withhold tax revenue from the state or side with their fellow villagers rather than the government in a tax dispute (Myers and Wang 2002, 596; Yamamoto 1999).

In the early nineteenth century, local governments in the Fujian area were not spared from the empirewide fiscal crisis, and the competition for resources between local officials and tax farmers escalated. In the fall of 1838, the magistrate of Fuqing county of Fuzhou prefecture, Huang Yaoshu, found that the Chen clan in Gaoxia village, which was under his jurisdiction, had accumulated more than 250 *taels* of tax arrears, despite the government's recurrent efforts to urge tax payment.

In the middle of October, Huang issued an ultimatum to the Chen clan and dispatched a team of government runners to collect the taxes household by household. Chen Maoliang, a tax farmer in the lineage who was responsible for submitting the tax payments of his fellow clansmen, gathered his brothers to deter the runners from entering their village. Citing widespread economic difficulty in the area, Chen Maoliang asked for a further delay of tax payment for the whole clan and told the runners to leave. Infuriated by Maoliang's disobedience, Huang sent another team of runners, headed by Weng Rui, to arrest Maoliang on October 20.

When the runners arrived at the Gaoxia village, Chen Maoliang attempted to resist arrest and cried out for help. His brothers and other angry clansmen encircled the government agents. The crowd attacked Weng Rui and his team with wooden poles, sharpened bamboo shafts, and thrown stones. Outnumbered, the arrest team dispersed and ran back to the county office. Weng Rui, however, ran to an adjacent village, where Huang and a few of his officers were investigating a homicide case. Having listened to Weng's report, Huang immediately led his officers to Gaoxia village.

Knowing that the county magistrate was coming in person to arrest him, Chen Maoliang urged more clansmen to defend the lineage. Some joined voluntarily; others joined under the threat of revenge by Maoliang and his brothers. A group of twenty-seven well-armed kinsmen was assembled. They barricaded the village entrance and waited for the magistrate to come. The arrival of Huang and his officers triggered an intense fight, and the well-organized clansmen injured several officers. Chen Maoliang threw stones at the magistrate and hit him in the back of his head. One of Maoliang's brothers, Chen Youyou, charged and pierced the magistrate's neck with a sharpened shaft. Amid the chaos, a group of villagers from a nearby rival lineage arrived and tried to stop the violence. The Chen clansmen immediately dispersed and hid.

Magistrate Huang, badly injured but alive, led his fellow officers to a garrison nearby, requesting the troops to organize a hunt for the twenty-seven Chen clansmen involved. The clansmen were all arrested in a few days and sent to the Fuzhou city for trial. Chen Maoliang was sentenced to immediate decapitation, and the government put his corpse on public display. Chen Youyou was sentenced to strangulation in the winter. Others were sentenced to different degrees of corporeal punishment, depending on the extent of their involvement in the resistance.

This case of tax resistance was initiated and organized by a strong local lineage group. The following case shows that a tax riot also could be initiated by a network of literati and consist of local residents from all walks of life who gathered spontaneously to support them.

A SPONTANEOUS TAX RIOT[2]

Jiangxi's Nan'an prefecture, bordering the northern part of Guangdong, was a mountainous and infertile region that survived on the commercial traffic between the international port of Guangzhou and the economically vibrant regions along the Yangzi River. It depended on the grain imported from other areas via the Gan River, which connected southern Jiangxi to the Yangzi River.

In the autumn of 1831, the upstream area of the Gan flooded, and grain output there dropped drastically. In the spring of 1832, when depleted grain storage from the previous year was exhausted and the new crop was not yet ready for harvest, Ganzhou and Nan'an prefectures, which were both located downstream of the Gan and relied on upstream regions for their food supply, suffered from soaring food prices. While Ganzhou was more accessible via the Gan, Nan'an was deeper in the mountains and was hit harder by the food shortage.

Long crippled by the populace's underpayment of taxes and tribute grain and incapable of organizing famine relief by itself, the prefecture government of Nan'an worried about the possible outbreak of rioting, as the area's residents were well known for their restlessness. Prefecture officials tried to preempt such unrest by asking wealthier families to donate their grain to the government to be used as famine relief. The response of the wealthiest elites, who apparently shared the government's fears, was enthusiastic. But the burden also fell on less well-to-do landowners, and the "donation" turned out to be compulsory rather than voluntary.

At the same time, local officials redoubled their efforts to pressure households that had not fulfilled their tax obligations. Wu Liyuan, an average peasant who had refused to pay his overdue tax for years, was one of the key targets. The government issued him an ultimatum for clearing all tax arrears. To resist, he gathered twenty-one of his friends, and on March 16 they traveled together to the prefecture government to request a hearing by the prefecture magistrate. Wu's friends included laid-off government clerks and soldiers, released prisoners, disqualified licentiates, and local ruffians. They shared Wu's resentment of the government's pressure for tax payment. They also were against the government's call for involuntary grain donation. They preferred universal relief through the release of official granary stock. The government clerk recognized Wu as a notoriously recalcitrant taxpayer and refused to let him and his companions in, but they managed to squeeze into the office anyway. The chaos attracted a large crowd of onlookers outside the government building.

When Wu and his friends met with the prefecture magistrate, they demanded the immediate termination of tax levies and the grain-donation drive. They also asked for universal famine relief. The magistrate turned down their request and explained the difficulties facing the government. The protesters refused to leave, and the crowd outside became restive. To avoid greater trouble, the magistrate backed down and promised to offer a sale of grain from the government granary at lower-than-market prices. But the crowd's major concern was the levies. When the magistrate wrote a notice about the details of the relief and instructed the clerks to post it at the main entrance of the government office, Wu quickly took hold of the board and smashed it to pieces. Realizing that their demands had been denied, the crowd threw stones at the building, and a riot ensued. It was swiftly terminated by government security forces, and forty to fifty of the most aggressive participants were arrested.

RETRIBUTION AGAINST UNPOPULAR POLICIES OR OFFICIALS

The state's deteriorating discipline and its fiscal crisis not only fueled tax resistance but also prompted other forms of violent confrontation between local communities and agents of the state. In the next case, we see how aggressive cost-cutting measures in the army triggered soldiers' violent retribution toward the general responsible for initiating such measures.

SOLDIERS' ASSAULT ON THEIR GENERAL[3]

The Gansu province was at the empire's northwestern frontier, bordering Mongolia and Xinjiang and deep in the barren Loess Plateau. Many imperial troops were stationed there for border defense and to monitor the local Mongolian and Muslim populations. The province's economy depended largely on subsidies from the imperial center. By the 1830s, the provincial government of Gansu was trapped in an alarming deficit, just as other provincial governments were. Corruption proliferated throughout the provincial bureaucracy. Some local officials made a living by charging high legal fees on litigants, some became indulgent opium smokers and let their undisciplined private housekeepers become de facto administrators of their county or prefecture, some thrived on embezzling soldiers' rations, and some raised special taxes to finance their luxurious private entertainments.

In 1830, the provincial government experimented with a new measure to alleviate the fiscal crisis. It lent most of the public granary stocks out to private merchants, who were to sell the grain at high profit margins and repay their debt in cash to the government with interest. According to the plan, the government would be able to use the repayment, together with the interest payment, to fill its coffer and restock the granaries. This optimistic assessment turned out to be unrealistic. The experiment aggravated the fiscal crisis, as many merchants failed to repay their grain debt, and the already deficient public granaries were left depleted.

The near bankruptcy of local governments contributed to a series of riots among the soldiers, whose livelihoods depended on government provisions. In 1833, Ye Changtai, a beloved general of the imperial troops stationed in Lanzhou, was accused of disobeying his superior and was cashiered. This offended many of Ye's loyal followers in the army. Yuan Gui, Ye's replacement, took a tough stance on army discipline. A large number of elderly soldiers were laid off to cut costs. The manufacture of military-used ropes, an established sideline activity and an important source of income for the soldiers, was banned.

These harsh measures and the desire to avenge Ye's dismissal triggered a troop mutiny. On a freezing night in late 1834, more than one thousand armed soldiers gathered outside the general office in Lanzhou city and set the building's entrance on fire. General Yuan Gui, who tried to suppress the unrest in person, fell from his horse and was slain. Yuan's residence in the building was burned to the ground. When reinforcements came, the rioters rushed to the eastern gate of Lanzhou city, killing a number of gatekeepers, and fled. A few rioters were arrested and tortured to death.

Suppression of the riot did not assuage the soldiers' discontent. Just a few months later, in April 1835, soldiers complained that their rationed grain was contaminated by impurities. They suspected that the authorities had replaced their original rationed rice with substandard rice and were pocketing the price difference. Hearing no response from the government, they stormed the prefecture government at Lanzhou. To avoid further trouble, the prefecture magistrate gave in and replaced their low-grade rations with better ones. The above two cases of state-resisting violence in Lanzhou were far from exceptional; many other cases of troop unrest were reported all over Gansu that year.

This type of militant retribution was not limited to soldiers. Below is a case of community-wide resistance against harassment by Manchu bannermen.

A COMMUNITY FIGHTS AGAINST MANCHU BANNERMEN[4]

The city of Fuzhou was the provincial capital of Fujian province, a coastal province known for rampant pirate activities and its historical propensity toward revolt. A large Manchu banner army was stationed in the city. On June 29, 1836, a few Manchu bannermen walked out from their camp to have lunch at Jinmenlou, a noodle restaurant located nearby, at the city's center, in the vicinity of the provincial government and provincial admiral's office. Drunk and refusing to pay, they harassed the waiters and other customers and beat those who resisted, smashing the furniture in the restaurant. Their actions angered those who lived and worked in the neighborhood. It is likely that the local residents had been frequently abused by them. The locals gathered rapidly to attack the bannermen and forcefully expel them from the area. Outnumbered and wounded by the furious street crowd, the bannermen retreated to their camp but soon returned with a dozen more armed companions. They were once more badly beaten by the locals and again fled. One bannerman was captured by the crowd, who dragged him to the Min county office to ask for his arrest and complain about the bannermen's abusive behavior.

The bannermen soon returned with nearly one hundred men, armed with swords and spears. They tied up and kidnapped a number of employees of the nearby restaurants and shops. All the shops in the neighborhood, which was the most prosperous district of the city, then closed down simultaneously in a market strike. To mediate the conflict, the Min county magistrate ordered a truce between the two parties. He also released the bannerman captured by the street crowd in exchange for the bannermen's release of the kidnapped employees. On the next day, the merchants still refused to open their shops. Only after intense persuasion from the county magistrate did the area's business return to normal.

As Mark Elliot (1990) points out, the ruling Manchus were never as Sinicized as has been previously supposed. Ethnic tension between Manchus and Han Chinese was persistent and at times manifested in overt conflicts between Manchu bannermen stationed in urban garrisons and local Chinese townsmen. The conflict in this case is surely ethnically tainted. But it also paralleled many other cases in which commoners defended themselves against the abuses by other agents of the state who were ethnic Chinese.

Retributive violence against agents of the state could not only be a direct reaction to their specific behavior but also a reaction to the general underperformance and corruption of the local government. In the following case, local residents mobilized to call for the ouster of an unpopular local official for his failure to maintain social order and for the tax abuse, corruption, and favoritism of the local government.

FIGHTING A NEPOTISTIC LOCAL MAGISTRATE[5]

Yongzhou was the southernmost prefecture of the Hunan province, bordering the Guangxi and Guangdong provinces. It was a mountainous region where Han Chinese and the ethnic minority Yao cohabited. Lin Zhuokui, who became the prefecture magistrate in 1832, was more than seventy years old. He was known in the prefecture for his greed and lethargy. He simply let the government be run by his house servants, who frequently traveled around the prefecture and extorted valuable gifts from county officials and local residents. Residents were, of course, not spared from the tax abuse.

During Lin's term of office, the conflict between Han and Yao cultivators intensified. For example, in Yongming county, deep in the mountains, a deadly feud broke out between Yao tribesmen and an alliance of four Han lineages over ownership of a tract of cultivable land. Neither the county nor the prefecture officials interfered, and the bloodshed escalated. Officials even imprisoned local literati who tried to stop the conflict by lodging plaints with higher levels of government, for fear that the litigation would alert the provincial or central government to the dreadful local conditions.

What finally revealed Lin's incompetence to the central authorities was an open confrontation between the local literati and the local government. In 1833, the prefecture government issued a notice to a handful of local gentry families well connected to Lin to inform them of several vacancies at the rank of government clerk. These posts were supposed to be filled through the formal procedure of open nominations and selections involving all local communities in the area.

A few educated elites in Dao zhou, under Lin's jurisdiction, detested his favoritism and had attempted several times to lodge plaints at the prefecture government against his abusive protégés, but the prefecture government repeatedly rejected them. The local elites, disgruntled by these officials protective of Lin, seized the opportunity of the outcry over the nepotism in government-clerk selection to openly express their anger. They inscribed a stone tablet with their demands for a comprehensive and fair replacement of all government runners and clerks. They erected the tablet at the entrance of the zhou office, immediately drawing a crowd of four hundred to five hundred bystanders. With their fury running high, the bystanders stormed the office building. Being indecisive and afraid of this popular rage, zhou officials consulted the prefecture government, which sent a representative to Dao zhou to smash the tablet and tame the angry crowd. But local tension persisted. A province-level official in Henan reported the event to Beijing through a secret memorial. In response, the central government decided to pacify the area by forcing Lin to step down from the post of magistrate.

In the above cases, violent resistance against the government was triggered by unpopular actions or policies initiated by the local authorities. Government inaction and failure to fulfill its proclaimed obligation of protecting its subjects could trigger violent retribution against specific officials as well. The following episode, in which hungry citizens smashed a local government office out of anger at the government's indifference to a local subsistence crisis and its alleged collusion with local merchants, is a case in point.

STORMING AN INDIFFERENT GOVERNMENT DURING A SUBSISTENCE CRISIS[6]

Fuzhou city, the provincial administrative seat of Fujian, relied on grain shipments from the Lower Yangzi Valley and Taiwan to feed its large population and the large number of Manchu troops stationed there. In the spring of 1832, the area was hit by a thunderstorm, and the river connecting the city to the ocean became so rough that grain ships from Taiwan and Jiangnan could not navigate it. The price of grain in the city shot up, rising from twenty *wen* per *sheng* to as high as fifty *wen* per *sheng*. In early April, Shi Liuhai, identified as a jobless thug by the local authorities, was shopping at the Yingfeng grain house. After the transaction, he complained to the seller that the change they gave him was in substandard copper coins. He demanded a discount on the purchased rice as compensation. In an emotional quarrel, Shi failed to persuade the seller.

In revenge, he gathered nine of his friends to revisit the Yingfeng grain house the next day. As grain prices continued to rise, the group made a scene by demanding that the shop owner lower his grain prices across the board. The owner ignored their demand, and they began to loot the grain shop, with bystanders joining in. Local guards were sent to the scene but were expelled. To establish the righteousness of their action and demand the authorities' intervention, Shi and his friends led the looting crowd on a march to the provincial governor's office. They tried to file a plaint against the Yingfeng grain house, accusing it of manipulating grain prices and bringing hardship to the commoners.

Apparently reluctant to get involved in the dispute, government officials kept the door of their office shut. Shi, together with his forty-some followers, was outraged at this cool reception. They accused local officials of being complicit with the grain merchants in raising prices to an unaffordable level. The protesters smashed the door of the government building and stormed the lobby. Someone even set the office on fire. After a while, imperial troops were dispatched from the local garrison. They arrived at the scene after most of the rioters had dispersed and managed to arrest only six participants.

Despite the crackdown, riots and looting in the city did not die off. The local government resorted to pacification and released the six arrested rioters. It even promised to work with local merchants to try to lower the grain price to thirty *wen* per *sheng*. Contrary to the government's expectation, this belated fulfillment of its obligations further empowered the angry citizens, who saw the governmental response as a sign of weakness and initiated another round of protests. Citizens from all corners rose up to loot nearby grain houses. In a matter of a few days, all the major grain houses in town were emptied. Worse, local residents were still angry at the government's initial indifference to its subjects' hardships and at its alleged collusion with grain sellers in letting prices rise unchecked. On one occasion, several hundred rioters (several thousand, according to a different account) gathered in front of the provincial-government office and threw stones at it. The unrest died down only after additional imperial troops were employed to disperse any gathering crowd.

This is an interesting case, as the first half of it resembles a state-engaging protest of the mid-eighteenth century, when commoners often sought help amid subsistence crises from local authorities in their conflicts with dominant classes such as grain merchants. But the second half of this case sets it apart from such state-engaging protests, as the inaction of the local government, as well as its alleged collusion with grain merchants, angered the protesters, who responded by attacking government buildings. The violence was a retribution against government indifference and corruption, and it carried no specific demand on the authorities.

In the mid-eighteenth century, local authorities were more responsive to popular demands for paternalist assistance during subsistence crises, which accounts for the prevalence of state-engaging protests in 1740–1759. In the early nineteenth century, local governments had much less capacity and will to respond to such popular demands. This case, together with cases in the previous chapter, offers crucial clues as to why state-engaging protests declined in the late eighteenth and early nineteenth centuries. When time and again the government remained aloof to popular requests for help during subsistence crises, the subjects naturally lowered their expectations of the state and became inclined to solve their problems themselves through such actions as grain looting.

However, there were still a handful of state-engaging protests in the early nineteenth century. While a few resembled filial-loyal protests of the mid-eighteenth century, many were much more antagonistic. In such state-engaging protests, as we see in the following two cases, protesters did not plead with the local government to perform its paternalist function but attempted to blackmail the state into action or even take over part of the state's functions themselves.

ENGAGING THE STATE ANTAGONISTICALLY

We saw in chapter 3 that most state-engaging protests in the mid-eighteenth century were peaceful, involving loyalist petitioners docilely pleading for the paternalist intervention of the state. This type of state-engaging protest was not nonexistent in the early nineteenth century. But more remarkably, a large number of state-engaging protests in this period involved violent attacks on government facilities and agents. In contrast to their respectful mid-eighteenth-century predecessors, many early nineteenth-century protesters sought to engage the state by forcing the government to take action in their favor or even by directly seizing state functions through violence. The following two incidents are representative of such protests.

BLACKMAILING THE STATE FOR FAMINE RELIEF[7]

By the early nineteenth century, the official granary system had been paralyzed and could no longer handle large-scale subsistence crises as effectively as it did in the mid-eighteenth century (Jones and Kuhn 1978; Will 1990, 289–301; Will and Wong 1991, 75–92). In the spring of 1831, the entire Jiangsu province was subjected to heavy rains and floods. Agricultural production was brought to a halt, and famines emerged in various locations, particularly in the relatively less prosperous northern parts of the province. The government delayed annual tribute-grain collection from the area as a famine-relief measure. But this only worsened the situation, as it reduced traffic on the Grand Canal (along which Jiangnan tribute grain was transported to the imperial capital), increasing unemployment among sailors working on tribute-grain boats.

Under these conditions, a large number of desperate and starving residents from various counties fled their home villages and traveled to better-off areas to ask for relief from wealthy households and local governments. These relief-seeking teams were widespread and destabilizing, as they were joined by local hooligans, salt smugglers, and reckless, unemployed sailors. The most notorious team at the time was led by Wang Yulin, a local ruffian who organized more than 3,600 starving peasants into an intimidating army of relief seekers. They successfully extorted large sums of cash from several county governments in northern Jiangsu.

Wang was a local resident of Yancheng county, which was seriously flooded in early July 1831. He gathered a number of his closest friends—including two disqualified licentiates and a few other local ruffians—into a squad to seek famine relief, urging local governments in the region to release stocked official grains. They called a meeting to plan the recruitment of famine victims and chart the route of their relief-seeking tour. Wang was elected as the chief famine-relief seeker (*zong zaitou*). Four deputy chiefs and one treasurer also were elected. After the meeting, they managed to attract thousands of desperate relief seekers from their respective villages or lineages.

On July 15, the highly organized and sizeable team started on their journey. Their first stop was the county seat of Yancheng. On July 16, they arrived at its city wall and asked the county government to provide sufficient food and cash to each of them. Wang exaggerated the total number of participants, claiming that there were ten thousand of them. Intimidated by their size, government clerks said that the county magistrate had left town for a famine survey. They allowed the crowd to enter the city and led them to meet with the county secretary. Arriving at the secretary's office, the crowd laughed at two wooden planks hanging by the entrance inscribed with the motto "To engage in hydraulic works enthusiastically, to protect the people's livelihoods perpetually" (*daxing shuili yongbao minsheng*). One of the famine-relief seekers suggested that it should be changed to "Flood breaking out relentlessly, and people's livelihood under threat perpetually" (*daxing shuihuan minsheng bubao*). In the burst of laughter, someone tore down and smashed the planks.

It turned out that the county secretary was out of town as well. But his housekeeper came to the lobby and promised that the relief seekers would receive forty thousand *wen* of copper cash but that they must wait for the relief outside the city gate. Wang agreed and left the office but was soon informed that the county magistrate was back in town. Wang immediately led the relief seekers back to the magistrate's office. He demanded that the magistrate give them 130,000 *wen* of copper cash on top of what the secretary's housekeeper promised, along with a sufficient number of boats so that they could return home swiftly, and intimating that he could not guarantee how his followers would react if their requests were refused. To avoid further trouble, the magistrate gave in to all of Wang's demands and led them to wait at a village outside the city wall.

When the cash and boats arrived, the money was distributed among the relief seekers. Wang turned one of the boats into a treasury office from which everybody received their share. But as planned, Wang did not return home, and they traveled to other counties via the river networks. They also stocked their boats with salt that they purchased locally at Yancheng, which was a salt distribution center, and then sold it illicitly wherever they went. On July 21, they arrived at the county seat of Dongtai. They repeated the trick that they had pulled in Yancheng, again reporting that there were nearly ten thousand of them, and they successfully extorted 209,000 *wen* of cash from the county government.

As Wang's group continued to defraud other cities, the provincial authorities conducted a clandestine investigation of the structure and leadership of Wang's relief-seeking team and prepared for a crackdown. Wang Yulin fell into a trap when his crowd reached southern Jiangsu. His coleaders were arrested one after the other. Finally, on September 11, Wang was arrested when he asked for famine relief in the county office of the Huating county of Songjiang prefecture.

Wang Yulin's strategy of seeking famine relief from local governments was quite different from the submissive petitions employed by most famine-relief seekers in the mid-eighteenth century. This case was not an isolated one; many similar cases in which protesters extorted or even looted grain and cash from local governments were documented in the early nineteenth century. We see in this case that local literati were involved in at least the planning stage of the action, and local communal bodies such as lineages were important building blocks in the plan. This increasing reliance on violence or threat of violence in forcing local governments to offer relief demonstrates that in the early nineteenth century, the perceived ability and responsiveness of local governments had become so low that protesters no longer expected a voluntary offering of relief. Famine-relief seekers in this case even openly ridiculed the paternalist proclamation of the local government by smashing the motto plank hanging over the office's entrance.

The same dynamics of popular disillusion with local governments are demonstrated in the next case. In contrast to many mid-eighteenth-century protests in which residents humbly petitioned local governments to open dike gates for flood control, flood victims in this case did not bother asking the government at all. Instead, they usurped the government's dike-management function by destroying part of a local official dike to release floodwater themselves.

SEIZING CONTROL OF PUBLIC INFRASTRUCTURE[8]

Huai'an prefecture, in the northern part of Jiangsu province and on the south bank of the Yellow River, was frequently troubled by flooding. In the late summer of 1832, the river level rose considerably, and local officials' attempts to prevent the water from overflowing were in vain. Agricultural land alongside the riverbank was flooded. In the southern part of Taoyuan county, heavily hit by the flood, a wealthy cultivator, Zhao Butang, and two other local literati met in a shack in the remote Xinji area to plot an action to rescue their community.

They decided that the government was unreliable and that they had to act on their own. They devised a plan to hire a number of landless vagrants, arm them, and send them to dismantle the part of the official dike that separated the Yellow River, the Hongze Lake, and the Grand Canal, into which the rising water of the river could be drained. The plan was carried out on August 21. The hired hands approached the dike, which was guarded by local troops, on a small boat from the Hongze Lake. They overpowered the guards, tied them up, and dug a hole of more than ninety *zhang* on the dike. Subsequently, the floodwater from the Yellow River rushed into the Hongze Lake and the Grand Canal. The fields along the southern bank of the Yellow River around the Taoyuan area were saved.

The destruction of the dike alarmed the emperor and high-ranking bureaucrats, as the subsequent flooding of vast areas surrounding the Hongze Lake and Grand Canal threatened the cultivators there. More important, the canal's rising water delayed the schedule of the tribute-grain ships that transported Jiangnan's grain to Beijing. This delay was a serious concern in the fall of 1832, when the North China Plain was hit by a growing famine. The bureaucracy swiftly arrested and executed those involved in breaking the dike. Local officials held responsible for dike security were demoted or even imprisoned.

This violent event in Taoyuan, identified as "unprecedented" by the emperor, was replicated in other parts of the empire. In the Pei county of Jiangsu's Xuzhou prefecture in the spring of 1834, and in the Wenshang and Shouzhang counties of Shandong's Yanzhou prefecture in the summer of 1833, local cultivators imitated the Taoyuan pioneers, destroying official dikes to release floodwater and save their fields.

These episodes stand in contrast to the petitions and organized protests that aimed to influence government action involving water control about a century earlier. The difference suggests that the government's capacity to regulate the hydraulic apparatus had declined to the point where local communities, when confronting a subsistence crisis, no longer expected the government to respond effectively. They resorted to self-rescue by seizing the state function of hydraulic management.

MUTED REBELLIONS, MOUNTING APPEALS

We see in the above eight cases, as well as in table 5.1, that collective resistance from 1820 to 1839 was at least as violent and confrontational as that between 1776 and 1795. On the other hand, while resistance in 1776–1795 helped fuel large-scale revolts against the dynasty, resistance in 1820–1839 did not. Armed revolts did occasionally flare up in 1820–1839, and the dynamics of their initial mobilization resembled the Tiandihui Rebellion and White Lotus Rebellion, which we discussed in the last chapter. These revolts were initiated mostly by persecuted heterodox sectarians or members of secret brotherhood organizations.[9] What made the early nineteenth century different from the late eighteenth century was that in all of these revolts, the initiators were not echoed by many others, even in areas plagued by local unrest. This represents a sea change from the late eighteenth century, when many disgruntled subjects and seasoned resisters responded enthusiastically to the call for arms by rebel organizers, helping to turn small-scale, sectarian revolts into large, sustained, popular actions.

Concomitant with the decline of large-scale rebellion in the 1820s and the 1830s was a surge in capital-appeal activities, in which aggrieved local communities sent representatives to Beijing to lodge plaints against local governments. In contrast to late eighteenth-century resistance, in which resentment against local governments extended to resentment against the imperial center, the rise in capital appeals signals that aggrieved subjects' resentment of local authorities was contained at the local level and that the people more or less believed in the central government's willingness to redress local injustice.

Most remarkably, the imperial center during the Jiaqing reign explicitly acknowledged that the subjects' grievances against local officials were legitimate and that the subjects would have blamed the imperial center for their plight, had the central government not addressed their grievances and offered them some measure of hope in the efficacy of the imperial center. In the midst of the White Lotus Rebellion in 1801, Jiaqing stated openly that local corruption was too rife to ignore and that encouraging his subjects to attack local officials by appealing to higher authorities was a viable alternative, one that could preempt revolt. He also lauded the institution of capital appeal, which, he said, could prevent any cover-up of misdeeds among local bureaucrats and give the throne direct access to the lives and voices of its subjects:

> Rebel leaders used the slogan "officials oppress the people, so the people revolt" as an excuse to justify their action and entice others to join. Local officials, who are supposed to be intimate with the people, are not as loving and as nourishing as they should [be] in ordinary times, and they even use the opportunity of persecuting heterodox sectarians to heighten their abuse of the commoners and arrest the innocents, therefore provoking the revolt.

> If the subjects were mistreated by local officials, why don't they lodge plaints at the provincial governments? If the provincial governments refuse to handle their cases, they could still travel to Beijing to lodge the plaint. Now we must reestablish the proper institutions [of capital appeal] so that we could firmly prevent the grievances and resentment of the downtrodden people from being covered up.
>
> (QSL-JQ 80, 8–9; MY TRANSLATION)

Lodging plaints at the imperial center against local officials was a long-established practice in Chinese history (Fang 2009). But during the Qing dynasty, it took on a much more institutionalized form when the state established elaborate rules governing the procedure of the practice. Under the Qing legal code, established in 1740, subjects who intended to complain about local-government officials or those who were not content with the adjudication of civil or criminal cases by county magistrates could lodge plaints at the government one level higher, that is, at the prefecture level. If adjudication at that level did not satisfy the plaintiffs, they could go further up to the provincial level. If plaintiffs were dissatisfied with all local rulings, they could lodge plaints at the imperial center in Beijing, where the office of the censorate and the capital gendarmerie within the imperial palace were authorized to receive appeals on behalf of the emperor.

Upon receiving the appeals, the responsible officials would report the cases to the emperor via secret palace memorial. For appeals that involved matters of great significance to the imperial order, such as an accusation of large-scale corruption, the emperor would assign special commissioners to investigate. For other cases, the emperor would send the case back to the provincial government and request that the provincial governor handle it in person. To raise the cost of filing capital appeals and to prevent the fabrication of charges against officials, the plaintiffs were taken into custody at the Justice Department in Beijing while the case was being processed. This could take months or even years. If the plaintiffs were found (or alleged) to be fabricating the case or were not following the proper appeal procedure, they would be subject to severe punishment such as flogging or banishment to the barren frontier (Ocko 1988).

The practice of capital appeal in Qing times reached all corners of the empire and all strata of commoners. They were aided by the swelling numbers of surplus literati who, not being able to find jobs in government, made a living by writing plaints for commoners. Many appellants saw the appeal as more than just a cold, formal procedure for attaining justice. They invested substantial moral meaning and emotional energy in the practice. In many documented cases, appellants employed emotionally charged symbolic acts such as kneeling upon two knees, banging one's head on the ground, and weeping publicly to impress the authorities with their misery and filial loyalty (e.g., QSL-DG 211, 13–15). Though not sanctioned by the legal code, some appellants would even submit their appeal by intercepting and kneeling in front of the imperial procession to catch the direct attention of the emperor while he was traveling outside the palace. Maintaining subservient and emotional expressions, the appellants acted as if they were children who had been abused by their parents and were looking to their grandparents for protection, justice, and consolation.

Tax abuse and other types of abuse by local officials were the grievances underlying most capital appeals (see table 5.3). Even cases in which appellants asked for arbitration of a civil dispute or criminal investigation from higher authorities usually included accusations that local officials were incompetent, biased, or complicit with the suspects.

Because capital appeals involved physical travel to the imperial capital of Beijing, one may wonder whether the practice would be concentrated in regions closer to Beijing. But figure 5.1 shows that this was not the case. Documented capital-appeal cases in the 1820s and 1830s were spread throughout different parts of the empire. This suggests that long distances and high travel costs did not deter subjects in distant provinces from lodging plaints at Beijing and that capital appeal had become a standard repertoire of action all across the empire by the early nineteenth century.

TABLE 5.3 Compositions of Documented Upward Appeals with Known Claims, 1820–1839

Claims	All Upward Appeals (%)	Capital Appeals (%)
Complaint against local officials or policies of local government	60.4	55.7
Seeking the action of higher-level authorities to deal with problems unresolved by local governments	39.6	44.3

Note: Number of all upward appeals: 222; number of all capital appeals among upward appeals: 131.

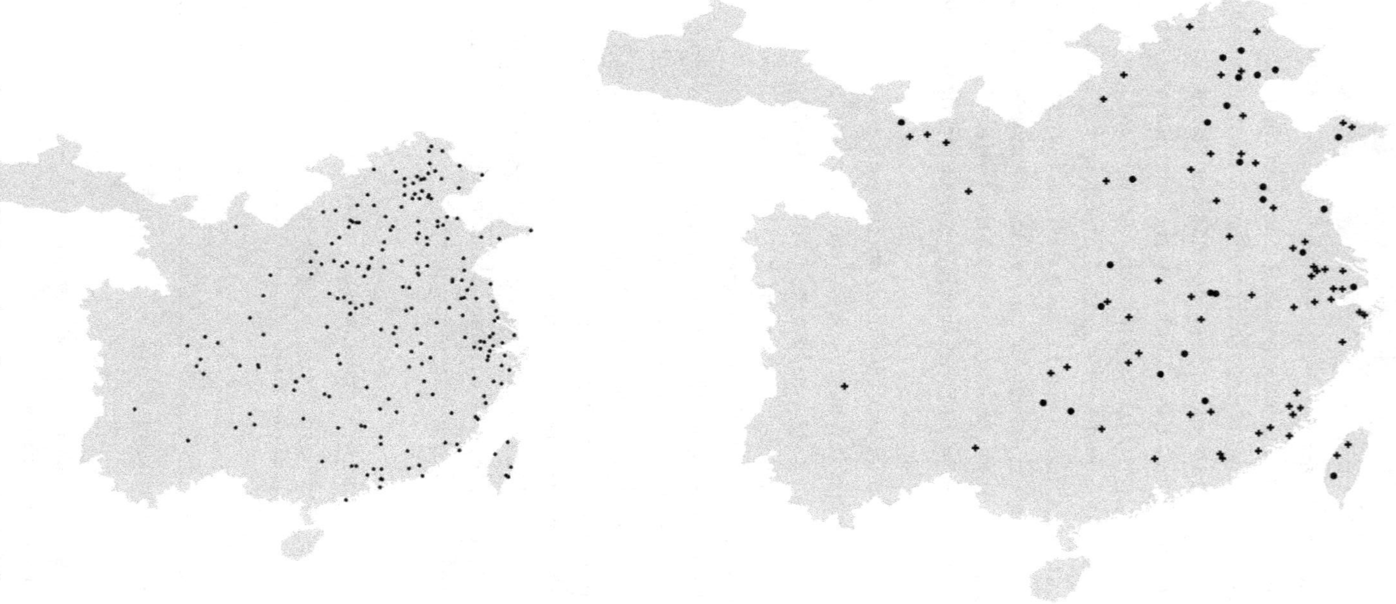

FIGURE 5.1 Geographical Distribution of Capital-Appeal Cases (*left*) Versus Geographical Distribution of Protest (*right*), 1820–1839 (background map: CHGIS)

It is noteworthy that documented protests for 1820–1839 were likewise evenly distributed across the empire.

Previous studies, based on circumstantial evidence such as the emperor's and officials' statements about the serious overloading of the capital-appeal system, agree that the Qing empire witnessed a surge in capital appeals in the early nineteenth century (Kuhn 2002; Ocko 1988; Wang 2009; Zhao 2001). This is supported by the number of cases of appeal documented in the QSL, which was a function of the total number of cases that the censorate and the capital gendarmerie reported to the emperor through the memorial system.

In figure 5.2, the number of capital-appeal cases at any point in time is divided by the total population of the time to control for the effect of population growth. As we can see from the unadjusted series, the index grew in the early nineteenth century. But the series is somewhat misleading, because after 1801, the criteria for cases being reported to the emperor changed. In 1801, the Jiaqing emperor, while further institutionalizing the capital-appeal system, instructed the offices to categorize all cases and report only

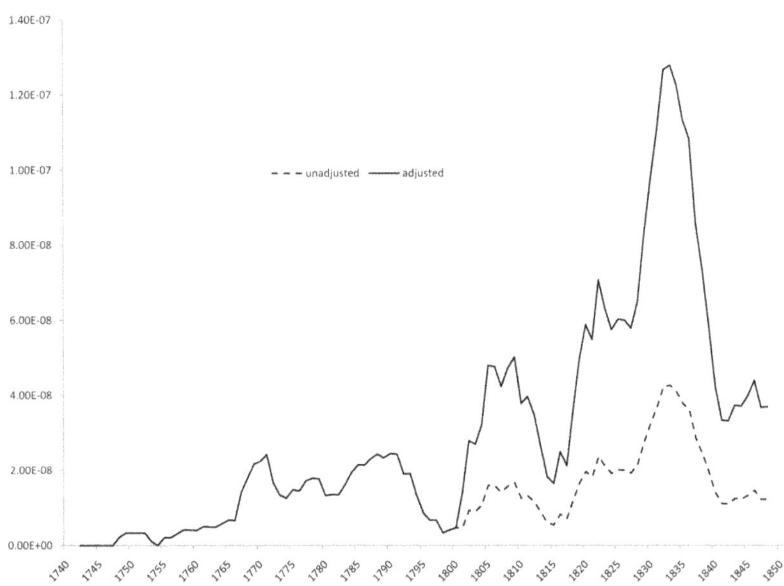

FIGURE 5.2 Per Capita Count of Cases of Capital Appeal, 1740–1850 (five-year moving average) (*source*: QSL)

those with both the most serious charges and clear evidence of unredressed grievances. They were to forward all other cases to the appropriate provincial governors without reporting them to the emperor on a case-by-case basic (Ocko 1988, 295–298). In other words, the number of cases documented after 1800 would have been much larger had it not been for the shift in reporting standards. Taking this into consideration, I increase the number of appeals after 1800 by a factor of three. This is a conservative approximation, as previous studies suggest that more than 80 percent of appeals received by the censorate and the capital gendarmerie were deemed inappropriate to be reported to the emperor under the new rule, suggesting that the number of reported cases could be lower than one-fifth of all cases (Ocko 1988, 298). Despite this conservative approximation, the adjusted series still shows that there was a large jump in the number of capital appeals in the 1800s and 1810s, followed by an even larger jump in the 1820s and 1830s.

One plausible reason for the simultaneous decline in large-scale rebellion and the surge in capital-appeal activities is the restoration of the throne's moral legitimacy following the Jiaqing emperor's resolution to revive the Qing state. As shown in many of the cases of petitioning in chapter 3, the state's paternalist ideology, through which the emperor–local officials–subjects relationship was conceptualized as that of grandfather-parents-children, was upheld by the imperial center and accepted by the subjects in the early Qianlong reign of the mid-eighteenth century. But in the late eighteenth century, the laxity of the aging Qianlong, together with the rise of Heshen and all the sexual rumors about the emperor, tarnished the moral legitimacy of the throne and helped empower whichever rebels were bold enough to claim the Mandate of Heaven. The Jiaqing emperor tried to resurrect this moral legitimacy by executing Heshen in 1800, purging his clique, and issuing a large number of imperial edicts to show his distaste for abusive local officials and his empathy for the plight of his subjects. This attempted moral regeneration continued into the early decades of the Daoguang reign (1821–1850). Under the prevalent neo-Confucianist ideology that had already diffused throughout all levels of Qing society, the emperor's renewed image as a loving and righteous patriarch could easily invoke the downtrodden subjects' filial loyalty toward him, dissuading them from rebellion and making them believe that they could gain the emperor's support once they obtained his attention to their plight.

Besides this hypothesis, which hinges on the moral legitimacy of the imperial center, there are other plausible explanations for the decline of rebellion and rise of capital appeal. For example, it might have something to do with the effectiveness of the capital-appeal system, strengthened under Jiaqing, in actually redressing local injustice before it escalated into rebellion. Alternatively, it might be related to the state's renewed coercive capacity in the aftermath of the White Lotus Rebellion to curb the growth of any rebellions. I revisit and compare all of these hypotheses after delving into the following cases of capital appeal.

THE PRACTICE OF CAPITAL APPEAL

The following four cases illustrate the underlying considerations, practices, and consequences of capital appeal among resisters or potential resisters to local officials. In the first two cases, local residents resentful of corrupt local governments decided to lodge plaints at the central government in lieu of open resistance against the local authorities. In the last two cases, local residents combined violent resistance toward local governments with capital appeals to advance their interests.

CAPITAL APPEAL AS AN ALTERNATIVE TO TAX RIOT[10]

In 1837, the county government of Guichi in Anhui province suddenly decided to impose a 40 percent tax surcharge on the original tax quota for each taxpayer. The reason behind the tax hike is not known, but the furious taxpayers accused county officials of corruption and intending to embezzle the extra tax. A large crowd of taxpayers gathered outside the county government to petition for a reduction in the tax rate. Fearing that the gathering might turn into a violent protest, Jin Mingguan, a respected literati who had once served in the local government, tried to defuse the tension by promising the crowd that he would persuade the county magistrate to revoke the surcharge.

But the magistrate ignored his plea. Jin then filed a plaint against the county government at the prefecture level and asked the prefecture magistrate to dictate a tax reduction. The prefecture magistrate arrested Jin by fabricating the absurd charge that he was a fugitive from justice who had changed his identity. Jin asked somebody in the prison (plausibly through bribery) to deliver a message to his fifteen-year-old son, Jin Qiteng, to ask him to lodge a plaint at the provincial government on his behalf. His son did this without hesitation.

The provincial government detained Jin Qiteng for half a year at the provincial capital while investigating the case at a glacial speed. The taxpayers in Guichi remained agitated during this prolonged period, but apparently they still expected that the higher-level government would bring them justice. When the provincial government sent an envoy to Guichi to check the local-government archive and interrogate local officials, hundreds of gentry and commoners greeted the envoy by kneeling, burning incense, and knocking their heads on the ground. The county clerks interviewed by the envoy acknowledged that the county government had imposed a huge tax surcharge on the taxpayers. Despite this testimony and other evidence, the provincial government, which was suspected of being complicit in the whole tax-abuse affair, declared the surcharge legitimate and fair. Subsequently, the prefecture government tortured Jin Mingguan to force him to confess that he had fabricated the embezzlement charges against the county government.

Even after all these twists and turns, Jin Mingguan and the taxpayers did not lose faith in the authorities. Jin sent another message to his son to urge him to travel all the way to Beijing to lodge a capital appeal. Local gentry and other taxpayers raised the funds to finance his travel. He lodged the plaint successfully, and this is how the case is concluded in the central-government archive. It is unclear how the central government handled the case. But given that not a single instance of violent tax resistance was documented in the area, we can assume that the prolonged process of upward appeal, despite the setbacks along the way, did help assuage the taxpayers' agitation and prevent a tax riot.

In this case, aggrieved taxpayers in Guichi chose capital appeal over a violent and extralegal tax riot to redress local injustice because of the persuasiveness and personal sacrifice of a respected literati. In the next case, angry taxpayers similarly resorted to capital appeal rather than protest to resist their predatory local government. They made this decision not because of the persuasion of any local elite but through collective deliberation among themselves.

DELIBERATING BETWEEN APPEAL AND PROTEST AGAINST TAX ABUSES[11]

In the autumn of 1829, tax collectors of Feicheng county of Shandong province urged Liu Wenzhao, who was late in submitting his family's tribute grain for the year, to convert his tribute-grain obligation into a monetary tax of 1,425 *wen* of copper, which was a disproportionately large amount. Liu's father, Liu Kexun, who was a respected local instructor, was exasperated and started contacting his fellow county residents who were also disgruntled with the local government. Liu soon collected a long list of the local government's wrongdoings, which included government clerks at a tax-collection station deliberately spilling submitted tribute grain on the ground during measurement so they could collect more than three times the quota for each taxpayer; government clerks closing tax-collection stations early and forcing the "late" payers to convert their original grain quota into copper cash payments at a usurious rate; education officers levying illegal fees on candidates taking the local examination; and official salt retailers adding an illegal thousand-*wen* surcharge for every fourteen *taels* of salt sold.

Liu and other angry neighbors, meeting publicly to deliberate what they should do, traded stories that they had heard about previous unsuccessful efforts in fighting tax abuse and other injustices. Several decades ago, during the late Qianlong reign, taxpayers in nearby Deping county had staged a tax riot against an arbitrary increase in the tribute-grain quota. And just two years before, in 1827, Laifu county's cultivators, in opposition to a similar hike in tax quota, had launched a strike by collectively handing all of their farming tools to the county office and threatening that they would stop tilling the land until the quota was lowered. The action planners were well aware that none of this resistance had successfully lowered the tax rate and that the problem of mounting tribute-grain quotas persisted.

They also discussed previous cases of capital appeal but found the results horrifying. Several years ago, Gao Junzhong, a representative from the nearby Gaotang zhou, had traveled to Beijing to lodge a plaint against an inflated tax rate and corrupt local government. He was, in the end, charged with fabricating the case and banished to serve the army at the frontier—and was tortured to death on the way. Another local literati from Changqing county lodged a capital appeal against the same taxation problem, and he encountered the same fate.

After carefully weighing different options, Liu and the other participants in the meeting still decided to bring the case to the gendarmerie office in Beijing through a capital appeal. But aware of the outcome of previous appeal attempts, they decided to slip a letter in a sealed envelope into the gendarmerie office rather than showing up in person. Qing legal code dictated that a sealed envelope, when received, had to be forwarded unopened to the highest responsible officials. Thus this warranted a better chance that the petition would circumvent the apparently corrupt and indifferent lower-level officials and reach the highest authorities of the justice system. But at the same time, Qing law also forbade this practice and ensured that a petition submitted this way would never be accepted. The drafter of the petition, if identified, would be severely punished. All of this meant that lodging a capital appeal via sealed letter was a nearly certain recipe for indifference to the appeal and heavy punishment for the appellants. This decision was thus a manifestation of desperation. They were hoping for a miracle: that the emperor, after reading their letter, would be touched enough to pardon them and redress the injustice.

Not surprisingly, the miracle did not occur. The capital gendarmerie office decided that the accusations in the letter were absurd. It also discovered that Liu was the one who had drafted it. The gendarmerie office reasoned that as most of the local authorities' wrongdoings cited in the plaint actually did not affect the plaintiff himself, either Liu made up the charges or there was a plot in the area to use them to blackmail local authorities. The office sentenced Liu to a severe punishment: they banished him to the empire's frontier, callous to the fact that he was more than seventy years old and likely to die of exhaustion on the way.

In this case, as in the previous one, potential tax rioters consciously chose capital appeal as an alternative to violent resistance against local authorities, even though they knew very well that their appeal was likely to be futile. The following two cases show a different way that disgruntled subjects used capital appeal. In these cases, aggrieved taxpayers adopted a two-pronged strategy, by combining violent resistance against local officials with capital appeal.

RIOT AND CAPITAL APPEAL AS A TWO-PRONGED STRATEGY[12]

De'an prefecture was located at the northern part of Hubei province and was cut off from major transportation networks such as the Yangzi and Han rivers. The prefecture's inaccessibility made it difficult to be monitored by the provincial government. Its prefecture administration and the county governments under it were infamous for corruption and abuse. There were plentiful excuses that local governments could use to levy extra taxes. For example, Fang Changqing, the prefecture magistrate, once raised a surtax allegedly for the construction of a government-run house for the poor, but the plan never materialized, and the funds ended up in local officials' purses. County governments in the prefecture regularly forced taxpayers to contribute special taxes for the purchase of grains to stock the public granary. These taxes were again used for officials' private gains; local granaries were never sufficiently stocked despite the extra funds.

In 1838, Magistrate Fang declared that the government was going to levy another new tax for the refurbishment of the prefecture academy. But local literati, probably tipped off by some government insiders, learned that the collected funds actually would be used to cover the maintenance of the prefecture salt factory, which was a significant source of income for government officials. Magistrate Fang traveled to Sui zhou, the wealthiest jurisdiction of the prefecture, to meet with the rich landowners there and urge them to pay the new taxes. Xu Xiling, a notorious government clerk and Fang's protégé, was given the responsibility of collecting the tax, and he actively recruited thugs to exact the levies village by village.

The new taxes created widespread grievances. In May 1838, angry rioters destroyed the salt factory in the prefectural capital. In the meantime, literati in Sui zhou initiated a capital appeal against the new tax and accused Fang of using Xu to extort taxpayers through brutal means. The plaint also listed all of Fang's previous wrongdoings. The plaint caught the attention of the emperor, who ordered Lin Zexu, then the governor-general of Hunan and Hubei, to investigate the corruption in the prefecture. After a few months of investigation, the provincial government released a report that rejected the plaintiffs' allegations. It found Fang innocent and that all the taxes that he had previously raised for a house for the poor, for restocking the public granary, and for the prefecture college were fair and appropriate. His only misdeed, if any, was his failure in disciplining Xu and his other agents.

The two-pronged strategy of the local resisters in this case is not exceptional. The following is another case in which villagers resorted to both local confrontation and capital appeal in an attempt to redress local injustice. The most noteworthy aspect is that rather than sending one representative to lodge the plaint, as in most other cases, the villagers lodged the plaint collectively by weeping and kneeling in front of the imperial palace in Beijing.

VIOLENCE AND APPEAL AGAINST THE APPROPRIATION OF A LOCAL TEMPLE [13]

In 1831, Liu Fengsan, a sojourner from the Cang zhou of Tianjin prefecture, came to Changping zhou, in the vicinity of Beijing within the Shuntian prefecture. He claimed that he was a grandson of Liu Jiang, a powerful eunuch in the imperial palace, and was the hereditary owner of a piece of local land where a popular temple had been erected. In collaboration with a local monk and a number of government officials, he occupied the temple, where many villagers prayed for good fortune. He demolished twenty-two residential buildings on the temple grounds and attempted to sell the wood and other building materials.

Local villagers, not convinced that Liu was what he claimed to be, were angered by his appropriation of the public land and the temple. They lodged a plaint against Liu in the zhou government. But the litigation was futile, and a number of residents who were involved in its initiation were arrested and tortured. With the failure of legal means of resistance, Ren Si, a government runner and local villager, struck a gong to gather a crowd to intercept Liu and his crews, who were transporting the building materials from the demolished temple for sale elsewhere. After the altercation, Liu lodged a capital appeal at the capital gendarmerie against the Changping residents. He charged them with refusing to accede to local-government arbitration and attempting to impede his legitimate business on his own property through violence.

Aware of Liu's appeal to the capital gendarmerie, Ren Si and other villagers fought back with their own capital appeal. A delegation of forty residents was organized, and they traveled to the imperial palace, lodging a joint plaint at the capital gendarmerie. To draw larger attention to their case, they knelt in the square outside the palace's main entrance and wept. This kind of collective action outside the palace was taboo, and the case immediately aroused the concern of high-ranking officials in the central government, who sent a special envoy to Changping to investigate the case. In the end, Liu's claim that he was a descendent of a court eunuch was found to be false and his occupation of temple land illegitimate. Ren Si was found guilty of lodging a capital appeal without filing a plaint with lower-level governments first. His action of organizing a collective appeal outside the palace was considered a serious offense. Both Liu and Ren received corporeal punishment, and Ren was detained to await the verdict on his offense of organizing the collective appeal.

THE SOURCE OF THE EARLY NINETEENTH-CENTURY TRANQUILITY

In most of the above four cases, as in many other documented cases, capital appeal failed to bring justice to the appellants. It even cost them their freedom or life. The futility of and tragic endings to these cases were not exceptional. A secret palace memorial drafted by the head of the capital gendarmerie in 1830 frankly admitted that, given the intentional neglect of appeal cases at different levels of government and the incapacity of the central government to handle the flood of new cases from the provinces, the backlog of appeals never ceased to grow. He lamented that "the faithful appellants would have rotted and only had their bones left by the time their cases were adjudicated" (LFZZ–FLL 3753-35, 649; my translation).

In fact, Jiaqing's encouragement of capital appeal was more rhetorical than real.[14] As discussed, more than 80 percent of all cases of capital appeal that were processed at the imperial capital were classified as fraudulent, trivial, or as cases that violated the appropriate appeal procedure. They were rejected outright or automatically forwarded back to lower-level governments (Ocko 1988, 298). For those rejected cases, the appellants either received severe punishment (which was often no less serious than the punishment of arrested protesters) from the central government or became the target of revenge by local officials, often involving torture or murder.[15] If a case was not rejected, the emperor would usually refer it to the governors of the provinces where the case originated. Provincial officials tended to protect their protégés in lower-level administrations or let them send ruffians to the provincial capital to torment the appellants while they were waiting for adjudication there (Ocko 1988, 299–300). There was only a very slim chance that the emperor would adjudicate the case himself and rule in the appellants' favor. But there were plenty of ways that the target of an appeal could avenge himself against the plaintiffs while the final verdict was pending. In addition, the whole process was very expensive, as local residents needed to raise a large sum of money to hire professional plaintiffs to draft the plaints, travel all the way to Beijing, reside there for a long time, and bribe different levels of officials, who would often dismiss the case otherwise (Ocko 1988, 298–304; Zhao 2001, 191–206). The speculation that the decline in revolt and rise in capital appeal stemmed from the effectiveness of the capital-appeal system is, therefore, groundless.

The risks and abuse that appellants faced in the appeal process, and local officials' vengeance against appellants, also invalidates the hypothesis that the rise in capital appeals resulted from a fear of state coercion that deterred its subjects from confrontations and rebellion against the state, because the punishments meted out on appellants who failed in their petitions was nearly as severe as the punishment that protesters or rebels faced. In addition, it is questionable whether the state commanded a higher coercive capacity in the early nineteenth century than in the late eighteenth century. The White Lotus Rebellion of 1796–1805 exposed the weakness of the state's coercive power, as it was the first in Qing history that the imperial army was unable to put down. The emperor had to hire mercenaries and rely on unofficial local militias organized by local gentry elites. After the rebellion, the status of the imperial army as a symbol of the might of Manchu rule was tarnished. It was also public knowledge that the army's counterinsurgency campaign, despite its embarrassing failure, had drained nearly all of the government's silver reserves accumulated during the prosperous eighteenth century (Jones and Kuhn 1978, 143–144; Kuhn 1970, 37–63). Worse still, the demobilized militias and mercenaries, now unemployed and often still awaiting back pay, had become a new source of protest and social disorder (QSL-JQ 124, 27–29; Kuhn 1970, 50).

The decline in revolt and the surge in capital appeal, therefore, had little to do with the effectiveness of the capital-appeal system in redressing injustice or the coercive capability of the state. The remaining plausible reason for the muted levels of rebellion and the increase in capital appeal is the popular perception that the emperor had regained his reputation for moral righteousness and compassion and was again ready to defend his subjects against injustices incurred by malicious local officials. As we saw in chapter 1, this moral regeneration was more symbolic than real, as the bureaucratic corruption and fiscal crisis worsened. In other words, while the collapsing moral legitimacy of the state in the late eighteenth century induced many state-resisting local protests to merge with open rebellion against the emperor, who was seen as the root of local injustices, protesters angry at local authorities in the early nineteenth century became more prone to submissive capital appeals to the presumably righteous and loving emperor, who was no longer seen as accountable for local ills.

The southwestern provinces, where the White Lotus Rebellion broke out, are a bellwether for this change in attitudes. The conditions that caused the rebellion—including local officials' abuses, endemic corruption, the local governments' declining social-control capabilities, and continuous expansion of vagrant populations and banditry—continued to deteriorate after the rebellion. Proposed plans in the central government to strengthen its control over the region through establishing new or upgraded administrative units were considered but scrapped because of the lack of financial resources (Macauley 2009). Despite the deterioration of local conditions, violent resistance declined in the region, in tandem with an escalation in plaint lodging against local officials at higher authorities. (Bai 1982, 245–246).

Finally, in the mid-eighteenth century, the Qianlong emperor's public condemnation of corrupt and incompetent local officials through imperial edicts was as frequent as was Jiaqing's and Daoguang's in the early nineteenth century (as seen in figure 1.3), and the popular acceptance of the moral legitimacy of the imperial center in the early Qianlong reign was at least as high as that in the early nineteenth century. This mid-eighteenth-century high moral legitimacy of the state did generate some petitions directed at higher authorities or the emperor himself. But during that period, local governments were often able to accommodate the demands themselves, and many aggrieved subjects managed to solve their problems by directly engaging local authorities. In other words, the high capacity of many local governments warranted local solutions to grievances, helping prevent the growth of upward appeal. But in the early nineteenth century, the high moral legitimacy of the central government stood in contrast to the crumbling capacity of local governments, prompting appeals in which appellants, with no hope in their local governments, turned to the imperial center as their first and last resort.

6

MID-QING PROTESTS IN COMPARATIVE PERSPECTIVE

To recapitulate, episodes of popular protest in the mid-Qing period of 1740–1839 were clustered in three waves: 1740–1759, 1776–1795, and 1820–1839. These waves of protest differed from one another in the predominant claims of the protesters and the common repertoires of actions they employed. Most protests in 1740–1759 were state engaging and nonviolent. The typical demands of protesters included an extension of paternalist care from the state amid subsistence crises, participation in governmental decisions on such issues as hydraulic management and bureaucratic appointments, and governmental arbitration of social conflicts. Rallies in front of government offices, market strikes, and parades were among the most frequently seen acts. In contrast, protests in both 1776–1795 and 1820–1839 were mostly state resisting and violent, involving as the most common elements tax riots, retribution against corrupt local officials or unpopular policies, and the expulsion of state agents who cracked down on social conflicts and other illicit activities such as smuggling and banditry. Many of these events included attacks on individual officials or government buildings. Comparing this change from state-engaging to state-resisting protests in the mid-Qing period to the salience of state-resisting protests in the seventeenth century, we see a cyclical pattern of protest transformation, as shown in figure 6.1.

Although most protests in 1776–1795 and 1820–1839 were similarly state-resisting and violent, they were connected to other political actions in different ways. Whereas violent resistances in the 1776–1795 period occasionally converged into large-scale rebellions against the Qing dynasty, growing antagonism against local officials in the second period was often seen in tandem with mounting humble petitions to the emperor through capital appeal, an institutionalized practice in which aggrieved subjects sent representatives to Beijing to lodge plaints at specific palace offices representing the emperor.

Underlying the differences in protest patterns in the three waves are the different identities that the protesters expressed in relation to the state.

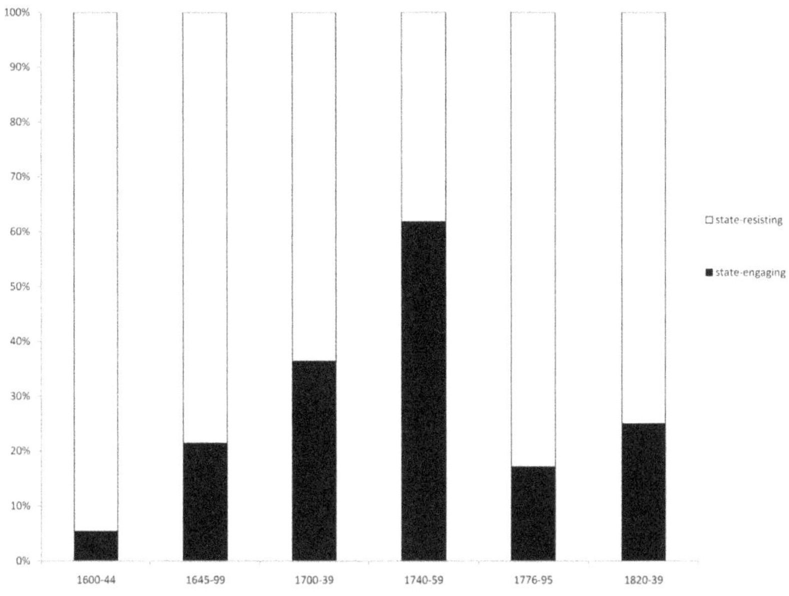

FIGURE 6.1 Changing Composition of Documented Protests with Known Claims, 1600–1839

Many state-engaging protesters in 1740–1759 acted as submissive, filial-loyal subjects of the paternalist authorities both local and central. State-resisting protesters in 1776–1795, in contrast, tended to be defiant and antagonistic to both local authorities and the dynastic ruler at the center. State-resisting protesters in 1820–1839, despite their antagonism to local government, generally acted as filial-loyal subjects when interacting with the imperial center.

CONTEXTUALIZING MID-QING PROTESTS

As we discussed briefly in the previous three chapters, the prevalent features of popular protest in the three waves are related to the political, economic, and cultural contexts of the corresponding three subperiods of mid-Qing China. The three subperiods are (1) the mid-eighteenth century, when the capacity, commercial prosperity, and moral legitimacy of the state were at their heights; (2) the late eighteenth century, when state capacity and the moral legitimacy of the imperial center were in decline but commercial prosperity was sustained; and (3) the early nineteenth century, when state capacity continued to crumble and the market economy was in crisis but the moral legitimacy of the imperial center revived. Juxtaposing the changing patterns and contexts of protest in the three subperiods to the predominantly reactive and violent protests during the turbulent dynastic transition between Ming and Qing, as discussed in chapter 1, we can readily see that the cyclical trajectory of protest transformation moved in tandem with the cyclical changes in the political economy and moral legitimacy of the early modern Chinese state.

We can explain this cyclical trajectory by extending G. William Skinner's (1971) classic theory about the cycle of peasant actions. Skinner finds that in Ming and Qing times, Chinese peasant communities followed a cyclical movement between normative closure and openness as a function of the dynastic cycle. During the dynastic heyday of the mid-eighteenth century, local communities benefited from maintaining a cozy relationship with

TABLE 6.1 Changing Contexts and Patterns of Protest From Late Ming to Mid-Qing China

	Seventeenth Century	Mid-Eighteenth Century	Late Eighteenth Century	Early Nineteenth Century
State capacity	low	high	low	low
Commercial prosperity	low	high	high	low
Imperial center's moral legitimacy	low	high	low	high
Protest claim	reactive	proactive	reactive	reactive
Protest action	violent	less violent	violent	violent
Protesters' identities vis-à-vis local authority	antagonistic	filial loyal	antagonistic	antagonistic
Protesters' identities vis-à-vis imperial center	antagonistic	filial loyal	antagonistic	filial loyal

diligent officials and conducting business with the outside world. To maximize their ability to take advantage of abundant external opportunities, local communities increased their "social and cultural versatility and enlarged the cultural repertoire from which they could draw on" by embracing "diverse customs, alien values, and exogenous norms . . . elements drawn not only from other little traditions but also from the great tradition of the imperial elite" (1971, 277).

However, during the phase of dynastic decline at the turn of the nineteenth century, when "developments external to the rural community led first to constricted political opportunities, then to constricted economic opportunities, and finally to endemic disorder" (Skinner 1971, 278), local communities became more aware of "the instrumental value of normative solidarity in the face of crisis" (279). Through "the reaffirmation of local norms" and the emphasis on "local pride and local-system loyalty" (278), local communities became "corporate, self-sufficient, introverted, particularized, encysted" entities. Many later studies of urban and rural histories of late imperial China attest to this theory of the cycle of openness and closeness, and they suggest that this theory applies not only to rural communities but also to urban ones (e.g., Perry 1980; Rowe 1989, 2007).

Viewed in this light, protesters' shifting dispositions toward local states, from confrontation in the seventeenth century to filial loyalty in the mid-eighteenth century and back to communal resistance in the late eighteenth and early nineteenth centuries, were functions of their strategic choice of action in the context of the changing capacity of the state. In the mid-eighteenth century, state capacity was high, and the economy was booming. In such a benign environment, local governments were generally capable of alleviating the hardships of local communities afflicted by natural disasters and other contingencies, as well as meeting whatever other demands local residents might have, if they were willing. Protesters seeking help from the state or intending to influence governmental policy would therefore have a better chance of success if they spoke the same language as the scholar-official elites and framed their demands as nonconfrontational and politically legitimate under the Confucianist political ideology. This also reduced the chance of harsh repression and hence increased the effectiveness of their mobilization efforts by allaying fear among participants. This sometimes could even draw the sympathy of higher-level officials or the emperor, who then put pressure on local governments to yield to protesters' demands. It is therefore not surprising that many protesters in the 1740–1759 wave presented themselves as filial subjects humbly asking for no more than a fulfillment or extension of the state's proclaimed paternalist obligation to nourish its subjects.

In the late eighteenth century and early nineteenth century (and in much of the seventeenth century as well), on the contrary, local governments were much weaker administratively and fiscally. The state was much less capable of alleviating the hardship of its subjects. As a result, victims of subsistence crises could no longer count on help from local governments. Worse, local governments, which became financially stringent, actually competed with local communities over shrinking resources by mounting tax levies and aggressively eliminating illicit (but profitable) activities that threatened state revenue, such as salt smuggling. When the state became part of the problem, to fend off predatory local-government agents, local communities invoked their communal solidarity in the form of tax riots, attacks on officials, and the like. The antagonism between local governments and grassroots communities was aggravated by the deflationary Daoguang Depression, which started in the 1820s, when commoners' declining income measured in silver made their tax dues and other government exaction even more unbearable.

This cyclical change in the capacity of the Ming-Qing government as depicted by Skinner explains the cyclical change in the predominant mode of protest, from state-resisting violence in the seventeenth century, to state-engaging demonstrations in the mid-eighteenth century, and back to state-resisting violence in the late eighteenth and early nineteenth centuries. However, it does not explain why the protesters' disposition toward the imperial center in the late eighteenth and early nineteenth centuries differed even though protesters in both periods were antagonistic to local authorities.

Local resisters' antagonism toward the imperial center in 1786–1795 and their filial loyalty toward the center in 1820–1839 should be understood in light of the changing moral legitimacy of the throne. Grassroots antagonism toward local government never automatically fostered antagonism toward the imperial center. In the late eighteenth century, Qianlong's delegation of most of his governing responsibilities to the corrupt and widely unpopular Heshen, together with the wild rumors about the emperor's promiscuous private life, promoted the popular perception that corruption and abuse in local governments originated in the moral decay at the apex of the ruling dynasty, which was losing its Mandate of Heaven. It was in this context that resisters' resentment of local government spilled over to become hatred of and even rebellion against the imperial order.

In the wake of the Jiaqing emperor's effort to cleanse the central government of Heshen's influence and to resurrect the rhetoric of benevolent rule and neo-Confucianist moral rigor, in the early nineteenth century the imperial center regained its moral legitimacy and was again seen as a loving grand patriarch. It was in this context that violent resisters, who fought tenaciously with local authorities, kept their anger at the local level and eagerly made use of the capital-appeal system to petition the emperor, who was expected to sympathize with the resisters' plight and to penalize corrupt local officials on their behalf, despite the well-known inefficacy of the system in redressing injustice.

QING CHINA, BOURBON FRANCE, AND TOKUGAWA JAPAN

China's cyclical trajectory from state-resisting protest to state-engaging protest and back to state-resisting protest during the early modern period stands in contrast to Europe's unidirectional trajectory from state-resisting to state-engaging protest during the same period. As we have just seen, the cyclical trajectory of Chinese protest can be explained by the cyclical change in state power, state legitimacy, and market dynamism from the seventeenth to the early nineteenth century, just as the unidirectional trajectory of Western European protests can be explained by the unidirectional expansion of state power and commerce there.

The implication of this China-Europe comparison to the world historiography of popular protest is twofold. First, early modern Europe's unidirectional path of protest transformation can no longer be seen as a universal and natural path applicable everywhere. Instead, this path should be particularized—or "provincialized," to paraphrase Chakrabaty (2000)—as no more than one special path brought about by the specific trajectories of state formation and market expansion in Western Europe. The case of early modern China shows that long-term transformation of protest patterns could follow a different path, given different trajectories of state and market development.

Second, reactive violence against the state in nineteenth-century China should no longer be seen as the *starting point* of the development of modern protest there. This study shows that state-resisting protests prevailing in China after it clashed with Western imperialism in the Opium War of 1839–1842 were in fact continuations of prior resistances, which marked the *endpoint* of a century-long transformation of protest away from mid-eighteenth-century proactive protests. At least as far as popular protest is concerned, the periods before and after the Opium War were related to each other as much by continuity as by rupture. The Opium War was far from the prime initiator of Chinese modernity, which had, in fact, already started to crystallize in the eighteenth century.

A question that follows is, if we can date the indigenous origins of modern popular protest in China to the mid-Qing period, as this study does, can we push back the origins even further, to the pre-Qing period? Whereas some claims and repertoires of mid-Qing protest, such as attacks on local officials in opposition to new taxes, unpopular policies, and various abuses, were continuations of claims and repertoires found in the preceding Ming dynasty or even earlier (Tong 1991; Wu 1996), many other claims and repertoires rarely had been seen before the mid-Qing period. They included many state-engaging claims that sought state action to protect or extend protesters' subsistence rights through the request for government regulation of grain prices, provision of universal famine relief, or dictation of rent reduction. They also included such repertoires as market strikes as a way to seek local officials' attention and direct appeals to higher-level officials or even the emperor by traveling to the provincial capital or Beijing.[1]

Many of these claims and repertoires would be difficult to materialize before the height of state centralization and market expansion of the eighteenth century. The rise of a centralized and activist state elevated the subjects' expectation that increasing state intervention would advance their interests and rights. For example, prior to the eighteenth-century development of the empirewide, centrally coordinated granary system and government regulation of the grain market, protests that asked the state to alleviate a local subsistence crisis through universal grain disbursal or price control would have been unlikely. In addition, expansion and deepening of the empirewide market economy fomented the advancement of long-distance travel networks via which commoners could visit distant places easily and cheaply. This enhanced the protesters' capability to travel to far-flung administrative seats to appeal directly to higher authorities or the central government. The increasing centrality of the market in local economies also explained protesters' frequent use of market strikes as a weapon to guarantee officials' attention to their demand. Rising popular literacy since the seventeenth century, as documented by Chow (2004, see also Meyer-Fong 2007), contributed to the proliferation of demonstrations and rallies that involved subjects of different socioeconomic backgrounds, as we saw from case to case in the significance of pamphlets, posters, and other means of written communication in mobilizing protesters from different communities and classes. Last but not least, the salience of lineage organizations in the mobilization process of many protests, especially state-resisting ones, was facilitated by the Qing policy of redoubling the Ming effort in institutionalizing lineage corporate bodies as the foundations of local societies and identities. The many "traditions" of mid-Qing protests as unveiled in this study, therefore, are not a continuation of some timeless traditions of Chinese protest originating from a distant past. Instead, they represent new developments in the culture of protest in the context of China's early modernity, which began in the late Ming and culminated in the mid-Qing dynasty.

Chinese protests in 1740–1759 were mostly proactive, nonviolent, cosmopolitan, and modular, not unlike the proactive petitions and rallies in England and France during the eighteenth century. This similarity is not surprising, given that the level of centralization of the mid-eighteenth-century Chinese state was as high as, if not higher than, the level in many agrarian bureaucracies in mid- and late-eighteenth-century Europe, such as the French absolutist state, as we saw in chapter 1. However, this similarity is accompanied by differences in protesters' specific claims on the state and their self-defined relation to the state. Mid-eighteenth-century protests in China, no matter how proactive, modular, and cosmopolitan they were, remained imbued in the neo-Confucianist orthodoxy of filial loyalty. Many protesters reinforced the pseudofamilial hierarchy among the emperor, local officials, and subjects in their protests. They posited themselves as filial sons seeking benevolent care or respect from the patriarch (local officials) or grand patriarch (the emperor). On the contrary, proactive protesters in eighteenth-century France and England, no matter how humble their rhetoric and how nonconfrontational their actions, became less and less subservient to the political status quo. Their claims often pointed to a transformation of the existing sociopolitical order, which was perceived to be unjust. This can be seen in both demonstrations directed at the English king that called for reforms to expand parliamentary power and humble petitions to the French monarch that called for the reduction or abolition of seigneurial rights. The identity expressed in these actions departed from that of loyal subjects of the divine monarch. On the contrary, the protesters started to position themselves as citizens, the real sovereign that the authorities served. This was indicative of the emergent ideology of popular sovereignty (e.g., see Chartier 1991, chap. 7; Zaret 2000).

Speaking of the century-long change in French political ideology before the Revolution, Roger Chartier notes that under the appearance of an invincible monarchial order and humble subjects, France witnessed a "new political culture that arose after 1750 . . . [that] substituted for an all-powerful authority, which decided in secret and without appeal, the public manifestation of individual opinions and the will to examine freely all established institutions. Thus a public was formed that, more sovereign than the sovereign, obliged the king to confront contrary opinions" (1991, 167). Decades before the Revolution, Chartier notes, literary discussions in urban salons and peasant petitions as reflected in *cahiers* compiled by rural intellectuals had already been soaked in the idioms of rights, liberties, and justice.

If we study the historical transformation of protest by confining our cases to France and England, we would easily be mistaken in thinking that centralizing state power and expanding markets alone could account for the emerging identity of citizens among protesters, as Charles Tilly and many other historical sociologists have suggested. But our analysis of mid-eighteenth-century China, where protesters contended as filial imperial subjects within the similar context of state and market expansion, has exposed the limits of this theory. Similar political-economic contexts can explain the similar protest claims in mid-eighteenth-century China and late eighteenth-century Europe at the most general level: protests on both sides were proactive. The subtle difference in the political identities and the concomitant demands expressed by the protesters, by contrast, has to be explained in terms of the different cultural milieus of the two places. While the identities expressed in French and British protests in the late eighteenth century were made possible by the emergent cultural schema of popular sovereignty, protesters in mid-eighteenth-century China, in the absence of such alternative schema, could constitute their collective identities only by drawing on the idioms of political filiality under the Confucianist orthodoxy.

Comparing China with other Asian states is equally important, as it lets us evaluate whether the pattern of China's early modern protest is unique or common across the continent. Among other Asian states, Japan often receives attention from students of early modern protest, thanks to the Aoki Koji catalog, which documented thousands of peasant protests, uprisings, and class conflicts throughout the Tokugawa period (1601–1867).

While the Tokugawa state was somewhat influenced by the Confucianist political ideology of paternalist and benevolent rule, it differed from the Ming and Qing states in that it was far more decentralized. The unified early modern Japan was divided into about two hundred domains, each of which was governed by a *daimyo*, or feudal lord. The political legitimacy of the *daimyo* originated from the recognition of the ruling Tokugawa Bakufu, which was equivalent to the central government of the time. The Tokugawa regime also devised a variety of practices (such as the *daimyos'* rotating residence in the capital city of Edo) that helped secure the loyalty of all *daimyos* to the Bakufu. Nevertheless, the Bakufu seldom administered each feudal domain directly, so this was left to the paternalist rule of the *daimyo*. Under this system of decentralized paternalism, the target of peasant protests, from peaceful petitions to forceful demonstrations to armed revolt, rarely transgressed the level of *daimyo* to reach the center of the Tokugawa regime, except for the peasants residing within the home domain of the Bakufu (e.g., Bix 1986; Ikegami and Tilly 1994; Vlastos 1986, 14–15; cf. White 1995).

Stephen Vlastos, working from the Aoki database and other sources, detailed the changing trajectory of protest in Tokugawa Japan from the seventeenth to the nineteenth century. In the first half of the Tokugawa period, from the seventeenth to the mid-eighteenth century, protests in different *daimyo* domains were predominantly nonviolent petitions involving such issues as appeals for lower taxes and requests for famine relief. At times, the peasants also would appeal to the *daimyo* to complain about abuses of village headmen. The *daimyos* often responded to these appeals favorably and acted on their paternalist, benevolent obligations toward their subjects—though repression of petitioners was not a rarity. In the second half of the Tokugawa period, during the late eighteenth and nineteenth centuries, extensive commercialization across Japan differentiated the peasants into rich and poor and precipitated increasingly frequent and violent class conflicts involving rent and land ownership. The peasants' violent clashes with the emergent merchant class, food merchants in particular, also were on the rise. In the meantime, commercialization eroded many *daimyos'* ability to govern their domains, as their revenue could no longer keep up with the increasingly marketized and complex society. As a remedy to this, *daimyos* across Japan increased taxes or shifted from cash taxes to tax in kind (usually rice) to avoid the risk of their cash revenue diminishing in purchasing power under inflation. As a result, many peasants, whose livelihoods were more volatile under the market economy, found it difficult to convert their cash income into grain. They often responded with violent tax resistance, which replaced peaceful petitions to become the dominant form of protest in the period (Vlastos 1986; see also Bix 1986; Ikegami and Tilly 1994; White 1995).

In Japan, the rise of state-engaging, peaceful protest in the sixteenth to mid-eighteenth centuries and its transition to state-resisting violence in the late eighteenth and nineteenth centuries, in juxtaposition with the consolidation of the Tokugawa political order from the seventeenth to mid-eighteenth centuries, as well as its erosion in the late eighteenth and early nineteenth centuries, shows that the cyclical transformation of protest patterns in Ming and Qing China was not unique. At the same time, we should bear in mind how protests in the two countries differed in their main targets, given the difference between Japan's decentralized feudal order and China's centralized imperial rule. While Japanese protesters rarely targeted or appealed to the Tokugawa Bakufu, except for those protesters actually residing in the domain that the Bakufu directly administered, Chinese protesters often appealed to higher-level officials or even to the emperor in their collective action contending with local officials. This difference, as we see later, is crucial to the development of mid-Qing protests into the modern social revolutions in the nineteenth and early twentieth centuries, in contrast to Japan's lack of such a revolution in its transition to modernity. Before turning to this issue, I discuss in the next section how the above comparison between Chinese and European protests could help resolve a recent theoretical debate between structuralists and culturalists in the historical study of protest.

STRUCTURE AND CULTURE IN THE MAKING OF PROTEST

The political-economy theory of protest transformation that was pioneered by Charles Tilly explained the changing pattern of protests in early modern Europe in terms of state centralization and commercialization, and it has been prevalent in the historical study of protest for decades, as I outlined in the introduction. Recently, more researchers of protest or of contentious politics in general have redirected their attention to such cultural processes as the creation of collective identities and the strategic framing of grievances and structural conditions. This cultural turn is concomitant with a "microturn," as most cultural analysts are currently more interested in the microdynamics of protest than in larger structural forces.

Dissatisfied with the alleged "structural bias" of the political-economic account, cultural analysts opine that favorable structural conditions such as expanding political opportunities under a centralizing state and dense, preexisting social networks in a commercial economy would not automatically bring about contention, unless action organizers managed to constitute a pervasive contentious discourse and an appealing contentious identity to motivate potential contenders. While the contentious discourse frames the contenders' grievances and goals and interprets the objective conditions as favorable to their action, the contentious identity serves as a dramaturgical presentation of self among the contenders to legitimize their actions and foster group solidarity (Benford and Snow 2000; Goodwin and Jasper 2003; McAdam 1996). Other analysts elaborate further that these framing activities are not totally voluntaristic but are constrained by the encompassing culture, as contenders always need to appropriate codes and meanings from the available (and often hegemonic) cultural schemas to assemble their discourse and identity (Steinberg 1999).

If the microstrategic construction of protest discourse and identity is enabled and constrained by the dominant cultural schema of the time, one may wonder how macrocultural forces would shape the macropattern of protest. William Sewell did offer us a clue based on his study of French contention at the turn of the nineteenth century. Paralleling the cultural sociological distinction between "cultural tool kit" and strategic action constructed by tools from the kit (Swidler 1986, 1995), Sewell distinguishes between cultural schema, which is an array of transposable codes and meanings that actors in different contexts can appropriate to make sense of the world and guide their actions, and cultural practice, through which actors constitute the symbolic dimension of their actions by applying codes and meanings drawn from the encompassing cultural schema (Sewell 2005). He argues that the new protest claims and repertoires in nineteenth-century France were outgrowths of new contentious discourses and identities, which can be regarded as new cultural practices stemming from a radical reconstitution of France's cultural hegemony. During this reconstitution, the originally dominant corporatist culture, which ensured people's collective loyalties to localistic corporate communities like villages and guilds and gave rise to reactive types of contention such as communal tax riots, was replaced by the ideology of social contracts, which offered "a powerful new associative idiom in whose terms French men and women could now act out their social loyalties" in proactive social movements (Sewell 1990, 546). The cultural reconstitution was touched off by the French Revolution as a contingent historical event.

This macrocultural explanation has been followed recently by scholars who attempt to identify the cultural origins of the rise of new national social movements in early nineteenth-century America and the revolutions of Eastern Europe in 1989 (Sharman 2003; Young 2006). This explanation is certainly at odds with the political-economy theories, according to which changing repertoires and claims of protest in early modern Europe originated in state centralization and the rise of market capitalism.

Judging between the two accounts by relying solely on Western cases, as most existing studies do, is not easy. Political-economic changes and cultural transformations were two concurrent processes in most European states during the eighteenth and early nineteenth centuries. It is difficult to tell whether the transformation of protest in that period was a result of the new dominant culture, new political-economic structures, or both. The case of mid-Qing China is useful in resolving this debate, as it witnessed sweeping commercialization and state centralization comparable to contemporaneous Europe, but alongside a relatively stable neo-Confucianist orthodoxy.

As we have seen, similar state centralization and commercialization in China and Europe fomented the rise of proactive protest, generally defined, to steer state action and expand people's rights. But Chinese and European proactive protests differed in their substantive claims and repertoires. Chinese protesters were inscribed in the schema of the Confucianist orthodoxy, defining their posture toward authorities in filial-loyal terms, making claims that never transgressed the plea for more effective paternalist intervention of the state as an expansion of their rights as imperial subjects. In contrast, European protesters were influenced by the emerging cultural schema of popular sovereignty, making claims associated with the new democratic rights of political participation.

In other words, the primary initiator of change in China's protest patterns is the changing political economy. The exact course of change in protest claims and identities, nevertheless, is always limited by what codes and meanings are available in the encompassing cultural schema. Though China witnessed no rupture in the cultural hegemony of neo-Confucianism in the mid-Qing period, the changing political economy at the turn of the nineteenth century did bring about change in protest patterns. As discussed, neo-Confucianism as a dominant cultural schema, like many cultural schema, is not monolithic but could contain multiple components, which included filial loyalty to the imperial state (i.e., "imperial Confucianism" in Rozman's characterization; see chapter 1) and loyalty to grassroots communal groups such as lineage organizations (i.e., Rozman's "mass Confucianism") at the same time. The decline of the state's ability to provide paternalist care and the rise of the predatory taxation of local governments at the end of the eighteenth century and in the early nineteenth century induced protesters, in order to maximize their chances of success or survival, to shift their preferential frame of action from imperial Confucianism to mass Confucianism, while remaining within the same Confucianist orthodoxy. This involved constructing different identities (universal imperial subjects or communal bodies), demands (request for paternalist care from the state or defending local communities against state interference and appropriation), and actions (humble petition or violent resistance).

These findings about China point to an integrated perspective according to which the macropattern of protest is not shaped by political economy or culture alone but by a combination of the two. The culturalists are right in pointing out that protest patterns are molded by the overarching cultural schema of a particular time and place. But we can add that protesters always have some room to choose what specific elements to borrow from the schema, and their choice is conditioned by the circumscribing political-economic settings. The structuralists are right in arguing that a changing political economy can induce change in protest repertoires and claims. But we need to bear in mind that the impact of political-economic change is always mediated by the codes and meanings available in the dominant cultural schema, which shaped protesters' discourses and identities.

What is unique to early modern Europe in comparison with mid-Qing China is that Europe's changing political economy, which motivated protesters to look for different codes and meanings in the first place, was coupled with the eighteenth-century crisis of the religious orthodoxy. This crisis delivered extra room to maneuver for the protesters, who could not only choose among long-established cultural idioms within the hegemonic culture but could also choose to borrow idioms from emerging new cultural schemas or even tailor new ideologies for their own actions. The same can be said with regard to the change in protest patterns in late nineteenth- and early twentieth-century China, when state decline and economic crisis deepened, the neo-Confucianist hegemony unraveled, and new schemas of radical ideologies began to be imported from the West. It is this nineteenth- and twentieth-century conjunction of ideological flux and accelerating political-economic changes in China to which I now turn.

FROM MID-QING PROTESTS TO TWENTIETH-CENTURY REVOLUTIONS

In the first three decades of the nineteenth century, the Jiaqing and Daoguang emperors successfully rejuvenated the moral legitimacy of the imperial center, reversing the late eighteenth-century popular perception that the Qing court was the source of moral decay and corruption. Although this moral rejuvenation motivated many aggrieved subjects to seek sympathy from the emperor through capital appeal in lieu of rebellion, it fell far short of arresting the state's deepening fiscal and administrative decay. The surge in capital appeals did not bring about the mitigation of any of the administrative malfeasances that motivated them. As we saw in chapter 5, an overwhelming majority of appeal cases were clogged in the system and never resolved.

The early nineteenth-century rise of capital appeal and fading of rebellion, therefore, does not represent an amelioration of popular grievances. It was no more than a shield that guarded the imperial center against the boiling anger at the bottom of society and offered the central government breathing room to address the fiscal and administrative crisis that caused the grievances in the first place, and discussion about remedies to resuscitate the state's fiscal strength, administrative rigor, and bureaucratic discipline did gather momentum in the central government in the first four decades of the nineteenth century (Kuhn 2002, 26–79; Lin 2006; Polachek 1992).

For example, Wei Yuan, a leading scholar representing the "statecraft school of thought," proposed to allow lower-ranked, unofficial literati with diversified views to advise on and even participate in the decision-making processes at different levels of government by serving as private advisers (*mu you*) to government officials. This was thought to be a way to revive the government's effectiveness and access to public opinion, and the proposal received wide support within the bureaucracy during the late Jiaqing and early Daoguang reign. During this period, proreform officials also started to form factions, transcending the taboo against factionalism imposed by the Yongzheng emperor. They became increasingly outspoken advocators of a bold administrative revamp, as shown by their debate over the liberalization of tribute-grain transportation and the proposed termination of the salt monopoly (Gao 2001, 548–578; Kuhn 2002, 27–53; Polachek 1976). Despite the pertinence of many of these reform proposals and the energy of the growing proreform factions, resistance to reform was strong enough that most of these proposals were not realized before time ran out in 1839–1842, when China's humiliating defeat in its clash with the British shattered the fragile legitimacy of the Manchu state.

After the Qing defeat in the war, tax resistances continued to surge all over the empire, and they started to transform into large-scale armed uprisings in the 1840s, just as they had done in the late eighteenth century. To be sure, social dislocation resulting from the forced trade liberalization following the war accounted partially for the resurgence of these uprisings. With the opening of Shanghai as a free-trade port in the 1840s, Westerners had direct access to the market and products of the Lower Yangzi Region. This immediately caused massive unemployment in the Guangdong–Lower Yangzi corridor of the Hunan and Jiangxi provinces, across which exports and imports had been transported between the Lower Yangzi Region and Guangzhou, which had been the only port city for foreign trade before the post–Opium War trade liberalization. The sudden collapse of the local economy aggravated the hardship and heavy tax burden in the region (Wakeman 1966, 133; Wang 1979, 444–445). It is not surprising that many tax resistances that turned into armed revolts in the 1840s were located here, as a catalog of major revolts in the decade illustrates (fig. 6.2).

The connection between social dislocations fostered by trade liberalization and the recurrence of uprisings in the 1840s and afterward seems convincing. But a closer look at individual revolts suggests that something else was involved in precipitating them. Many of these revolts originated as routine tax resistance or as capital appeal against abusive local officials, not unlike most resistances and appeals in the 1820s and the 1830s. While tax resisters were audacious in seeking the emperor's sympathy despite repeated setbacks and repression by local governments before the 1840s, many of them seemed to have lost their patience in the 1840s, as shown by the precipitous drop in documented appeal cases in figure 5.2. Some tax resisters disillusioned with the capital-appeal process even engaged in open revolt, such as those involved in the Leiyang Rebellion in 1844.

In the winter of 1842, Duan, a respected literati in the Leiyang county of Hunan, traveled to Beijing on behalf of the Leiyang taxpayers to lodge a plaint against the county clerks, whose extortion and illegal tax levies created widespread grievances in the community. The central government refused to handle the plaint and accused Duan of fabricating the charges. Duan was sent back to Leiyang in 1843 and imprisoned, pending banishment

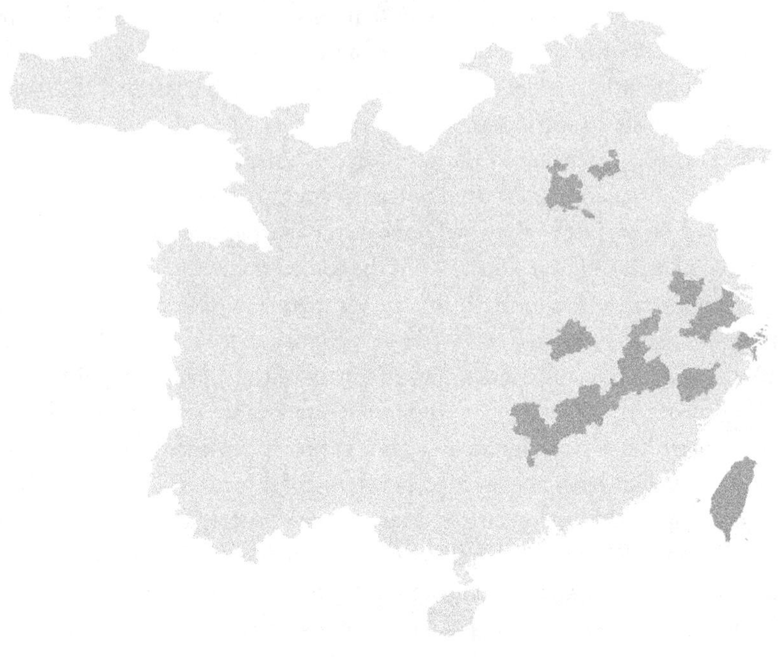

FIGURE 6.2 Location of Major Protests-Turned-Revolts in the 1840s (shaded areas) (*Source*: Chen 1980; background map: CHGIS)

to the western interior of the empire. Knowing that the county clerks were avenging Duan's appeal attempt by abusing him in prison, Leiyang residents stormed the prison and set him free. In the months that followed, government clerks were occasionally beaten and their houses sacked by angry taxpayers. Local literati repeatedly petitioned the local government for lower tax rates and sanctions against abusive clerks, but nothing changed, and tax levies continued to soar.[2]

In the summer of 1844, a number of local gentry abruptly decided to take an unusual action, one that had not been a component of similar tax resistances anywhere in the empire in the preceding decades. They established a new public office, a de facto local government, to replace the original county office. The public office began to run local affairs and levy taxes on the residents. Founding an alternative power center amounted to a declaration of war on the ruling dynasty. Anticipating a showdown, the rebels employed their tax revenue to make weapons and accumulate gunpowder.

Imperial troops swiftly arrived in Leiyang to demolish the building where the office was housed. This triggered an armed uprising. More than a thousand villagers armed with homemade cannons marched toward the county seat and attempted to seize the city. Imperial reinforcement outnumbered the inexperienced rebel army and easily decimated it.

These events in 1842 and 1843 were initially undistinguishable from other cases of capital appeal and tax resistance in the 1820s and 1830s—until the moment when the aggrieved resisters decided, in 1844, to openly rebel against the dynasty. This sudden propensity to revolt in the aftermath of the Opium War might have had something to do with the radical change in the popular perception of the imperial center's moral legitimacy.

The Qing defeat in the war shattered the image of the Manchu rulers as the grand patriarchs of the empire, and nationalist sentiment began to boil among the Chinese elite, who blamed the weakness and moral decay of the Manchus for China's humiliating defeat. The damage to the legitimacy of Manchu rule was even greater than during the Heshen regency of the late eighteenth century (see Bernhardt 1992, 55–62; Chen 1980, 7–12; Wakeman 1966).

Remarkably, the first uprising that erupted after the outbreak of the Opium War was an anti-British action that turned into an anti-Manchu movement in South China in 1841. The uprising's leaders (mostly local gentry elite) and participants (ranging from cultivators to urban dwellers) "despised the Manchus for their weakness before the barbarians" (Kuhn 1978, 269). They denounced the Manchu rulers' reluctance to prepare for war despite repeated warnings by Chinese officials since the 1820s. Worse, the Manchus were eager to make peace with the British by allowing them to occupy the city of Guangzhou and to repress anti-British militias (Wakeman 1966, chaps. 7, 12). In the wake of this anti-British, anti-Manchu movement was a general rise in anti-Manchuism among the scholar-official class. A Qing historian notes that "commencing in late 1843 or thereabouts, a literati-bureaucratic opposition did, in fact, begin to galvanize and acquire a highly visible organizational form: the so-called Ku Yen-wu [Gu Yanwu] Shrine Association" (Polachek 1992, 206). It is noteworthy that the association was named after Gu Yanwu, a seventeenth-century anti-Manchu intellectual who, unlike many other Chinese literati defecting to the nascent Manchu state, steadfastly maintained his loyalty to the Ming dynasty and refused to accept the Manchus as China's legitimate rulers following the dynastic transition.

THE TAIPING REBELLION AND THE COLLAPSE OF EMPIRE

The growth of anti-Manchu sentiment turned into the popular and elite perception that the Qing state had lost the Mandate of Heaven and that new rulers were about to emerge. This perception emboldened many tax resisters, such as those in Leiyang, to opt for the path of open revolt, a path never taken in the 1820s and the 1830s. It also enabled Hong Xiuquan and Yang Xiuqing, two obscure heterodox sectarians who had been entrenched in the mountains of South China, to attract a large number of followers in the 1850s and launch the Taiping Rebellion (1850–1864). Their call for restrengthening the Chinese by exterminating the Manchu rulers as the "Manchu demons" and "mortal enemy of us Chinese" echoed the popular sentiment about the dynasty. In the declaration of the rebels, the Manchu emperor was no longer referred to as the grand patriarch of the Chinese subjects but as a "Tartar dog," an immoral, alien ruler who came from a race "inferior" to the Chinese (Spence 1996, 116, 160). The initial unfolding of the Taiping Rebellion was reminiscent of the outbreak of the White Lotus Rebellion in the mid-nineteenth century, during which sectarians persecuted by the authorities engaged in open revolt and happened to attract a large following of nonsectarians, who also despised Manchu rule and had been resisting the state on their own.

The leadership of the Taiping Rebellion mostly originated in the Hakka migrant communities in the mountainous regions of northern Guangdong and Guangxi. God-worshipping societies operating after the model of Buddhist religious sects were founded in the 1840s by Hong Xiuquan, who obtained a copy of the Bible from a foreign missionary in the port city of Guangzhou (Kuhn 1977; Spence 1996). He told his followers that he was a reincarnation of a son of Jehovah and that in a dream Jehovah had given him a sacred sword and told him to cleanse the world of corruption and suffering. Despite Hong's use of Biblical language, the genre of this story is very similar to the White Lotus legend that the Venerable Mother would send the Maitreya Buddha to earth through reincarnation and create a new world free of corruption and suffering.

When the Qing government aggressively cracked down on the god-worshipping societies and went after Hong, the sectarians, now well armed, moved north and entered the Guandong–Lower Yangzi corridor, which in the 1840s had already been plagued by tax resistance and revolts such as the

1844 Leiyang Revolt. Along the way, the rebels expanded by recruiting seasoned tax resisters and by allying with preexisting secret brotherhood societies in the region (Yang 1961, 225–227). The army grew rapidly and eventually captured most of the major cities in the Lower Yangzi area. The victory of the Taiping rebels from south to north was made possible not only by the expanding recruitment of aggrieved peasants but also by the indirect aid of protesters launching parallel resistances against local officials, as they "fought alongside rebel troops in battles against Qing armies and loyalist militia . . . [and] took a toll on the defenses and the spirit of the region's protectors, thereby expediting the Taiping advance." Many aggrieved commoners welcomed the invading rebels by offering them food, drink, and local intelligence (Bernhardt 1992, 89–90). Some gentry elites even expressed their hatred of the Qing government by leading their militias to join the rebels (Zheng 2009).

After Hong's army conquered Qing's southern capital of Nanjing and established the "Peaceful Heavenly Kingdom" (*Taiping tianguo*) there, he declared that:

> when disorder reaches its extreme, then there is order, when darkness reaches its extreme, then there is light; this is the Way of Heaven. Now, night has fled and the sun has risen! We only wish that all our brothers and sisters on earth would rush from the demon's treacherous gate and follow God's true Way . . . they would one and all improve themselves and improve the world . . . enjoying universal tranquility.
>
> (*TAIPING IMPERIAL DECLARATION,* CITED IN KUHN 1977, 360)

Upon enacting the above time-honored script of dynastic transition, the Taiping rebels also adopted policies to foster levels of gender and social equality unprecedented in previous Chinese rebellions. Because of these reformist programs, apparently influenced by Western social thought, which was entering the Qing empire via missionaries after the Opium War, twentieth-century revolutionaries and scholars alike consider the rebellion the first modern revolution in Chinese history (Skocpol 1979). What the Taiping Rebellion represented was, in fact, an amalgam of indigenous ideologies and repertoires of mid-Qing protest and the Western ideologies newly imported into the empire.

The Qing state, already weakened considerably by the Opium War, relied on Western military aid and Han provincial officials, who built private armies autonomous from the central government, to put down the Taiping movement. In post-Taiping China, the regional military regimes that emerged during the anti-Taiping campaign continued to thrive and proliferate, becoming the de facto rulers of many parts of China. The professionalization and accelerated growth of regional military regimes, however, did not deter the growth of sectarian activism, the politicization of the secret brotherhood societies, and the explosive growth of violent, state-resisting protests such as tax riots. Some brotherhood associations—having long been active in South China and overseas Chinese communities, such as the Tiandihui, which ignited the Tiandihui Rebellion in Taiwan in 1785–1788—became major supporters of Sun Yat-sen's Republican revolutionary movement in the late nineteenth and early twentieth centuries. These secret societies provided the movement with manpower and financial and organizational support. Sun and many of his comrades were actually core members of one of these secret societies themselves (Chesneaux 1972).

Sun's revolutionary movement was led by a group of Westernized intellectuals who combined Western ideas of popular sovereignty and nationalism with racialist anti-Manchuism, which originated among the literati class amid the seventeenth-century Manchu conquest and went dormant under the heyday of eighteenth-century Manchu rule, to foster a plan of overthrowing the Manchu imperial state and establishing a modern Chinese republic grounded on Han Chinese leadership. With the support of secret societies, the revolutionaries diligently instigated or participated in many kinds of local unrest to weaken Qing rule in hotspots of escalating social disturbance across the empire. In 1911, they were eventually successful in toppling the Qing dynasty.

Japan also witnessed the intensification of violent resistance and popular revolts in the latter half of the nineteenth century, following its subjugation by Western imperial powers and the subsequent decline in the legitimacy of the Tokugawa Bakufu. But under the decentralized political system of the Tokugawa regime, these revolts remained regional, targeted at the *daimyos* and other local elites. The Tokugawa regime was, in the end, toppled not by any revolutionary forces from below but instead by an imperial army formed in the aftermath of a coup, in which a group of young samurai seized state power and erected a modern, centralized bureaucracy under the revived emperorship of Meiji, in 1868.

The escalating peasant protests in the late Tokugawa period contributed to this political transformation in two ways. First, the adamant tax resistance of the peasants starved many *daimyos* of revenue and led to the impoverishment of the samurai class that they patronized. The pauperization of the samurai was a key factor in their radicalization and participation in the coup leading to the Meiji Restoration. Second, the peasant resistance weakened *daimyo* rule, making some of them vulnerable to attack by the imperial army and urging others to shift their allegiance to the Meiji state as a more reliable guarantor of social order. In other words, the localized revolts helped destroy the power base of the local feudal elite of the Tokugawa regime, clearing the path for centralizing reform of the nascent Meiji state as a revolution from above (Hung 2008, 581–582; Ikegami and Tilly 1994, 453–454; Vlastos 1986, 142–167).

The puzzle about Japan in comparison with China, as noted by Vlastos, is that "the destruction of feudalism and subsequent modernization was not accompanied by social revolution, but by a shift of power within elite political classes" (1986, 167). Some explain this by arguing that strong social control exercised by Japan's landowning elite at the village level restrained peasants' ability to mobilize (Skocpol 1979), while others attribute it to the relatively low population-to-land ratio in Japan, which generated fewer landless vagrants susceptible to mobilization for rebellions like those in Qing China (Goldstone 1991). These two explanations are both convincing but not adequate, as Vlastos' and other studies do show that nineteenth-century Japan was in fact plagued by large-scale peasant rebellions. The key is therefore not the lack of rebellions but that most rebellions remained regionally segmented and never converged into movements aimed at seizing national state power like the Taiping Rebellion and Republican Revolution in China.

More serious work that compares protests and revolts in nineteenth-century Japan and China is needed. But we can hypothesize that the Japan-China difference lies principally in the difference between Japan's decentralized feudal system and China's centralized imperial system. Under Japan's decentralized system, based on *daimyo* rule, rebels tended to see *daimyos* as the highest source of their plight and targets of action, and they were less prone to framing their grievances and demands with reference to the higher-level power at the Bakufu. In China, the centralized imperial state, self-portrayed as the grand patriarch of the empire, easily became the galvanizing point of variegated protesters and rebels, who, under the leadership of either the god-worshipping societies, in the case of the Taiping Rebellion, or the westernized Republican revolutionaries, in the case of the 1911 Revolution, converged into an empirewide coalition that confronted the very center of the Manchu regime head on.

FROM REPUBLICAN TO COMMUNIST REVOLUTION

After the success of the 1911 Republican Revolution, China entered into a prolonged period of civil war. The convergence of violent state-resisting protests, heterodox movements, and secret-brotherhood activism continued, creating a breeding ground for the Communist movement. This movement gestated in the aftermath of Russia's October Revolution, in 1917, and took on the regional warlords and later the Guomindang (Nationalist Party) founded by the original Republican revolutionaries. After local warlords were subjugated by a united front between the Guomindang (GMD) and the Chinese Communist Party (CCP) in the late 1920s, the two parties split. While the struggle between the two intensified in the coastal metropolises, violent resistance against local tax bullies and peasant wars against GMD regional lords never ceased in the vast inland area. As early as 1926, a group of CCP activists—including Mao Zedong—proposed developing a Communist rural movement by allying with the contentious peasants. Initially, the proposal faced stern stricture by the Party's Central Committee, which had been fixated on an urban-based working-class movement (Selden 1971, 25–27; Bianco 1971). But after the Party finally decided to turn to the countryside in the wake of their all-out defeat by the GMD in the coastal big cities in 1927, the Communists immediately found themselves at home there, where they "encountered a peasantry well schooled in the art of collective violence" (Perry 1980, 208).

To be sure, the Communists, once they established their foothold in the countryside, were quick to introduce social reforms that were unfamiliar to their rural supporters and were modeled after an ideal "modern society" based on translated revolutionary texts from Europe. These reforms included gender equality in work and education, grassroots elections, and rural cooperatives, among others (Selden 1971). But at the same time, the CCP also adapted their program to the long-standing demand for rent and tax reduction among the peasants and retribution against local notables and officials. In fact, the first Red base areas following the Communists' rural turn in the late 1920s were located in Jiangxi and southern Hunan along the Guangdong–Lower Yangzi corridor, where tax resistance had escalated into armed revolts in the 1840s and the Taiping movement had expanded rapidly by recruiting local resisters in the 1850s. Besides cooperating with preexisting heterodox sects and brotherhood organizations, the CCP expanded popular support by presenting themselves as resourceful outside allies against abusive local bullies, which the peasants had been resisting assiduously on their own for a century or more. The CCP recruited many of these resisters and sectarians into the Soviet government and Red Army (see Averill 2006). Outside the areas controlled by the Communists, localized resistance against taxes and other policies of the GMD government converged under the open or underground leadership of CCP activists, becoming another crucial building block of the Communist movement (e.g., Bianco 2001; Duara 1988; Thaxton 1997). In this light, despite the Western modernist ideals that their leaders employed to frame their action, the twentieth-century Chinese revolutions, including both the Republican Revolution, which toppled the Qing government in 1911, and the Communist Revolution, which ousted the GMD in 1949, were in part continuations of mid-Qing antistate resistance that recurrently grew into large-scale rebellions, first in the late eighteenth century and again in the mid-nineteenth century.

A caveat is that the culmination of violent state-resisting protests from the mid-nineteenth century to the twentieth century, as well as their connections with the revolutionary movements, does not mean that filial-loyalist, state-engaging protests that prevailed in the mid-eighteenth century, together with the practice of capital appeal that became popular in the early nineteenth century, completely disappeared in the age of revolution. In the early twentieth century, the Republican and Communist Revolutions were far from the only choices for social and political movements. In fact, during the last decade of Qing rule, the Republican revolutionaries faced fierce competition from the loyalist reformist movement, which defied the revolution and sought to retain the Qing imperial rule by modifying it into a constitutional monarchy. Among the landmark activities of the movement was the "Protect the Railroad Campaign" (*baolu yundong*), which appealed to local and central governments to prevent Chinese railroads from falling into the hands of foreign powers. The dominant repertoires employed by this movement, such as humble petitions at government offices by "kneeling and praying with incense" and lodging plaints at Beijing, were strikingly similar to many mid-Qing state-engaging protests (see illustration 2 in the appendix, for example; see also Rankin 2002).

In a similar vein, the student movements and other mass movements during the warlord period and the GMD period were perennially divided into radical factions, which called for the overthrow of the existing regime, and loyalist factions, which sought to improve the existing regime through nonantagonistic appeal. Studies of early twentieth-century Chinese student movements repeatedly confirmed that filial repertoires such as kneeling upon two knees were often employed by protesters to invoke the sympathy of the authorities (Solinger 1989; Strand 1990; Wasserstrom 1991, 227–229).

Humble petition was a common action not only for loyalist students but also for leftist ones mobilized by underground Communist cells, with the wave of petitions requesting the GMD to resist Japanese invasion in the 1930s and those requesting the GMD to negotiate with the Communists in the late 1940s as examples. Other social groups not directly involved in the GMD-CCP struggle occasionally petitioned the GMD government to advance their interests. A case in point is the mass petition of salt-transportation boatmen in 1932, in which several thousands of them traveled to the GMD government in Nanjing to petition for protection of their employment against the use of railroads and steamships (Sun 2005). Another example is the decade-long movement in which residents of Wuyuan county, which was part of Anhui province in Qing times but was annexed to the Jiangxi province by the GMD government in the Republican period, petitioned for a return to Anhui by appealing to establishment figures of Anhui origins, such as Hu Shi (Xu 2007).

Some of these state-engaging petitions were in fact organized by the CCP. For example, in the rural areas of the Jiaxing region of Jiangsu in 1926, the local CCP cadres responded to local peasants' demands for rent reduction amid economic hardship by mobilizing them for a protracted "kneeling and praying with incense" (*guixiang*) movement. As we have seen, this was a very common repertoire of state-engaging protest in the mid-eighteenth century. The movement, which was orchestrated by a CCP-led "*guixiang* struggle committee" (*guixiang douzheng weiyuanhui*), lasted for weeks and was successful in forcing local authorities, controlled by local landlords, to declare an across-the-board reduction in land rent (JXSDASZW). It shows that the CCP was open to letting their appeals and actions be shaped by preexisting protest claims and repertoires (many originating in the mid-Qing period, if not earlier) among local populations whom the CCP was wooing, even though these claims and repertoires might be seen by the revolutionaries as "feudal and superstitious."[3]

To emphasize the continuities between twentieth-century revolutions and state-resisting and state-engaging protests in mid-Qing China is not to downplay the transformative role played by the revolutionary movements.

The new demands and institutions that the revolutionaries introduced, such as liberty and democracy, national liberation, and centralized mass organizations, were undoubtedly imported from Western social and political movements by Westernized intellectuals of the time. But by highlighting these transformative aspects of the movements, existing studies tend to overlook their connection with the past. Choosing between an emphasis on continuity and an emphasis on change is like the choice between characterizing a glass of water as half empty or half full. The main point is that continuity and change have always coexisted.

As such, twentieth-century revolutions and other social movements in China manifested a hybridization of Western modernity, which was introduced in China after the 1840s, and the indigenous early modernity of China that crystallized in the mid-Qing period. China's modern popular protests, therefore, were never pure replications of modern Western protests. Instead, they were modern protests with Chinese characteristics.

5.

EPILOGUE: THE PAST IN THE PRESENT

The mid-Qing traditions of protest persisted not only into the late Qing and Republican periods but also into contemporary China. Repertoires of many protests in today's China are marked by the protesters' propensity to restrict their confrontation and violence, if any, to specific local officials. At the same time, they are keen to seek sympathy from higher-level officials through submissive petitions at different central-government organs, above all Beijing's "letter and visit" (*xinfang*) bureau, which specializes in receiving complaints from grassroots citizens against the wrongdoings of local cadres. In some cases, protesters invoke symbols of central authorities, such as copies of the constitution, to put pressure on local cadres by such acts as citing and reading policy documents from the central government that support their claims (Bernstein and Lu 2003; O'Brien and Li 2006). These repertoires of individualizing the source of injustice to particular officials, together with actual or symbolic appeal to higher authorities, remind us of the mid-Qing practices of assaulting individual officials in revenge for unpopular policies, lodging capital appeals, and demonstrating with statues of city gods as localized symbols of the imperial center.

The claims of today's Chinese protesters echo those of many mid-Qing protests, as well. Most recent demands have involved subsistence rights. They include protests against corrupt officials who threaten protesters' livelihoods through excessive tax levies or the illegal appropriation of farmland. Some protests request that the government protect or extend the protesters' subsistence rights by redressing injustices or removing menaces that threaten those rights. Petitions that ask the government to put pressure on a factory that contaminated a local water source or an enterprise that laid off workers without proper compensation are cases in point (Hurst 2009, chap. 5; Jun 2000; Lee 2007; Zweig 2000). These demands echo many mid-Qing protests that sought universal famine relief from the government amid subsistence crises, government action to pressure exploitative merchants, or retribution against corrupt and abusive local officials.

These long-standing protests that seek to protect or advance people's subsistence rights and that restrict their confrontation to individual local officials while manifesting subservience to the political center are shrewdly described by Elizabeth Perry (2008, 45) as "moral economy protests":

> China's pervasive moral economy protests, framed in a language of "rights," have often demanded (sometimes successfully) the removal of unpopular lower-level officials. Rarely, however, have they questioned the ruling authority of either the Communist Party or its ideology. In this respect, contemporary protesters bear some resemblance to imperial-era rebels. The endemic unrest that punctuated the history of imperial China often led to the replacement of particular officials (and very occasionally even of dynasties), while at the same time retaining and reinforcing certain basic principles of the Confucian order. . . . Today's pattern of protest . . . may prove more system-supportive than system-subversive.

Today's moral-economy protests have proliferated not only in the impoverished countryside. They also can be found among the supposedly Westernized, modernist, and urban student protesters. For example, in the 1989 student movement, before the final weeks of radicalization and bloody showdown, most students' demands were restricted to opposition to individual corrupt officials who aggravated inflation and threatened the livelihoods of the common people. They empathetically expressed their loyalty to the CCP through such acts as kneeling in front of the Great Hall of People to request dialogue and the penalization of corrupt cadres (Wasserstrom 1991; Zhao 2001). These acts displayed the protesters' faith in higher-level leaders as a righteous force that they could count on to combat corruption and restore morality in the People's Republic.

Characterizing as "rightful resistance" cases of peasant protest in which protesters confronted local officials by appealing to higher-level authorities or employing CCP official ideology as their weapon, Kevin O'Brien and Li Lianjiang (2006) see their particular claims and repertoires as consequences of the protesters' rational strategies to maximize their chances of success and minimize the chance of repression within the context of authoritarian rule. They find parallels to these rightful resistances in the "consentful contention" of former East Germany, where protesters used the official language of dutiful socialist citizens to protest the expulsion of a satirical singer-songwriter. They also find a South African parallel in the antiapartheid strategy of using the ruling party's language of "rule of law" and "liberal tradition" against the ruling party. Despite these parallels, O'Brien and Li do not neglect the uniqueness of China's rightful resistances. This uniqueness lies in their emphasis on subsistence issues (as opposed to liberty and equality) and in their submissive appeal to the central authorities against local officials.

Protesters' emphasis on subsistence issues can be explained using Elizabeth Perry's (2008) view about the deep-seated, distinct Chinese conception of rights, which has persisted from classical Confucianist canons to Mao Zedong's thought and contemporary protest. In contrast to Western conceptions of rights, the Chinese conception emphasizes livelihood over liberty and collective subsistence over individual freedom. To Perry, today's Chinese protests are mostly "framed in a language more reminiscent of Mencius or Mao than of Locke and Jefferson" (43). Corresponding to this conception of rights is an exceptional conception of authority, in which rulers' primary obligation is to benevolently and sympathetically protect and enhance the subsistence rights of the ruled as a collective good. Officials who neglect the plight of the people are seen as immoral, as they let their individual greed overshadow the collective good, and they are subject to rectification or expulsion by agents of superior moral forces.

Moreover, protesters' propensity to submissively appeal to higher authorities against local ones can be explained by the Confucianist conception of political hierarchy as an extension of familial hierarchy. In this conception, the highest rulers, local officials, and commoners were linked in a hierarchical relationship resembling a grandfather, father, and son, which is delimited by the seniors' paternalist and benevolent obligation to the juniors and the juniors' absolute subservience to the seniors. This grandfather-father-son analogy sometimes was made explicit in Qing official discourses. We have already seen how this Confucianist-familial conception of political power motivated protesting subjects to appeal to higher authorities against local officials in mid-Qing times. The salience of similar appeals among today's protesting citizens suggests that this conception of power continues to prevail.

Given the above cultural continuities that are found in claims and repertoires in popular protest from mid-Qing to today's China, the next questions are how these continuities are possible and what processes and institutions have helped transmit these particular conceptions of rights and power from past to present. Although I do not intend to reach any definitive answer here, circumstantial evidence in the literature does lead us to some viable hypotheses.

First and foremost, many twentieth-century state builders in China, despite their proclaimed modernist and revolutionary aspirations, never totally exonerated themselves from the Confucianist schema of political legitimation and institution building. By reinvoking this schema in their state-making activities to varying extents, they ineluctably reproduced the Confucianist conceptions of rights and authority and reinscribed these conceptions in society. According to Perry's observation, Mao's Confucianist discourse that people have the "right to rebel" when the state fails to protect their subsistence rights, as well as successive Communist leaders' emphasis on the merit of securing these subsistence rights as the source of their legitimacy, is an example of the subterranean salience of the Confucianist morality within the CCP regime (Liu 2000; Perry 2008). The ruling Communists' reiterated priority of maintaining the righteousness of cadres and their dedication to nourishing the people echo the Qing emperor's view, as well as the view of the 1930s GMD government that Frederic Wakeman (2000) characterized as a Confucian Fascist regime, that the state should serve as a paternalist, moralizing agent (Thornton 2007).

On some occasions, Confucianist ideas even surfaced without disguise in revolutionary writings and speeches. In *How to Be a Good Communist (Lun gongchan dangyuan de xiuyang)*, the must-read text for all CCP members, Liu Shaoqi, the organization czar of the CCP during its revolutionary years and the state chairman of the People's Republic from 1959 to 1966, invoked the names of Confucius and Mencius repeatedly to elaborate on the necessity of repressing one's personal interests for the sake of the peoples' collective good and the party's discipline in one's pursuit of highest morality. This text echoes in some ways the Yongzheng emperor's *Discourses on Friends and Parties*, which was a must-read of mid-Qing officials and literati and pitted officials' vicious private interests against their virtuous filial loyalty to the emperor and benevolent nourishment of the people. The official Communist policy of "critical inheritance" of traditional Chinese culture and "sinicization of socialism," which spanned the revolutionary years to today, is more than just empty talk (Zhang and Schwartz 2003).

At times, Communist leaders legitimized their authority by propagandizing their close, familial relationship with the people. During the height of the Cultural Revolution, the slogan "our familial intimacy with our parents never matched our familial intimacy with Chairman Mao" (*dieqin niangqin bugou mao zhuxi qin*), which was promoted by the Maoist leaders to the Red Guards, was reminiscent of the Yongzheng emperor's requirement that his officials place their filial loyalty to the emperor above their filiality toward their biological parents. In a different context, today's Premier Wen Jiabao recurrently and comfortably refers to himself as "Grandpa Wen" (*Wen yeye*), a title that many petitioners use when they address him.

The Communist state elite not only reproduced the Confucianist-familial conception of authority and its purported moral obligation to nourish the people at the discursive level but also injected it into many institutional practices of the state. The paternalistic characteristics of the Chinese socialist state were unseen in most other socialist states during the Cold War. The patron-client relation between cadres and workers in urban work units in Mao's China was quite well known; there were few other socialist states in which cadres would routinely arrange marriages and prepare birthday presents for the workers (Walder 1986). These Chinese cadres actually acted more like lineage elders than ironhanded Stalinists. Moreover, the central government and local state companies in both the Mao and post-Mao periods were characterized by what Dorothy Solinger labeled a "paternalistic relationship between state and firm" whereby the "state considers the firm its 'own child'" (Solinger 1993, 153). Under this paternalist relation, "Chinese local systems and local bureaucracies are oriented toward the state . . . and are comfortable with dependence on the center when the center can provide parenting" (154). As "the imperial Chinese state and the centralized socialist regime are neatly comparable to each other," the ideology of the post-1949 party-state is in fact "the grand concept of the state that universal cosmopolitan Confucianism helped uphold appear[ing] in a new guise under socialism" (154–156). Given this implicit Confucianist orientation of the Communist state, it is not surprising at all that the CCP resurrected the imperial capital-appeal system almost immediately after it seized national power, in 1949, by establishing the *xinfang* system to encourage ordinary citizens to petition higher authorities and complain about the local cadres' wrongdoings (Minzner 2006).

Alongside the state-making elite as highly visible agents who reproduced the Confucianist conceptions of rights and authority in a top-down manner, there were also agents in society that inadvertently reproduced the conceptions from the ground up. Explaining the centuries-long continuity of petitions, riots, and the notion of righteous protest (not unlike China's moral-economy protests) among Japanese peasants, Anne Walthall (1986; Eisenstadt

1995; cf. Swider 1986) employs the concept of "cultural reservoirs." This refers to the plurality of popular-culture vehicles that embodied the memories of past protest in one place at one time and transmitted those memories to other times and places. Of these reservoirs, legends and tales about protest heroes and martyrs as told in oral or written vernacular literature are the most significant, as far as Tokugawa peasant protests are concerned.

As for Chinese protest, there is no reason not to presume the existence and salience of similar cultural reservoirs in perpetuating claims and repertoires of mid-Qing protests into the twentieth century and beyond. One plausible candidate for such reservoirs in China could be the colorful historical tales told by grassroots storytellers and local operas, which persisted despite the revolutionary ferments of the twentieth century (Hung 1993). Though further research is needed to decipher how exactly these oral traditions helped shape protest forms, what we do know is that many of these tales are saturated with stories about the plight of commoners under evil officials, miserable subjects appealing to benevolent and parent-like higher authorities, and how the bad officials were penalized and avenged in the end. The local operas occasionally include scenes of confrontational protests and humble petitions (e.g., see illustration 10 in the appendix).

To be sure, to emphasize the relevance of some traditions in the present is far from asserting that traditions could survive and persist in a static and perennial manner and that those traditional practices and consciousnesses never underwent meaningful transformations over time. As Edward Shils points out in his classic *Tradition* (1981), traditional practices and institutions, when reproduced in the present, are rarely exact replicas of what they had been in the past. They often interact or merge with other, exogenous traditions to form new, hybridized traditions, and they also constantly undergo change in response to changing circumstances or pressures from other traditions.

Into the twentieth century, what was available to Chinese protesters was a hybridized cultural reservoir constituted by the indigenous reservoir of protest tradition inherited from the mid-Qing period and a new reservoir of imported protest traditions originating in the West. Provided with such a hybridized reservoir, forms and appeals of protest within any movement were often a manifestation of syncreticism, simultaneously carrying traits of different traditions, East and West, old and new. In the early twentieth century, recalcitrant intellectuals, who were at the forefront of most social and political movements, did frequently engage with the authorities in nonthreatening, loyalist, and docile ways and invoked the ideal of righteous literati to establish their moral superiority, just as their mid-Qing predecessors did. At the same time, they also recurrently initiated strikes and sit-ins and harnessed the languages of liberty and democracy to legitimize their demands on the authorities. In the late twentieth century and today, many protesters often replicate, consciously or unconsciously, the pattern of mid-Qing protests by personalizing the source of injustice and pleading with higher authorities for sympathetic intervention. However, when conditions allow, they are equally eager to make use of the ideology of the rule of law, the state's judicial apparatus, and the attention of international human-rights organizations in making their case.

Existing cultural reservoirs of protest never shape the forms and appeals of protest in a deterministic way. As the analysis in chapters 3 through 5 illustrates, mid-Qing protesters, in response to changing political-economic opportunities and perceived legitimacy of the authorities, kept assembling and reassembling pertinent claims and repertoires by choosing different available elements from the reservoir, deciding whether and how to attack or to petition local officials, whether and how to seek help from the authorities or to loot official granaries, and whether and how to revolt against or appeal to the emperor. The coming of the traditions of Western protest and revolution in the twentieth century only enriched the range of claims and repertoires from which protesters could choose.

Given the fluidity of protesters' strategic choices from existing cultural reservoirs in formulating their actions, we should not expect today's prevalence of moral-economy protest to be naturally perennial. This type of protest represents only one among the many possible protest patterns in contemporary China, and we should not be surprised if some contingent events in the near future, such as a protracted economic crisis or defeat in a geopolitical conflict, dramatically shatter the perceived legitimacy of the CCP government and, in turn, urge these moral-economy protests to give way to radical movements or revolts seeking systemic political change.

By transgressing the presumption that historical transformation of protest in the non-Western world can only unfold in a unilinear fashion and by displacing traditional protest forms with modern forms originating in Europe, this study suggests that non-Western protests follow their own rhythms of change and are delimited by their own traditions of claims and repertoires. The "traditional" pattern of Chinese protests, as they culminated at the height of China's early modernity in the mid-Qing period, continues to constitute significant elements in the modern cultural reservoir of protest. Western traditions of protest introduced in twentieth-century China did change this cultural reservoir—but by *enriching* rather than by *replacing* the indigenous elements in it.

This study does not intend to decipher the structure and history of this cultural reservoir. Nor can it tell us how exactly today's protesters decide which elements from the reservoir to select. To answer these questions, we must examine anthropologically the cultural milieus, habitus, and strategies of the protesters in concrete, contemporary cases with the aid of the historical lens developed in this study. One thing is sure: the development of Chinese protest never follows a linear path along which the present continually supersedes the past. Instead, the past is always a constitutive part of the present, and it will continue to be part of the future. The persistence of the Confucianist ideology and practice of filial loyalty toward authorities among dissenters helps explain the durability of paternalist and authoritarian politics in China despite a century of revolution since 1911. These ideologies and practices are likely to continue their influence in the twenty-first century. They are what future reformers or revolutionaries aspiring to establish sustainable democratic institutions in China have to reckon with, adapt to, and overcome.

NOTES

INTRODUCTION

1. See also Weller and Guggenheim (1982).
2. A competing view, popular in literature and cultural studies, defines modernity not as a process but as a consciousness that privileges the present over the past and espouses a linear, progressive conception of time (Berman 1988; Kant 1784; see also Struve 2004 for the discussion about the applicability of such a conception of "early modernity" to Ming-Qing China). This is doubtless an indispensable aspect of modernity, but it is also an epiphenomenal aspect. After all, it was the universalization and rationalization of political economy and identities that made the rise of such modern consciousness possible.

1. MARKET EXPANSION, STATE CENTRALIZATION, AND NEO-CONFUCIANISM IN QING CHINA

1. For updated discussions on the Smithian dynamics in early modern China, see Arrighi, Hui, Hung, and Selden (2003, 266–281) and Arrighi (2007); cf. Wong (1997, part 1) and Pomeranz (2000).
2. See Rowe (1998), Xu (1999), Wu (2001), Naquin and Rawski (1987, 214–216), Li (1999), and Fan (1992) for general descriptions of interregional trade and Chen (1996) for the "uneven development" of the Qing empire; Marks (1996, 1998) for the division of labor between Guangdong and Guangxi; and Fan (1998, chap. 2) for the interregional trade between the Lower Yangzi region and other areas.
3. The emergence of an empirewide integrated market was also illustrated by the synchronism of the movements of rice prices in different regions in the eighteenth century (Quan 1996d).
4. In the eighteenth century, there was a number of documented cases in which local gentry and commoners mobilized others for tax resistance and other

collective actions by presenting fabricated imperial edicts to show the emperor's support of their contentious claims. The fact that this trick could work means that these edicts did reach grassroots society and were accepted as a routine way for the emperor to communicate with his subjects (QSL-QL 935, 12–13, 21–22).

5. The number shown in the figure is based on the edicts from the "admonishing the officials" (*xun chengong*) section of the collection.

2. DOCUMENTING THE THREE WAVES OF MID-QING PROTEST

1. For a discussion of these rebellions and their relation to political protests of the period, see Kuhn (1970), Naquin (1976, 1981), Ownby (1996), and Hung (2004, 2005).
2. For a thorough discussion of China's inner Asia frontier in the Qing dynasty, see Fletcher (1978a, 1978b) and Millward (2007). For a discussion of social formations in Qing Manchuria, see Isett (2007).
3. The reliability tests in these studies are usually done by comparing the records of unrest events in a subsample of spatial-temporal units with the corresponding records in local gazetteers, a supposedly more detailed source of information on local histories down to the county level.
4. Although in his recent writings Tilly seems to have abandoned the use of the "reactive-proactive" typology altogether, others continue to regard this classification as useful (e.g., Sewell 1990, 528–530; O'Brien 2002).
5. It is noteworthy that for the fifty-plus years that this survey overlaps with mine, the general trajectory of conflicts that it documents is roughly the same as what I find, although the survey covers only events occurring in urban centers and its typology of protest is different from the one used here.

3. FILIAL-LOYAL DEMONSTRATIONS, 1740–1759

1. Description of this case is based on the following primary sources: ZPZZ-GZD QL 13, 473–474; QSL-QL 502, 33–34.
2. This case is based on QSL-QL 281, 10.
3. E.g., QSL-QL 313, 24; 389, 29.
4. This case is based on QSL-QL 171, 1; 173, 6–7, 13–4, 33; 185, 6–9; ZPZZ-KYQ 563–564; QSG 291, *lie zhuan* 78.
5. This case is based on SYD-QL 3, 26–36, 41–42, 47–49, 69–70; QSL-QL 536, 4–9, 15–19, 28–31.

6. This case is based on ZPZZ-KYQ, 564–565; NGDK, 044739; QSL-QL 287, 17; 289, 9–11; 304, 10–11.
7. This case is based on LFZZ-NMYD 9706–014, 9706–021; QSL-QL 141,15; 147, 26.
8. This case is based on QSL-QL 212, 4–5; 215, 22–23.
9. This case is based on QSL-QL 127, 32; 267, 24; 269, 21–22; 275, 16–17.
10. This case is based on QSG 337, *lie zhuan* 124; QSL-QL 145, 24–25; 146, 10–11; 147, 12; 155, 24; 169, 26.
11. This case is based on ZPZZ-KYQ 583–584; SZFZ 149, 6; QSL-QL 313, 24; 314, 12–14, 25–26, 31–35; 315, 2–8; SLXK 29, 511–516.
12. XXXJZC, 42.
13. This case is based on QDTD, 657–673; ZPZZ-KYQ, 29–31; QSL-QL 151, 20–21; 153, 23.
14. This case is based on ZPZZ-NMYD 0282–052, 0283–001, 0283–004; ZPZZ-KYQ 103–104; SHXZ 12, 5–6; DHXL-QL 24, 8; QSL-QL 273, 26–28; 274, 2, 9; 289, 9.
15. This case is based on QDDASL 13, 302–43; QSL-QL 288, 3, 7, 15–16; 289, 2–3, 8–11, 31–32.

4. RIOTS INTO REBELLION, 1776–1795

1. Description of this case is based on ZPZZ-LSDA 1997.2, 19–27; QSL-QL 1266, 6–7, 11–12, 14–15; Ha 2002. I am grateful to Wu Jen-shu for bringing my attention to this case.
2. This case is based on ZPZZ-GZDQL 49, 171–172, 219–220, 289–291; QSL-QL 1142, 24, 27; 1143, 18–19.
3. This case is based on ZPZZ-GZDQL 43, 241–247, 456–457; QSL-QL 1055, 22–23; 1056, 16–17.
4. This case is based on ZPZZ-GZDQL 53, 264–266, 315–317, 336–338, 454–457, 655–656, 665–666, 667–668; 54, 17–18, 34–36, 453–455, 562–563, 577–578; 55, 365–367, 451–453, 819–820, 851–856, 863–868; 57, 669–670; 60, 265–266; QSL-QL 1167, 16–18, 23–24; ZPZZ-LSDA 1996.1,20–37; see also Ownby 1990.
5. This case is based on QSL-QL 1405, 1–4; 1406, 10–11, 25–26, 30; 1407, 11–16.
6. This case is based on ZPZZ-GZDQL 55, 69–72.
7. This case is based on ZPZZ-GZDQL 60, 337–339; QSL-QL 1208, 21–22.
8. One example is the incident of organized salt smugglers attacking government inspectors in Shangdong's Ze county in 1777. See ZPZZ-GZDQL 40, 621–622, 663–665, 832–852; 41, 50–51, 73–74, 182–188, 243–245, 285–287, 290–291, 469–471; QSL-QL 1043, 20–24; 1044, 14–15; 1045, 6–9, 28–29; 1046, 14–15, 22–23; 1047, 10–11.

9. This case is based on ZPZZ-GZDQL 48, 453–456, 597–600, 839–840; 49, 28–31, 69–70, 73–74, 173–174, 208–210, 379–380, 576–577, 597–598; 611–613, 695–697, 188–190, 381–382; ZPZZ-KYQ, 636–639; QSL-QL 1136, 12–14, 20–23.
10. QSG is the comprehensive history of the Qing dynasty, compiled in the early twentieth century based on multiple archival materials. Its chronological section provides a succinct summary of the most significant events during the dynasty, including all episodes of armed revolts. If a given year witnessed an uprising that lasted three months (which could be an uprising that erupted in the preceding year and continued into the year in question for three months) and another uprising that lasted six months, then the event months of armed rebellion of that year would be $(1 \times 3) + (1 \times 6) = 9$.

5. RESISTANCE AND PETITIONS, 1820–1839

1. This case is based on ZPZZ-GZDDG 7, 315–318.
2. This case is based on LFZZ-NMYD 8919, 2–4; SYD-JQDG 37, 203; QSL-DG 211, 30–31.
3. This case is based on QSL-DG 277, 16–19; 261, 7–8; 262, 30–31; NGDK 174426, 209354; SYD-JQDG 39, 471.
4. This case is based on QSL-DG 288, 12–14; ZPZZ-FLL, DG 16, 58 (DG 21.12.16); SYD-JQDG 41, 379.
5. This case is based on SYD-JQDG 40, 226; QSL-DG 267, 12–13; 271, 35–36.
6. This case is based on ZPZZ-NMYD 8920–8958; SYD-JQDG 37, 238–239; QSL-DG 212, 2–3, 17–18.
7. This case is based on ZPZZ-FLL DG 11, 14 (DG11.11.27); SYD-JQDG 36, 389–390; QSL-DG 196, 16–18, 20–21.
8. This case is based on NGDK 131659; SYD-JQDG 37, 458–462; QSL-DG 220, 7–8, 25–26; 222, 21–22, 24–26, 31–32; 228, 37.
9. Rebellions of the period included the Celestial Principles sect uprising in Zhili in 1813, the Blue Lotus sect uprising in Taiwan in 1826, the Tiandihui uprising in Taiwan in 1832, and the Prebirth sect uprising in Shanxi in 1835 (Yang 1975, 209–210; see also Hung 2005).
10. This case is based on LFZZ-FLL 3799, 29[1822]–30[1825]; NGDK 162546.
11. This case is based on LFZZ-FLL 4039, 12[1208]; SYD-JQDG 35, 149–150; QSL-DG 168, 8–9.
12. This case is based on LFZZ-FLL 3789, 14 [176]; SYD-JQDG 43, 353; QSL-DG 314, 19; 315, 27–28; 318, 9–10.
13. This case is based on LFZZ-FLL 3767, 5 [2997]; SYD-JQDG 37, 199–200; QSL-DG 211, 13–15.

14. Some argue that the increasing number of capital appeals in the early nineteenth century is attributable to the 1800 order of the Jiaqing emperor that the censorate and the capital gendarmerie should not reject any case of capital appeal (Wang 2009). But this order should not have been a major cause behind the sustained increase in cases, as the emperor himself revoked the order a few months later in 1801, after which the two offices had to reject cases that had not yet been adjudicated by lower-level governments (Ocko 1988, 297–298).

15. Under Qing legal code, organizers of confrontational protest faced banishment to the empire's frontier, flogging, or decapitation as the highest penalty. The penalties faced by appellants alleged of fabricating cases or not following the formal appeal procedures included banishment to the frontier and more than one hundred lashes (which was often tantamount to a death penalty).

6. MID-QING PROTESTS IN COMPARATIVE PERSPECTIVE

1. *Scripta Sinica*, the most comprehensive electronic database covering all major official chronologies of China's dynasties, as well as other historical writings by officials and literati, enables us to search when particular terms describing particular types of protests started to be mentioned in historical writings. Using *qiuzhen* (requesting famine relief), *bashi* (market strike), and *jingkong* (capital appeal) as examples, I find they were mostly never documented before the Qing period, while records containing those terms soared in the eighteenth and nineteenth centuries. The only exception is *qiuzhen*, which showed up as far back as the records of the Tang dynasty. The practice of requesting relief before the Qing period, however, involved only individual local officials or gentry who sought governmental relief on behalf of the people. Popular participation of collective action for famine relief was seldom mentioned before Qing times, with only a few exceptions in the Ming dynasty.

2. Description of this case is based on ZPZZ-NMYD 980–03; LFZZ-NMYD 3390–3392; QL-DG 393, 4; 406, 4; LYXZ 8, 7–13; Kuhn 2002, 80–90.

3. Lu Xun, the leftist writer who was widely acclaimed as the cultural icon of the New Culture movement in early twentieth-century China, once derogatorily referred to "kneeling and praying with incense" petitions as a major means through which submissive subjects begged for their rulers' mercy in the old times. He believed that such petitions would eventually be replaced by modern demonstrations (Lu Xun 1934).

REFERENCES

PRIMARY MATERIALS

CHGIS: *China Historical GIS Version 1.0: Qing Dynasty (1820) Dataset.* 2002. Harvard Yenching Institute and Center for Historical Geography, Fudan University.

DHXL: *Donghua xulu* [Continued records from within the Eastern Gate]. 1884 edition.

DQSCSX: *Daqing shichao shengxun* [Sacred imperial edicts of the ten reigns of the Qing]. Taipei: Wenhai chubanshe.

JXSDASZ: Jiaxing shi dang'an shi zhi [Archival documentation of the history of Jiaxing city]. http://www.jxdasz.com/web/fwb/disp.asp?id=2122&cateid=37.

KYQ: Zhongguo renmin daxue qingshi yanjiusuo dangan yanjiushi, ed. 1979. *Kongyongqian shiqi chengxiang renmin fankang douzheng ziliao* [Materials on the people's struggle in city and countryside during the reigns of Kangxi, Yongzheng, and Qianlong]. Beijing: Zhonghua shuju.

LFZZ-FLL: *Junjichu lufu zouzhe—falü lei* [Grand council copies of secret palace memorial—legal affairs category]. Beijing: The First Historical Archive of China.

LFZZ-NMYD: *Junjichu lufu zouzhe—nongmin yundong lei* [Grand council copies of secret palace memorial—peasant movement category]. Beijing: The First Historical Archive of China.

LYXZ: *Guangxu Leiyang xianzhi* [Gazetteer of Leiyang county]. 1886 edition.

NGDK: Neige daku dang [Grand secretariat archive]. Taipei: Fu Ssu-nien Library, Academia Sinica.

QCYSDG: *Qingchao yeshi daguan* [A grand overview of unofficial history of the Qing]. Vol. 1. 1959 edition. Taipei: Zhonghua shuju.

QDDASL: Gugong bowu yuan Mingqing dang'an bu, ed. 1978–. *Qingdai dang'an shiliu congbian* [Collections of archival sources in the Ming and Qing periods]. Beijing: Zhonghua shuju.

QDTD: Zhongguo diyi lishi dang'an guan, ed. 1988. *Qingdai tudi zhanyou guanxi yu diannong kangzu kangzheng* [Materials on land tenure and tenants' anti-rent struggles in Qing times]. Beijing: Zhonghua shuju.

QSG: *Qing shigao* [Draft history of the Qing]. 1976 edition. Beijing: Zhonghua shuju.

QSL-DG: *Daqing shuanzong shilu* [Veritable record of the Qing at the reign of Daoguang]. Beijing: Zhonghua shuju.

QSL-JQ: *Daqing ruizong shilu* [Veritable record of the Qing at the reign of Jiaqing]. Beijing: Zhonghua shuju.

QSL-QL: *Daqing gaozong shilu* [Veritable record of the Qing at the reign of Qianlong]. Beijing: Zhonghua shuju.

QZQ: Zhongguo shehui kexue yuan lishi yanjiu suo qingshi yanjiu shi, ed. *Qing zhongqi bailian jiao qiyi ziliao* [Archival materials on the White Lotus Rebellion in five provinces in mid-Qing]. Vol. 4. Suzhou: Jiangsu renmin chubanshe.

SHXZ: *Qianlong Shanghang xianzhi* [Gazetteer of the Shanghang county in the Qianlong reign].

SLXK: *Shiliao xunkan* [Compilation of historical materials]. Taipei: Guofeng chubanshe

SYD-JQDG: *Jiaqing Daoguang chao shangyu dang* [Imperial edicts archive in the Jiaqing and Daoguang reign]. Guilin: Guangxi shifan daxue chubanshe.

SYD-QL: *Qianlong chao shangyu dang* [Imperial edicts archive in the Qianlong reign]. Beijing: Dang'an chubanshe.

SZFZ: *Guangxu Suzhuo fuzhi* [Gazetteer of the Suzhou prefecture of Guangxu reign].

XXXJZC: Gu Gongbian. N.d. (Qing dynasty). "Xiaoxia Xianji Zaichao [Selected summer notebook]," in *Congshu jicheng xubian*, vol. 96. Shanghai: Shanghai Shudian, 1994.

YZPDL: Yongzheng Emperor. 1724. *Yuzhi pengdang lun* [Imperial discourse on friendship and cliques].

ZPZZ-FLL: *Gongzhongdang zhupi zouzhe—falu lei* [Secret palace memorial—legal affairs category]. Beijing: The First Historical Archive of China.

ZPZZ-GZDDG: *Gongzhongdang Daogang chao zouzhe* [Secret palace memorial in the palace archive in Daoguang reign]. Taipei: National Palace Museum.

ZPZZ-GZDJQ: *Gongzhongdang Jiaqing chao zouzhe* [Secret palace memorial in the palace archive in Jiaqing reign]. Taipei: National Palace Museum.

ZPZZ-GZDQL: *Gongzhongdang Qianlong chao zouzhe* [Secret palace memorial in the palace archive in Qianlong reign]. Taipei: National Palace Museum.

ZPZZ-KYQ: *Gongzhongdang zhupi zouzhe* [Secret palace memorials in the palace archive]. Excerpted in KYQ.

ZPZZ-LSDA: *Gongzhongdang zhupi zouzhe* [Secret palace memorials in the palace archive]. Excerpted in *Lishi Dang'an*.

ZPZZ-NMYD: *Gongzhongdang zhupi zouzhe—nongmin yundong lei* [Secret palace memorial in the palace archive—peasant movement category]. Beijing: The First Historical Archive of China.

SECONDARY MATERIALS

Abu-Lughod, Janet L. 1989. *Before European hegemony: The world system* A.D. *1250–1350*. New York: Oxford University Press.

Adas, Michael. 1989. *Machines as the measure of men: Science, technology, and ideologies of Western dominance*. Ithaca, N.Y.: Cornell University Press.

——. 1992. From avoidance to confrontation: Peasant protest in precolonial and colonial southeast Asia. In *Colonialism and Culture*, ed. Nicholas B. Dirks, 175–208. Ann Arbor: University of Michigan Press.

Anderson, Perry. 1979. *Lineages of absolutist state*. London: Verso.

Antony, Robert. 2003. *Like froth floating on the sea: The world of pirates and seafarers in late imperial South China*. Berkeley: University of California, Institute of East Asian Studies, China Research Monographs.

——. 2006. State, community, and pirate suppression in Guangdong province, 1809–1810. *Late Imperial China* 27, no. 1: 1–30.

Arrighi, Giovanni. 2007. *Adam Smith in Beijing: Lineages of the twenty-first century*. New York: Verso.

Arrighi, Giovanni, Po-keung Hui, Ho-fung Hung, and Mark Selden. 2003. Historical capitalism, east and west. In *Resurgence of East Asia*, ed. Giovanni Arrighi, Takeshi Hamashita, and Mark Selden, 259–333. London: Routledge.

Atwell, William S. 1986. Some observations on the "seventeenth-century crisis" in China and Japan. *Journal of Asian Studies* 45, no. 2: 223–244.

——. 1998. Ming China and the emerging world economy c.1470–1650. In *The Cambridge history of China*, vol. 8., *The Ming dynasty*, ed. Dennis Twitchett and Frederick Mote, 8:376–416. Cambridge: Cambridge University Press.

Auyero, Javier, and Timothy Patrick Moran. 2007. The dynamics of collective violence: Dissecting food riots in contemporary Argentina. *Social Forces* 85, no. 3: 1341–1367.

Averill, Stephen C. 2006. *Revolution in the highlands: China's Jinggangshan base area*. Lanham, Md.: Rowman and Littlefield.

Bai Gang. 1982. Lun qing zhongqi bai lian jiao qiyi de shehui houguo [On the social consequences of the White Lotus Rebellion in mid-Qing]. In *Henan renmin bianweihui*, ed. Zhongguo nonmin zhanzheng shi luncong, vol. 4 Kaifeng: Henan renmin chubanshe.

Bartlett, Beatrice S. 1991. *Monarchs and ministers: The grand council in mid-Ch'ing China, 1723–1820*. Berkeley: University of California Press.

Benford, Robert D., and David A. Snow. 2000. Framing processes and social movements: An overview and assessment. *Annual Review of Sociology* 26: 611–639.

Berman, Marshall. 1988. *All that is solid melts into air: The experience of modernity*. New York: Penguin.

Bernhardt, Kathryn. 1992. *Rents, taxes, and peasant resistance: The lower Yangzi region, 1840–1950*. Stanford, Calif.: Stanford University Press.

Bernstein, Thomas, and Lu Xiaobo. 2003. *Taxation without representation in rural China*. Cambridge: Cambridge University Press.

Berry, Mary Elizabeth. 2001. Public life in authoritarian Japan. In *Public spheres and collective identities*, ed. Shmuel Noah Eisenstadt, Wolfgang Schluchter, and Björn Wittrock Brunswick, 133–165. New Brunswick, N.J.: Transactions.

Bianco, Lucien. 1971. *Origins of the Chinese revolution, 1915–1949*. Stanford, Calif.: Stanford University Press.

———. 2001. *Peasants without the party: Grassroots movements in twentieth-century China*. Armonk, N.Y.: M. E. Sharpe.

Bix, Herbert P. 1986. *Peasant protest in Japan, 1590–1884*. New Haven, Conn.: Yale University Press.

Blaut, J. M. 1993. *The colonizer's model of the world: Geographical diffusionism and Eurocentric history*. New York: Guilford.

Bonney, Richard, ed. 1999. *The rise of the fiscal state in Europe, c. 1200–1815*. Oxford: Oxford University Press.

Braudel, Fernand. 1992. *Civilization and capitalism, 15th–18th century III: The perspective of the world*. Berkeley: University of California Press.

Brenner, Robert, and Christopher Isett. 2002. England's divergence from China's Yangzi delta: Property relations, microeconomics, and patterns of development. *Journal of Asian Studies* 61, no. 2: 609–662.

Brook, Timothy. 1990. Family continuity and cultural hegemony: The gentry of Ningbo, 1368–1911. In *Chinese local elites and patterns of dominance*, ed. Joseph W. Esherick and Mary Backus Rankin, 27–50. Berkeley: University of California Press.

Buoye, Thomas, M. 2000. *Manslaughter, markets, and moral economy: Violent disputes over property rights in eighteenth-century China*. Cambridge: Cambridge University Press.

Cai Shaoqing. 1984. On the origin of the Gelaohui. *Modern China* 10, no. 4: 481–508.

Chakrabaty, Dipesh. 2000. *Provincializing Europe: Postcolonial thought and historical difference*. Princeton, N.J.: Princeton University Press.

Chang Chung-li. 1959. *The Chinese gentry: A study of their role in nineteenth-century Chinese society*. Seattle: University of Washington Press.

——. 1962. *The income of the Chinese gentry*. Seattle: University of Washington Press.

Chang, Michael G. 2007. *A court on horseback: Imperial touring and the construction of Qing rule, 1680–1785*. Cambridge, Mass.: Harvard University Asia Center.

Chao Zhongchen. 1993. Wanming baiying dalian liuru jiqi yingxiang [The massive inflow of silver in late Ming and its influences]. *Shixue yuekan* 1: 33–39.

Chartier, Roger. 1991. *The cultural origins of the French revolution*. Durham, N.C.: Duke University Press.

Chen Hua. 1996. *Qingdai quyu shehui jingji yanjiu* [Regional socio-economic development in Qing dynasty]. Beijing: Renmin daxue chubanshe.

Chen Xuewen. 1991a. Mingqing shiqi minyuetai diqu de zhetangye [The sugar business of Fujian, Guangdong, and Taiwan in Ming and Qing] In *Mingqing shehua jinji shi yanjiu* [Studies of social and economic history of Ming and Qing], 67–86. Taipei: Hedao chubanshe.

——. 1991b. Mingdai zhongye gongshang yiweiben sichaode chuxian [The emergence of the thought of "industry and commerce are also the fundamentals" in mid Ming], in *Mingqing shehua jingji shi yanjiu* [Studies of social and economic history of Ming and Qing], 365–370. Taipei: Hedao chubanshe.

Chen Zaizheng. 1980. Shijiu shiji sishi niandai guonei jieji maodunde jihua yu taiping tianguo geming [Intensification of class contradiction in the 1840s and the Taiping rebellion]. *Xiamen daxue xuebao* 1: 1–19.

Chesneaux, Jean, ed. 1972. *Popular movements and secret societies in China, 1840–1950*. Stanford, Calif.: Stanford University Press.

Chiu Peng-sheng. 2002. You fangliao dao gongchang: Qingdai qianqi mianbu zihao de jingji yu falu fenxi [From putting-out system to factory system: A legal and economic analysis of cotton-textile workshops in Qing Suzhou]. *Lishi yanjiu* 1: 75–87.

Chow, Kai-wing. 1994. *The rise of Confucian ritualism in late imperial China*. Stanford, Calif.: Stanford University Press.

——. 2004. *Publishing, culture, and power in early modern China*. Stanford, Calif.: Stanford University Press.

Ch'u T'ung-tsu. 1962. *Local government in China under the Ching*. Cambridge, Mass.: Harvard University East Asian Center.

Crossley, Pamela K. 1999. *A translucent mirror: History and identity in Qing imperial ideology*. Berkeley: University of California Press.

De Bary, William Theodore. 1981. *Neo-Confucian orthodoxy and the learning of the mind-and-heart*. New York: Columbia University Press.

Deng Gang. 1999. *The premodern Chinese economy: Structural equilibrium and capitalist sterility*. London: Routledge.

——. N.d. The origins of a fiscal state, its continuation, and changes in China. http://www.dse.unive.it/summerschool/papers/Deng%20-%20outline.pdf.

Duara, Prasenjit. 1988. *Culture, power, and the state: Rural north China, 1900–1942*. Stanford, Calif.: Stanford University Press.

Dunstan, Helen. 2006. *State or merchants? Political economy and political process in 1740s China*. Cambridge, Mass.: Harvard Asia Center.

Dutton, George. 2006. *Tay Son uprising: Rebellion and society in eighteenth-century Vietnam*. Honolulu: University of Hawaii Press.

Earl, Jennifer, Andrew Martin, John D. McCarthy, and Sarah A. Soule. 2004. The use of newspaper data in the study of collective action. *Annual Review of Sociology* 30: 65–80.

Ebrey, Patricia Buckley, and James L. Watson, eds. 1986. *Kinship organization in late imperial China, 1000–1940*. Berkeley: University of California Press.

Eisenstadt, Shmuel N. 1995. *Japanese civilization: A comparative view*. Chicago: University of Chicago Press.

——, ed. 2002. *Multiple modernities*. New Brunswick, N.J.: Transaction.

Eisenstadt, Shmuel N., Wolfgang Schluchter, and Bjorn Wittrock, eds. 2001. *Public spheres and collective identities*. New Brunswick, N.J.: Transaction.

Elliot, Mark. 1990. Bannerman and townsman: Ethnic tension in nineteenth-century Jiangnan. *Late Imperial China* 11, no. 1.

Elman, Benjamin. 1989. Imperial politics and Confucian societies in late imperial China: The Hanlin and Donglin academies. *Modern China* 15, no. 4: 379–418.

——. 2000. *A cultural history of civil examination in late imperial China*. Berkeley: University of California Press.

——. 2001. *From philosophy to philology: Intellectual and social aspects of change in late imperial China*. Berkeley: University of California Press.

——. 2002. The social roles of literati in early to mid Ch'ing. In *The Cambridge history of China*, ed. Willard J. Peterson, 9:360–427. Cambridge: Cambridge University Press.

Elvin, Mark. 1973. *The pattern of the Chinese past*. Stanford, Calif.: Stanford University Press.

——. 1998. The environmental legacy of imperial China. *The China Quarterly* 156: 733–756.

Entenmann, Robert Eric. 1982. Migration and Settlement in Sichuan, 1644–1796. Unpublished Ph. D. dissertation, Harvard University.

Esherick, Joseph, and Jeffrey Wasserstrom. 1990. Acting out democracy: Political theatre in modern China. *Journal of Asian Studies* 49, no. 4: 835–865.

Fan I-chun. 1992. *Long-distance trade and market integration in the Ming–Ch'ing period, 1400–1850*. Ph. D dissertation, Stanford University.

Fan Jinmin. 1998. *Mingqing jiangnan shangye de fazhan* [The development of commerce in Jiangnan in the Ming–Qing period]. Nanjing: Nanjing daxue chubanshe.

Fang Qiang. 2009. Hot potatoes: Chinese complaint systems from early times to the late Qing (1898). *Journal of Asian Studies* 68, no. 4: 1105–1135.

Faure, David. 2007. *Emperor and ancestor: State and lineage in south China*. Stanford, Calif.: Stanford University Press.

Feuerwerker, Albert. 1984. The state and economy in late imperial China. *Theory and Society* 13, no. 3: 297–326.

Fletcher, Joseph. 1978a. Ch'ing inner Asia, c. 1800. In *The Cambridge history of China*, ed. John K. Fairbank ed., 10:35–106. Cambridge: Cambridge University Press.

——. 1978b. The heyday of the Ch'ing order in Mongolia, Sinkiang, and Tibet. In *The Cambridge history of China*, ed. John K. Fairbank, 10:351–408. Cambridge: Cambridge University Press.

Flynn, Dennis O. and Giraldez Arturo. 1995. Born with "silver spoon": The origin of world trade in 1571. *Journal of World History* 6, no. 2: 201–211.

Frank, Andre Gunder. 1998. *ReOrient: Global economy in the Asian age*. Berkeley: University of California Press.

Fuma, Susumu. 1993. Late Ming urban reform and the popular uprising in Hangzhou. In *Cities of Jiangnan in late imperial China*, ed. Linda Cooke Johnson, 47–80. Albany: SUNY Press.

Furth, Charlotte. 1990. The patriarch's legacy: Household instructions and the transmission of orthodox values. In *Orthodoxy in late imperial China*, ed. Kwang-ching Liu, 187–211. Berkeley: University of California Press.

Gao Wangling. 1995. *Shiba shiji zhongguo de jingji fazhan he zhengfu zhengce* [Economic development and government policies in eighteenth-century China]. Beijing: Zhonggu shehui kexue chubanshe.

——. 2005. *Zudian guanxi xinlun: dizhu, nongmin he dizu* [New perspectives on tenant relation: Landlords, peasants, and land rent]. Shanghai: Shanghai shudian chubanshe.

Gao Xiang. 1995. *Kong Yong Qian sandi tongzhi shixiang yanjiu* [A study of the governing philosophies of Kongsi, Yongzheng, and Qianlong emperors]. Beijing: Renmin daxue chubanshe.

——. 2001 *Jindai de chushu shiba shiji zhongguo guanlian bianqian yu shehui fazhan* [The dawn of modernity: Transformations of ideas and social change in eighteenth-century China]. Beijing: Shehui kexue wenxian chubanshe.

——. 2002. Qing chu lixue yu zhengzhi [The school of principles and politics in early Qing]. *Qingshi luncong* 7: 178–210.

Gaustad, Blaine. 2000. Prophets and pretenders: Intersect competition in Qianlong China. *Late Imperial China* 21, no. 1: 1–40.

Giesen, Bernhard. 2001. Cosmopolitans, patriots, Jacobins, and romantics. In *Public spheres and collective identities*, ed. Shmuel N. Eisenstadt, Wolfgang Schluchter, and Bjorn Wittrock, 221–250. New Brunswick, N.J.: Transaction.

Goldstone, Jack A. 1991. *Revolution and rebellion in the early modern World.* Berkeley: University of California Press.

——. 2000. The rise of the West or not? A revision to socio-economic history. *Sociological Theory* 18, no. 2: 175–194.

——. 2002. Efflorescence and economic growth in world history: Rethinking the "rise of the West" and the industrial revolution. *Journal of World History* 13, no. 2: 323–389.

Goodwin, Jeff, and James M. Jasper. 2003. Caught in a winding, snarling vine: The structural bias of political process theory. In *Rethinking social movements: Structure, meaning, and emotion*, ed. Jeff Goodwin and James M. Jasper, 3–30. New York: Rowman and Littlefield.

Gorski, Philip S. 2003. *The disciplinary revolution: Calvinism and the rise of the state in early modern Europe.* Chicago: University of Chicago Press.

Guo Chengkang. 1996. Zhongguo shiba shiji wujia wanti yu zhengfu duice [The price question and government remedy in eighteenth-century China]. *Qingshi yanjiu* 1: 8–19.

Ha Enzhong. 2002. Qianlong chao fuhu huomai qiangliang nongmin an [The case of rich household burying food-looting peasants alive in Qianlong reign]. *Zijincheng* 2: 20–22.

Habermas, Jurgen. 1985. Modernity: An incomplete project. In *Postmodern culture*, ed. Hal Foster, 3–30. London: Pluto.

Hamilton, Gary H. 1990. Patriarchy, patrimonialism, and filial piety: A comparison of China and western Europe. *The British Journal of Sociology* 41, no. 1: 77–104.

——. 2006. *Commerce and capitalism in Chinese societies.* New York: Routledge.

Harrell, Steven, and Elizabeth J. Perry. 1982. Syncretic sects in Chinese society. *Modern China* 8, no. 3: 283–304.

Ho Ping-ti. 1959. *Studies on the population of China, 1368–1953.* Cambridge, Mass.: Harvard University Press.

Hobsbawn, Eric. 1959. *Primitive rebels: Studies in archaic forms of social movement in the nineteenth and twentieth centuries.* New York: W. W. Norton.

Huang, Philip C. C. 1985. *The peasant economy and social change in north China*. Stanford, Calif.: Stanford University Press.

——. 1996. *Civil justice in China: Representation and practice in the Qing*. Stanford, Calif.: Stanford University Press.

Huang, Ray 1969. Fiscal administration during the Ming dynasty. In *Chinese government in Ming times*, ed. Charles O. Hucker, 73–128. New York: Columbia University Press.

Human Rights Watch. 2005. *"We could disappear at any time": Retaliation and abuses against Chinese petitioners*. New York: Human Right Watch.

Hung Chang-tai. 1993. Reeducating a blind storyteller: Han Qixiang and the Chinese communist storytelling campaign. *Modern China* 19, no. 4: 395–426.

Hung Ho-fung. 2001. Imperial China and capitalist Europe in the eighteenth-century global economy. *Review (Fernand Braudel Center)* 24, no. 4: 473–513.

——. 2003. Orientalist knowledge and social theories: China and the European conceptions of east-west differences from 1600 to 1900. *Sociological Theory* 21, no. 3: 254–279.

——. 2004. Early modernities and contentious politics in mid-Qing China, c. 1740–1839. *International Sociology* 19, no. 4: 478–503.

——. 2005. Contentious peasants, paternalist state, and arrested capitalism in China's long eighteenth century. In *The historical evolution of world-systems*, ed. Christopher Chase-Dunn and Eugene N. Anderson, 155–173. New York: Palgrave.

——. 2008. Agricultural revolution and elite reproduction in Qing China: The transition-to-capitalism debate revisited. *American Sociological Review* 73: 569–588.

——. 2009. Cultural strategies and the political economy of protest in mid-Qing China, 1740–1839. *Social Science History* 33, no. 1.

Hurst, William. 2009. *Chinese workers after socialism*. Cambridge: Cambridge University Press.

Ikegami, Eiko. 1995. *The taming of the samurai: Honorific individualism and the making of modern Japan*. Cambridge, Mass.: Harvard University Press.

Ikegami, Eiko, and Charles Tilly. 1994. State formation and contention in Japan and France. In *Edo and Paris: Urban life and the state in the early modern era*, ed. James L. McClain, John M. Merriman, and Ugawa Kaoru, 430–454. Ithaca, N.Y.: Cornell University Press.

Isett, Christopher. 2007. *State, peasant, and merchant on the Manchurian frontier, 1644–1862*. Stanford, Calif.: Stanford University Press.

Jing Junjian. 1982. Hierarchy in the Qing dynasty. *Social Sciences in China: A Quarterly Journal* 3, no. 1: 156–192.

Johnston, Hank, and Bert Klandermans, eds. 1995. *Social movements and culture.* Minneapolis: University of Minnesota Press.

Jones, Susan Mann, and Philip Kuhn. 1978. Dynastic decline and the roots of rebellion. In *The Cambridge history of China*, ed. John K. Fairbank, 10:107–162. Cambridge: Cambridge University Press.

Jun Jing. 2000. Environmental protest in China. In *Chinese society: Change, conflict, and resistance*, ed. Elizabeth Perry and Mark Selden, 143–161. New York: Routledge.

Ka Chih-ming. 2003. *Fantoujia: Qingdai Taiwan zuquan zhengzhi yu shoufan diquan* [Aboriginal landlords: Ethnic politics and land rights of assimilated aborigines in Qing Taiwan]. Nankang, Taiwan: Academia Sinica.

Kahn, Harold L. 1971. *Monarchy in the emperor's eyes: Image and reality in the Ch'ien-lung reign*. Cambridge, Mass.: Harvard University Press.

Kant, Emmanuel. 1784. *What is enlightenment?* Trans. Mary C. Smith. http://www.columbia.edu/acis/ets/CCREAD/etscc/kant.html.

Kishimoto-Nakayama Mio. 1984. The Kangxi depression and early Qing local markets. *Modern China* 10, no. 2: 226–256.

Kuhn, Philip A. 1970. *Rebellion and its enemies in late imperial China: Militarization and social structure, 1796–1864*. Cambridge, Mass.: Harvard University Press.

——. 1977. Origins of the Taiping vision: Cross-cultural dimensions of a Chinese rebellion. *Comparative Studies in Society and History* 19, no. 3: 350–366.

——. 1990. *Soulstealers: The Chinese sorcery scare of 1768*. Cambridge, Mass.: Harvard University Press.

——. 2002. *The origins of the modern Chinese state*. Stanford, Calif.: Stanford University Press.

Kutcher, Norman. 1999. *Mourning in late imperial China: Filial piety and the state.* Cambridge: Cambridge University Press.

Lamley, Harry. 1977. Hsieh-tou: The pathology of violence in southeastern China. *Ch'ing-shih wen-t'i* 3, no. 7: 1–39.

Lavely, William, and Wong R. Bin. 1998. Revising the Malthusian narrative: The comparative study of population dynamics in late imperial China. *Journal of Asian Studies* 57, no. 3: 714–743.

Lee, Ching-Kwan. 2007. *Against the law: Labor protests in China's rustbelt and sunbelt*. Berkeley: University of California Press.

Lee, James Z., and Wang Feng. 1999. *A quarter of humanity: Malthusian myth and China's reality*. Cambridge, Mass.: Harvard University Press.

Leong, Sow-theng. 1997. *Migration and ethnicity in Chinese history: Hakkas, Pengmin, and their neighbors*. Stanford, Calif.: Stanford University Press.

Le Roy Ladurie, Emmanuel. 1976 [1974]. Rural revolts and protest movements in France from 1675 to 1788. In *Studies in eighteenth-century culture*, ed. Ronald C. Rosbottom, 423–442. Madison: University of Wisconsin Press.

Li Bozhong. 1999. Zhongguo chuanguo shichang de xingcheng, 1500–1840 [Formation of national market in China, 1500–1840]. *Qinghua daxue xuebao* 4: 48–54.

Li, Tana. 1998. *Nguyen Cochinchina: Southern Vietnam in the seventeenth and eighteenth century*. Ithaca, N.Y.: Cornell University Press.

Li Xiangjun. 1995. *Qingdai huangzheng yanjiu* [A study of famine policy in the Qing dynasty]. Beijing: Nongye chubanshe.

Lieberman, Victor B. 1999. *Beyond binary history: Re-imagining Eurasia to c. 1830*. Ann Arbor: University of Michigan Press.

Lin Manhoung. 1991. Two social theories revealed: Statecraft controversies over China's monetary crisis, 1808–1854. *Late Imperial China* 12, no. 2: 1–35.

——. 2006. *China upside down: Currency, society, and ideologies, 1808–1856*. Cambridge, Mass.: Harvard Asia Center.

Liu, James T. C. 1973. How did a neo-Confucian school become the state orthodoxy? *Philosophy East and West* 23, no. 4: 483–505.

Liu Kwan-ching. 1988. Cong dang'an cailiao kan yiqi jiuliu nian hubei sheng bailianjiao qiyi de zongjiao yinsu [Religion in the White Lotus Rebellion in 1796 in Hubei as seen in archival sources]. In *Zhongguo diyi lishi dang'an guan. ed. Mingqing dang'an yu lishi yanjiu*. Beijing: Zhonghua shuju.

——. 2004. Religion and politics in the White Lotus Rebellion of 1796 in Hubei. In *Heterodoxy in late imperial China*, ed. Liu Kwan-ching and Richard Shek, 281–321. Honolulu: University of Hawaii Press.

Liu Xiaofeng. 2000. *Rujia geming jingshen yuanliu kao* [On the origins of Confucian revolutionary spirit]. Shanghai: Shanghai sanlian shudian.

Lu Xun. 1934. *Nanqiang beidiao ji* [Ascents and rhythm north and south]. Shanghai: Tongwen shudian.

Ma, Laurence J. C. 1971. *Commercial development and urban change in Sung China (960–1279)*. Ann Arbor: University of Michigan Press.

Macauley, Melissa. 2009. Small-time crooks: Opium, migrants, and the war on drugs in China, 1819–1860. *Late Imperial China* 30, no. 1: 1–47.

Mair, Victor H. 1985. Language and ideology in the written popularization of the sacred edict. In *Popular culture in late imperial China*, ed. David Johnson, Andrew J. Nathan, and Evelyn S. Rawski, 325–359. Berkeley: University of California Press.

Man-cheong, Iona D. 2004. *The class of 1761: Examinations, state, and elites in eighteenth-century China*. Stanford, Calif.: Stanford University Press.

Mann, Susan. 1997. *Precious records: Women in China's long eighteenth century.* Stanford, Calif.: Stanford University Press.

Markoff, John. 1996. *The abolition of feudalism: Peasants, lords, and legislators in the French revolution.* University Park: Pennsylvania State University Press.

Marks, Robert B. 1984. *Rural revolution in south China: Peasants and the making of history in Haifeng county, 1570–1930.* Madison: University of Wisconsin Press.

——. 1996. Commercialization without capitalism: Processes of environmental change in south China, 1550–1850. *Environmental History* 1, no. 1: 56–82.

——. 1998. *Tigers, rice, silk, and silt: Environment and economy in late imperial south China.* Cambridge: Cambridge University Press.

Marsh, Robert M. 2000. Weber's misunderstanding of traditional Chinese law. *American Journal of Sociology* 106, no. 2: 281–302.

Marx, Karl. 1951. Revolution in China and in Europe. In *Marx on China: 1853–1860,* ed. Dona Torr, 1–10. London: Lawrence and Wishart.

Marx, Karl, and Frederick Engels. 1972. The communist manifesto. In *The Marx-Engels reader,* ed. Robert C. Tucker, 331–362. New York: W. W. Norton.

Masatoshi Tanaka. 1984. Popular uprisings, rent resistance, and bondservant rebellions in the late Ming. In *State and society in China: Japanese perspectives on Ming-Qing social and economic history,* ed. Linda Grove and Christian Daniels, 165–214. Tokyo: University of Tokyo Press.

McAdam, Doug. 1996. The framing function of movement tactics: Strategic dramaturgy in the American civil-rights movements. In *Comparative perspectives on social movements: Political opportunities, mobilizing structures, and cultural framings,* ed. Doug McAdam, John D. McCarthy, and Mayer Zald, 338–355. New York: Cambridge University Press.

McCaffrey, Cecily Miriam. 2003. *Living through rebellion: A local history of the White Lotus uprising in Hubei, China.* Unpublished dissertation, Department of History, University of California at San Diego.

McMahon, Daniel. 2005. The Yuelu academy and Hunan's nineteenth-century turn toward statecraft. *Late Imperial China* 26, no. 1: 76–109.

——. 2008. Dynastic decline, Heshen, and the ideology of the Xianyu reforms. *Tsing Hua Journal of Chinese Studies,* n.s., 38, no. 2: 231–255.

——. 2009. Qing reconstruction in the southern Shaanxi highlands: State perceptions and plans, 1799–1820. *Late Imperial China* 30, no. 1: 85–118.

Merrick, Jeffrey. 1990. *The desacralization of the French monarchy.* Baton Rouge: Louisiana State University Press.

Meyer-Fong, Tobie. 2007. The printed world: Books, publishing culture, and society in late imperial China. *Journal of Asian Studies* 66, no. 3: 787–817.

Michelson, Ethan. 2007. Climbing the dispute pagoda: Grievances and appeals to the official justice system in rural China. *American Sociological Review* 72, no. 3: 459–485.

Millward, James A. 2007. *Eurasian crossroads: A history of Xinjiang.* New York: Columbia University Press.

Mingqing dang'an tongnan bianweihui, ed. 2000. *Mingqing dang'an tongnan* [A general introduction to Ming-Qing archives]. Beijing: Dongan chubanshe.

Minzner, Carl F. 2006. Xinfang: An alternative to formal Chinese legal institutions. *Stanford Journal of International Law* 42: 103–179.

Muhlhan, Klaus 2009. *Criminal justice in China: A history.* Cambridge, Mass.: Harvard University Press.

Myers, Ramon H., and Yeh-chien Wang. 2002. Economic developments, 1644–1800. In *The Cambridge history of China*, ed. Willard J. Peterson, 9:563–645. Cambridge: Cambridge University Press.

Naquin, Susan. 1976. *Millenarian rebellion in China: The Eight Trigrams uprising of 1813.* New Haven, Conn.: Yale University Press.

——. 1981. *Shantung rebellion: The Wang Lun uprising of 1774.* New Haven, Conn.: Yale University Press.

Naquin, Susan, and Evelyn S. Rawski. 1987. *Chinese society in the eighteenth century.* New Haven, Conn.: Yale University Press.

O'Brien, Kevin. 2002. Collective action in the Chinese countryside. *China Journal* 48: 139–154.

O' Brien, Kevin J., and Li Lianjiang. 2006. *Rightful resistance in rural China.* New York: Cambridge University Press.

Ocko, Jonathan K. 1988. I'll take it all the way to Beijing: Capital appeals in the Qing. *Journal of Asian Studies* 47, no. 2: 291–315.

——. 1990. Hierarchy and harmony: Family conflict as seen in Ch'ing legal cases. In *Orthodoxy in late imperial China*, ed. Kwang-ching Liu, 212–230. Berkeley: University of California Press.

Olzak, Susan. 1989. Analysis of events in the study of collective action. *Annual Review of Sociology* 15: 119–141.

Overmyer, Daniel. 1976. *Folk Buddhist religion: Dissenting sects in late traditional China.* Cambridge, Mass.: Harvard University Press.

——. 1981. Alternatives: Popular religious sects in Chinese society. *Modern China* 7, no. 2.

Ownby, David. 1990. The ethnic feud in Qing Taiwan: What is this violence business, anyway? An interpretation of the 1782 Zhang-Quan Xiedou. *Late Imperial China* 11, no. 1.

——. 1996. Brotherhoods and secret societies in early and mid-Qing China: The formation of a tradition. Stanford, Calif.: Stanford University Press.

——. 1999. Chinese millenarian traditions: The formative age. *American Historical Review* 104, no. 5: 1513–1530.

——. 2003. A history for Falun Gong: Popular religion and the Chinese state since the Ming dynasty. *Nova Religio* 6, no. 2: 223–243.

——. 2008. *Falun Gong and the future of China*. Oxford: Oxford University Press.

Pandey, Gyanendra. 1988. Peasant revolt and Indian nationalism. In *Selected subaltern studies*, ed. Ranajit Guha and Gayatri Chakravorty Spivak, 233–287. Oxford: Oxford University Press.

Park, Nancy E. 1997. Corruption in eighteenth-century China. *Journal of Asian Studies* 56, no. 4: 967–1005.

Parsons, J. B. 1970. *Peasant rebellions of the late Ming dynasty*. Tucson: University of Arizona Press.

Perdue, Peter C. 1986. Insiders and outsiders: The Xiangtan Riot of 1819 and collective action in Hunan. *Modern China* 12, no. 2: 166–201.

——. 1987. *Exhausting the earth: State and peasant in Hunan, 1500–1850*. Cambridge, Mass.: Harvard University Press.

——. 2005. *China marches west: The Qing conquest of central Eurasia*. Cambridge, Mass.: Harvard University Press.

Perry, Elizabeth J. 1980. *Rebels and revolutionaries in north China, 1845–1945*. Stanford, Calif.: Stanford University Press.

——. 2002. *Challenging the mandate of heaven: Social protest and state power in China*. Armonk, N.Y.: M. E. Sharpe.

——. 2008. Chinese conceptions of "rights": From Mencius to Mao—and now. *Perspectives on Politics* 6, no. 1: 37–50.

Perry, Elizabeth J., and Mark Selden. 2000. Introduction to *Chinese society: Change, conflict, and resistance*, ed. Elizabeth J. Perry and Mark Selden, 1–19. London: Routledge.

Polachek, James. 1992. *The inner opium war*. Cambridge, Mass.: Harvard Asia Center.

Pomeranz, Kenneth. 2000. *The great divergence: Europe, China, and the making of the modern world economy*. Princeton, N.J.: Princeton University Press.

Qin Baoqi and Zhang Yan. 1999. *Shiba shijide Zhongguoyu shijie: shehui juan* [China and the world in the eighteenth century: Society]. Shenyang: Liaohai chubanshe.

Qin Guojing. 2004. *Zhongguo dixia shehui* [Underground Society in China]. Vol. 1. Beijing: xueyuan chubanshe.

Quan Hansheng. 1996a. Mingqing jian meizhou baiyin de shuru zhongguo [Import of American silver into Ming-Qing China]. In *Essays on Chinese economic history*, by Quan Hansheng, 435–450. Taibei: Hedao chubanshe.

——. 1996b. Meizhou baiyin yu zhongguo shiba shiji de wujia geming [American silver and the price revolution in eighteenth-century China]. In *Essays on Chinese economic history*, by Quan Hansheng, 475–508. Taibei: Hedao chubanshe.

——. 1996c. Qianlong shisanniande migui wenti [The question of high price rice in 1748]. In *Essays on Chinese economic history*, by Quan Hansheng, 547–566. Taibei: Hedao chubanshe.

——. 1996d. Qing yongzheng nianjian (1723–35) de mijia [The rice price in the reign of Yongzheng (1723–1735]. In *Essays on Chinese economic history*, by Quan Hansheng. Taibei: Hedao chubanshe.

Rankin, Mary B. 2002. Nationalistic contestation and mobilization politics: Practice and rhetoric of railway-rights recovery at the end of the Qing. *Modern China* 28, no. 3: 315–361.

Rawski, Evelyn S. 1979. *Education and popular literacy in Ch'ing China*. Ann Arbor: Center for Chinese Studies, University of Michigan.

——. 2004. The Qing formation and the early-modern period. In *The Qing formation in world-historical time*, ed. Lynn A. Struve, 207–241. Cambridge, Mass.: Harvard University Asia Center.

Robinson, David. 2001. *Bandits, eunuchs, and the son of heaven: Rebellion and the economy of violence in mid-Ming China*. Honolulu: University of Hawai'i Press.

Rosner, Erhard. 1987. The strikes of merchants in the Qing period. *Journal of the Economic and Social History of the Orient* 30, no. 1: 95–113.

Rowe, William T. 1989. *Hankow II: Conflict and community in a Chinese city, 1796–1895*. Stanford, Calif.: Stanford University Press.

——. 1990. Modern Chinese history in comparative perspective. In *Heritage of China: Contemporary Perspectives on Chinese Civilization*, ed. Paul S. Ropp, 242–262. Berkeley: University of California Press.

——. 1992. Success stories: Lineage and elite status in Hanyang county, Hubei, c. 1368–1949. In *Chinese local elites and patterns of dominance*, ed. Joseph W. Esherick and Mary Backus Rankin, 51–81. Berkeley: University of California Press.

——. 1998. Domestic interregional trade in eighteenth-century China. In *On the eighteenth century as a category of Asian history: Van Leur in retrospect*, ed. Leonard Blusse and Femme Gaastra, 173–192. Aldershot: Ashgate.

——. 2001. *Saving the world: Chen Hongmou and elite consciousness in eighteenth-century China*. Stanford, Calif.: Stanford University Press.

——. 2002. Social stability and social change. In *The Cambridge history of China*, ed. Willard J. Peterson, 9:473–562. Cambridge: Cambridge University Press.

——. 2007. *Crimson rain: Seven centuries of violence in a Chinese county.* Stanford, Calif.: Stanford University Press.

Rozman, Gilbert. 1991. Comparisons of modern Confucian values in China and Japan. In *The East Asian region: Confucian heritage and its modern adaptation*, ed. Gilbert Rozman, 157–203. Princeton, N.J.: Princeton University Press.

——. 2003. Center-local relations: Can Confucianism boost decentralization and regionalism? In *Confucianism for the modern world*, ed. Daniel A. Bell and Hahm Chaibong, 181–200. Cambridge: Cambridge University Press.

Rude, George. 1980. *Ideology and popular protest.* New York: Pantheon.

Scott, James C. 1976. *The moral economy and the peasants: Rebellion and subsistence in Southeast Asia.* New Haven, Conn.: Yale University Press.

——. 2000. The moral economy as an argument and as a fight. In *Moral economy and popular protest: Crowds, conflict, and authority*, ed. Adrian Randall and Andrew Charlesworth, 187–208. London. McMillan.

Selden, Mark. 1971. *The Yenan way in revolutionary China.* Cambridge, Mass.: Harvard University Press.

Sewell, William H. 1990. Collective violence and collective loyalties in France: Why the French revolution made a difference. *Politics and Society* 18, no. 4: 481–526.

——. 2005. *Logics of history: Social theory and social transformation.* Chicago: University of Chicago Press.

Sharman, J. C. 2003. *Repression and resistance in communist Europe.* London: Routledge.

Shen Daming. 2007. *Daqing luli yu qingdai de shehui kongzhi* [Qing legal code and social control in the Qing]. Shanghai: Shanghai renmin chubanshe.

Shepherd, John. 1993. *Statecraft and political economy on the Taiwan frontier, 1600–1800.* Stanford, Calif.: Stanford University Press.

Shiba, Yoshinobu. 1970. *Commerce and society in Sung China.* Trans. Mark Elvin. Ann Arbor: Center for Chinese Studies, University of Michigan.

——. 1983. Sung foreign trade: Its scope and organization. In *China among equals: The middle kingdom and its neighbors, tenth–fourteenth centuries*, ed. Morris Rossabi, 89–115. Berkeley: University of California Press.

Shils, Edward. 1981. *Tradition.* Chicago: University of Chicago Press.

Silver, Beverly. 2003. *Forces of labor: Workers' movements and globalization since 1870.* Cambridge: Cambridge University Press.

Skinner, William. 1971. Chinese peasants and the closed community: An open and shut case. *Comparative Studies in Society and History* 13: 270–281.

Skocpol, Theda. 1979. *States and social revolutions: A comparative analysis of France, Russia, and China*. Cambridge: Cambridge University Press.

Solinger, Dorothy. 1989. Democracy with Chinese characteristics. *World Policy Journal* (Fall): 621–632.

——. 1993. *China's transition from socialism: Statist legacies and market reforms, 1980–1990*. Armonk, N.Y.: M. E. Sharpe.

Sommer, Mathew H. 2000. *Sex, law, and society in late imperial China*. Stanford, Calif.: Stanford University Press.

Spence, Jonathan D. 1990. *The search for modern China*. New York: W. W. Norton.

——. 1996. *God's Chinese son: The Taiping heavenly kingdom of Hong Xiuquan*. New York: W. W. Norton.

Steinberg, Marc C. 1999. *Fighting words: Working-class formation, collective action, and discourse in early nineteenth-century England*. Ithaca, N.Y.: Cornell University Press.

Stone, Lawrence. 1965. *The crisis of the aristocracy, 1558–1641*. Oxford: Oxford University Press.

Strand, David. 1990. Protest in Beijing. *Problems of Communism* 39: 1–19.

Struve, Lynn. 2004. Chimerical early modernity: The case of "conquest generation" memoirs. In *The Qing formation in world-historical time*, ed. Lynn Struve, 335–380. Cambridge, Mass.: Harvard University Asia Center.

Sun Wenguang. 2005. Chong shangfang dao qingyuan shiwei [From capital appeal to petition and demonstration). Boxun. http://news.boxun.com/news/gb/pubvp/2005/07/200507100012.shtml.

Swidler, Ann. 1986. Culture in action: Symbols and strategies. *American Sociological Review* 51: 273–286.

——. 1995. Cultural power and social movements." In *Social movements and culture*, ed. Hank Johnston and Bert Klandermans, 25–40. Minneapolis: University of Minnesota Press.

Tarrow, Sidney. 1994. *Power in movement: Social movements, collective action, and politics*. Cambridge: Cambridge University Press.

Thaxton, Ralph. 1997. *Salt of the earth: The political origins of peasant protest and communist revolution in China*. Berkeley: University of California Press.

Thompson, E. P. 1991. *Customs in common*. New York: Penguin.

Thornton, Patricia. 2007. *Disciplining the state: Virtue, violence, and state-making in modern China*. Cambridge, Mass.: Harvard Asia Center.

Tilly, Charles. 1978. *From mobilization to revolution*. Englewood Cliffs, N.J.: Prentice-Hall.

——. 1986. *The contentious French*. Cambridge, Mass.: Harvard University Press.

——. 1990. *Coercion, capital, and European states,* A.D. *990–1992*. Oxford: Blackwell.

——. 1993. Contentious repertoires in Great Britain, 1758–1834. *Social Science History* 17, no. 2: 253–280.

——. 1995. *Popular contention in Great Britain, 1758–1834*. Cambridge, Mass.: Harvard University Press.

——. 2002. *Stories, identities, and political change*. New York: Rowman and Littlefield.

——. 2006. *Regimes and repertoires*. Chicago: University of Chicago Press.

Tong, James. 1991. *Chaos under heaven: Collective violence under the Ming*. Stanford, Calif.: Stanford University Press.

Vlastos, Stephen. 1986. *Peasant protest and uprising in Tokugawa Japan*. Berkeley: University of California Press.

von Glahn, Richard 1991. Municipal reform and urban social conflict in late Ming Jiangnan. *Journal of Asian Studies* 50, no. 2: 280–307.

——. 1996. *Fountain of fortune: Money and monetary policy in China, 1000 to 1700*. Berkeley: University of California Press.

Wakeman, Frederic. 1966. *Strangers at the gate: Social disorder in south China, 1839–1861*. Berkeley: University of California Press.

——. 1972. The price of autonomy: Intellectuals in Ming and Ch'ing politics. *Daedalus* 101 (Spring): 42–43.

——. 1985. *The great enterprise: The Manchu reconstruction of imperial order in seventeenth-century China*. Berkeley: University of California Press.

——. 1998. Boundaries of the public sphere in Ming and Qing China. *Daedalus* 27, no. 3: 167–189.

——. 2000. A revisionist view of the Nanjing decade: Confucian fascism. In *Reappraising republican China*, ed. Frederic Wakeman and Richard L. Edmonds, 141–178. Oxford: Oxford University Press.

Walder, Andrew. 1988. *Communist neotraditionalism: Work and authority in Chinese industry*. Berkeley: University of California Press.

Wallerstein, Immanuel. 1974. *The modern world-system I: Capitalist agriculture and the origins of the European world-economy in the sixteenth century*. New York: Academic Press.

Walthall, Anne. 1986. *Social protest and popular culture in eighteenth-century Japan*. Tucson: University of Arizona Press.

Wang, Wensheng. 2009. Social crises and political reform during the Jiaqing reign of Qing China, 1796–1810s. In *From early Tang court debates to China's peaceful rise*, ed. Friederike Assandri and Dora Martins, 33–52. Amsterdam: Amsterdam University Press.

Wang Yeh-chien. 1973. *Land taxation in imperial China, 1750–1911*. Cambridge, Mass.: Harvard University Press.

——. 1979. Evolution of the Chinese monetary system, 1644–1850. In *Modern Chinese economic history: Proceedings of the Conference on Modern Chinese Economic History, August 26–29, 1977*, ed. Hou Chi-ming and Yu Tzong-shian. Taipei: Academia Sinica.

——. 1980. The secular trend of prices during the Ch'ing period, 1644–1911. In *Zhongguo jingji fazhanshi lunwenji*, ed. Yu Zongxian et al, 1541–1577. Taipei: Lianjing chubanshe.

——. 1992. Secular trends of rice prices in the Yangzi delta, 1638–1935. In *Chinese history in economic perspective*, ed. Thomas G. Rawski and Lillian M. Li, 35–68. Berkeley: University of California Press.

Wasserstrom, Jeffrey. 1991. *Student protests in twentieth-century China: The view from Shanghai*. Stanford, Calif.: Stanford University Press.

Weber, Max. 1946. *From Max Weber: Essays in sociology*. Oxford: Oxford University Press.

Weller, Robert P., and Scott E. Guggenheim, eds. 1982. *Power and protest in the countryside: Studies of rural unrest in Asia, Europe, and Latin America*. Durham, N.C.: Duke University Press.

White, James W. 1995. *Ikki: Social conflict and political protest in early modern Japan*. Ithaca, N.Y.: Cornell University Press.

Wickham, Carrie Rosefsky. 2002. *Mobilizing Islam*. New York: Columbia University Press.

Will, Pierre-Etienne. 1990. *Bureaucracy and famine in eighteenth-century China*. Stanford, Calif.: Stanford University Press.

Will, Pierre-Etienne, and Bin R. Wong. 1991. *Nourish the people: The state civilian granary system in China, 1650–1850*. Ann Arbor: University of Michigan Press.

Wills, John E. 1979. Maritime China from Wang Chih to Shih Lang: Themes in peripheral history. In *Conquest, region, and continuity in seventeenth-century China*, ed. Jonathan D. Spence and John E. Wills, 203–238. New Haven, Conn.: Yale University Press.

Wittfogel, Karl. 1957. *Oriental despotism: A comparative study of total power*. New Haven, Conn.: Yale University Press.

Wolf, Eric. 1982. *Europe and the people without history*. Berkeley: University of California Press.

Wong, R. Bin. 1982. Food riots in the Qing dynasty. *Journal of Asian Studies* 41, no. 4: 767–788.

——. 1997. *China transformed: Historical change and the limits of European experience.* Ithaca, N.Y.: Cornell University Press.

——. 2006. Detecting the significance of place. In *The Oxford handbook of contextual political analysis*, ed. Robert E. Goodwin and Charles Tilly, 534–546. Oxford: Oxford University Press.

Woodside, Alexander. 1990. State, scholars, and orthodoxy: The Ch'ing academies, 1736–1839. In *Orthodoxy in late imperial China*, ed. Kwang-ching Liu, 158–186. Berkeley: University of California Press.

——. 2002. The Ch'ien-Lung reign. In *The Cambridge history of China*, ed. Willard Peterson, 9:230–309. Cambridge: Cambridge University Press.

——. 2006. *Lost modernities: China, Vietnam, Korea, and the hazards of world history.* Cambridge, Mass.: Harvard University Press.

Wu Chengming. 2001. *Zhongguo de xiandai hua* [China's modernization: Market and society]. Beijing: Sanlian shudian.

Wu Jen-shu. 1996. *Mingqing chengshi minbian yanjiu: chuantong zhongguo jiti xingdong zhi fenxi* [A study of urban unrest in Ming-Qing cities: Analyzing collective actions in traditional China]. Unpublished dissertation, National Taiwan University.

——. 2000. Festival, cult, and protest: The city-god cult and the collective protests of urban people in Ming and Qing times. *Journal of Academia Sinica* 34 (December): 149–210.

Wu H. L. Silas. 1967. The memorial systems of the Ch'ing dynasty (1644–1911). *Harvard Journal of Asiatic Studies* 27: 7–75.

Xu Jianping. 2007. Hudong: Zhengfu yizhi yu minzhong yiyuan: yi minguo shiqi wuyuan huiyuan yundong wei li [Intercommunion: The purpose of the government and the desire of the mass of common people—Case analysis on "Wuyuan back to Anhui movement" in Republic of China]. *Zhongguo lishi dili luncong* 22, no. 1: 39–50.

Xu Tan. 1999. Qingdai qianqi shangpin liutong geju de bianhua [The change in the pattern of commodity circulation in early Qing]. *Qingshi yanjiu* 3: 1–13.

Yamamoto Ei'shi'. 1999. Tax farming by the gentry: Reorganization of the tax collection system in the early Qing. *Memoirs of the Research Department of the Toyo Bunko* 57.

Yang, C. K. 1961. *Religion in Chinese society: A study of contemporary social functions of religion and some of their historical factors.* Berkeley: University of California Press.

——. 1975. Some preliminary statistical patterns of mass actions in nineteenth-century China. In *Conflict and control in late imperial China*, ed. Frederic Wakeman, Jr. and Carolyn Grant, 174–211. Berkeley: University of California Press.

Yang Guobin. 2005. Environmental NGOs and institutional dynamics in China. *China Quarterly* 181 (March): 46–66.

——. 2009. *The power of the Internet in China: Citizen activism online.* New York: Columbia University Press.

Ye Gaoshu. 2002. *Qing qianqide wenhua zhengce.* Taipei: Daoxiang chubanshe.

Young, Michael P. 2006. *Bearing witness against sin: The evangelical birth of the American social movement.* Chicago: University of Chicago Press.

Yu Songqing. 1987a. Ming Qing bailian jiao yanjiu [Research on the White Lotus teachings of the Ming and Qing dynasties]. In *Ming Qing bailian jiao yanjiu*, by Yu Songqing, 1–116. Chengdu: Sichuan renmin chubanshe.

——. 1987b. Ming Qing shiqi mimi zongjiao zhongde nuxing [Women in the secret societies during the Ming-Qing period. In *Ming Qing bailian jiao yanjiu*, by Yu Songqing, 295–311. Chengdu: Sichuan renmin chubanshe.

Yu Yingshi. 2004. *Song Ming lixue yu zhengzhi wenhua* [Philosophy of principle and political culture in Ming and Qing]. Taipei: Yunchen wenhua.

Yuan, Tsing. 1979. Urban riots and disturbances. In *From Ming to Ch'ing*, ed. Jonathan D. Spence and John E. Wills. New Haven, Conn.: Yale University Press.

Zaret, David. 2000. *Origins of democratic culture: Printing, petition, and the public sphere in early modern England.* Princeton, N.J.: Princeton University Press.

Zelin, Madeleine. 1984. *The magistrate's tael: Rationalizing fiscal reform in eighteenth-century Ch'ing China.* Berkeley: University of California Press.

——. 2005. *The merchants of Zigong: Industrial entrepreneurship in early modern China.* New York: Columbia University Press.

Zhang, Tony, and Barry Schwartz. 2003. Confucius and the cultural revolution: A study in collective memory. In *States of memory: Continuities, conflicts, and transformations in national retrospection*, ed. Jeffrey K. Olick, 101–127. Durham, N.C.: Duke University Press.

Zhang Zuoliang. 2003. *Qianlong chao shehui dongluan ji zhengfu duice yanjiu* [A study of social unrest and government response in the Qianlong reign]. Unpublished master's thesis, Institute of History, Chinese Academy of Social Sciences.

Zhao, Dingxin. 2001. *The power of Tiananmen: State-society relations and the 1989 Beijing student movement.* Chicago: University of Chicago Press.

——. 2009. The mandate of heaven and performance legitimation in historical and contemporary China. *American behavioral scientist* 53, no. 3: 416–433.

——. 2010. *The rise of the Confucian-legalist state and patterns of Chinese history.* Unpublished manuscript. Department of Sociology, University of Chicago.

Zhao Xiaohua. 2001. *Wanqing songyu zhidu de shehui kaocha* [A social observation of the criminal-justice system in late Qing China]. Beijing: Zhongguo renmin daxue chubanshe.

Zheng Xiaowei. 2009. Loyalty, anxiety, and opportunism: Local elite activism during the Taiping rebellion in eastern Zhejiang, 1851–1864. *Late Imperial China* 30, no. 2: 39–83.

Zheng Yongchang. 1994. *Mingmo Qingchu yingui qianjian xianxiang yu xiangguan zhengzhi jingji sixiang* [The "expensive silver and cheap copper" phenomenon in late Ming and early Qing, and the related political economic thoughts]. Taipei: Guoli taiwan shifan daxue lishi yanjiu suo.

Zhongguo diyi lishi dang'an guan, ed. 1985. *Zhongguo diyi lishi dang'an guan guancang gaishu* [A concise description of the holdings in the Chinese Number One Historical Archives]. Beijing: Dangan chubanshe.

Zhou, Zhenke. 2006. Shengyu, shengyu guangxun jiqi xiangguang de wenhua xianxiang [Sacred edits, amplified instructions of the sacred edicts, and related cultural phenomenon]. In *Shengyu guangxun: jijie yu yanjiu*, ed. Zhou Zhenke, 351–632. Shanghai: Shanghai shudian.

Zito, Angela R. 1987. City gods, filiality, and hegemony in late imperial China. *Modern China* 13, no. 3: 333–371.

Zweig, David. 2000. The "externalities of development": Can new political institutions manage rural conflict? In *Chinese society: Change, conflict, and resistance*, ed. Elizabeth Perry and Mark Selden, 120–142. New York: Routledge.

GLOSSARY

An Ning	安寧
Anhui	安徽
Anyi	安邑
ba	八
baolu yundong	保路運動
Baoshan	寶山
Baoying	寶應
baozhang	保長
Bashan xiucai	巴山秀才
bashi	罷市
bashi weicheng	罷市未成
Beijing	北京
Bengang	笨港
bujin shi baixing	不盡是百姓
Cai Qian	蔡搴
Cang zhou	滄州
Changde	常德
Changping cang	常平倉
Changping zhou	昌平州
Changqing	長清
Changsha	長沙
Changzhou (prefecture)	常州
Changzhou (county)	長州
Chaozhou	潮州
Chen Faqing	陳發清
Chen Jie	陳傑
Chen Maoliang	陳茂亮
Chen Youyou	陳佑佑
Chengdu	成都
Cheng-Zhu	程朱
chiying baotai	持盈保泰
Chongming	崇明
Dao zhou	道州
Daoguang	道光
Daqing lüli	大清律例
Daqing shichao shengxun	大清十朝聖訓
Dasheng	大乘
daxing shuihuan minsheng bubao	大興水患民生不保
daxing shuili yongbao minsheng	大興水利永保民生
De'an	德安
Deping	德平
dianpu	佃僕
dibao	地保
dieqin niangqin bugou mao zhuxi qin	爹親娘親不夠毛主席親

Dinghai 定海
Dong Kaifu 董開富
Dong wu 東悟
Dongtai 東臺
dou 斗
Duan 段

falü lei 法律類
Falun Gong 法輪功
fang 方
Fang Changqing 方長慶
Fanzaigou 番仔溝
Feicheng 肥城
fen 分
Fengqiao 鳳橋
Fengyang 鳳陽
Fu Song 福崧
Fu zhou 涪州
Fujian 福建
Fuqing 福清
Fuzhou 福州

Gan 贛
Gansu 甘肅
Ganzhou 贛州
Gao Junzhong 高均中
Gaotang zhou 高唐州
Gaoxia 槔下
Gaoyou 高郵
Gongyang 公羊
Gongzhong dang 宮中檔
Gu 鼓
Gu Cong 顧琮
Gu Jiejie 谷介節
Gu Yanwu 顧炎武
Gu Yaonian 顧堯年
Gu Youcheng 谷有成
guanbi minfan 官逼民反
Guangdong 廣東
Guangxi 廣西
Guangzhou 廣州
Guichi 貴池
guixiang 跪香
guixiang douzheng weiyuanhui 跪香鬥爭委員會
Guizhou 貴州
Guolu 嘓嚕
Guomindang 國民黨

Haizhou 海州
Han 漢
Hangzhou 杭州
Hanlin 翰林
Hanshan 寒山
He zhou 合州
Hejuchang 河堨場
Henan 河南
Heshen 和珅
Hong Liangji 洪亮吉
Hong Xiuquan 洪秀全
Hongze 洪澤
Hu Fannian 胡範年
Huai'an 淮安
Huang 黃
Huang Yaoshu 黃燿樞
Huating 華亭
Hubei 湖北
Hunan 湖南

Jiading 嘉定
Jiang 蔣
Jiang Shunjiao 姜順蛟
Jiangnan 江南
Jiangsu 江蘇
Jiangxi 江西
jianshang 奸商
Jiaqing 嘉慶

jie	劫
Jie zhou	解州
jin	斤
Jin Mingguan	金銘館
Jin Qiteng	金啓騰
Jingjiang	靖江
jingkong	京控
Jinmenlou	津門樓
Jinshachang	金沙場
Jinzhou	錦州
jipu rulai tian you yan lushan buqu di wu pi	吉甫如來天有眼 祿山不去地無皮
Junji chu lufu zouzhe	軍機處錄副奏摺
juzhong hongtang	聚衆哄堂
Kai	開
Kangxi	康熙
koutou	叩頭
Kunshan	崐山
Laifeng	來鳳
Laifu	萊撫
Lanzhou	蘭州
Leiyang	耒陽
li	里
li	釐
li	理
Li Bozhong	李伯重
Li Tinghan	李廷翰
liang fang	糧房
Liangshan	梁山
Liao	廖
lie zhuan	列傳
Lin Fengming	林鳳鳴
Lin Shuangwen	林爽文
Lin Zexu	林則徐
Lin Zhuokui	林倬奎
Liu Fengsan	劉鳳三
Liu Jiang	劉江
Liu Jinli	劉金利
Liu Kesun	劉克遜
Liu Laosi	劉老四
Liu Mianxiao	劉勉孝
Liu Shaoqi	劉少奇
Liu Shishu	劉師恕
Liu Wenzhao	劉文照
lixue	理學
Lu Xun	魯迅
Lu Zhuo	盧焯
Lun gongchandang yuan de xiuyang	論共產黨員的修養
Luo Riguang	羅日光
Luzaigang	鹿仔港
manjie shi shengren	滿街是聖人
Mao Zedong	毛澤東
Mayang	麻陽
Mei Diaoyuan	梅調元
Meijiawan	梅家灣
Mile fo	彌勒佛
Min	閩
Ming	明
Ming shilu	明實錄
moushi yicheng	謀事已成
mu	牧
mu	畝
muyou	幕友
Nan'an	南安
Neige	內閣
Neige daku	內閣大庫
Ni Yuyu	倪玉玉

Ningguo	寧國
niu	牛
nongmin yundong lei fan qing douzheng xiang	農民運動類反清鬥爭項
nupu	奴僕
Pei	沛
peng	朋
peng	棚
Pi Xueli	皮學禮
Piqiaodiao	皮橋吊
puzhen	普賑
Qianlong	乾隆
Qing	清
Qing shigao	清史稿
Qing shilu	清實錄
Qingchao yeshi daguan	清朝野史大觀
Qingpu	青浦
qiuzhen	求賑
Quan Hansheng	全漢昇
Quanzhou	泉州
qunyan feiteng	群言沸騰
Randeng jiao	燃燈教
ren'ai	仁愛
Ren Si	任四
Shaanxi	陝西
Shandong	山東
shangcheng qiukuan	上城求寬
Shanghai	上海
Shanghang	上杭
Shangyu	上諭
Shangyu dang	上諭檔

Shanxi	山西
Shaoxing	紹興
Shehong	射洪
sheng	升
Sheng	嵊
Shengyu	聖諭
shenjin zhijia	紳衿之家
Shi Liuhai	施六害
Shi'er	施二
Shouzhang	壽張
Shuntian damengzhu	順天大盟主
Sichuan	四川
Song Lian	宋璉
Songjiang	松江
Sui zhou	隨州
Suqian	宿遷
Taicang	太倉
Taiping	太平
Taiping tianguo	太平天國
Taiwan	台灣
Taiyuan	太原
Taizhou	台州
Tangjia	唐家
Taoyuan	桃源
Teng	籐
Tiandihui	天地會
Tianjin	天津
Tingzhou	汀州
Tongren	銅仁
tongsheng huyu qiumian kaizha	同聲呼籲 求免開閘
Tongzhou	通州
Wang	王
Wang Huizu	汪輝祖
Wang Kaijing	王開經

Wang Lun	王倫
Wang Qiude	王求德
Wang Sanbao	王三豹
Wang Shidan	王施旦
Wang Shikui	王士魁
Wang Taihe	王太和
Wang Wei	王偉
Wang Yangming	王陽明
Wang Yulin	王玉林
Wang Yuying	王育英
Weng Hualong	翁化瀧
Wenjiang	溫江
Wenshang	汶上
Wei Yuan	魏源
weifu buren	爲富不仁
weiguo weimin fei weiji	為國為民非為已
wen	文
Wen Jiabao	溫家寶
Wen yeye	溫爺爺
Weng Rui	翁瑞
Wu Liyuan	伍哩沅
Wu Shiying	吳士映
Wu Yueqian	吳曰謙
wuqian maimi qiongmin nanguo	無錢買米 窮民難過
wulai bufa zhitu	無賴不法之徒
Wuling	武陵
Wusheng laomu	無生老母
wuye zhitu	無業之徒
Wuyuan	婺源
Xiaogan	孝感
Xiaojing	孝經
Xiayi	夏邑
xiezhi guanli	挾制官吏
xinfang	信訪
Xinghua	興化
Xinji	新集
Xinjiang	新疆
xinxue	心學
Xu Xiling	徐錫齡
Xuancheng	宣城
xuanyu huadao shi	宣諭化導使
Xue Wei	薛渭
Xue Zi	薛滋
xun chengong	訓臣工
xunfu	巡撫
Xuzhou	徐州
Yan Chengxia	嚴承夏
Yancang	鹽倉
Yancheng	鹽城
yang	養
Yang Xiuqing	楊秀清
Yanggu	陽穀
Yangqu	陽曲
yangmin	養民
Yangzhou	楊州
Yangzi	楊子
Yanzhou	兗州
Yao	猺
Ye Changtai	葉昌泰
yi xiao zhi tianxia	以孝治天下
Yin Jishan	尹繼善
Yingfeng	盈豐
Yongchun	永春
Yongquan	湧泉
Yongzheng	雍正
Yongzhou	永州
youyang zhou	酉陽州
Yuan Gui	袁貴
yuhu	漁戶

yumin 愚民
Yunnan 雲南
Yuzhi pengdang lun 禦制朋黨論

zaicheng jumin youli zhi jia 在城居民 有力之家
zaozuo fuyan 造作浮言
Ze 澤
Zeng Lao'er 曾老二
Zeng Laoyan 曾老巖
zhang 丈
Zhang Baotai 張保太
Zhang Laoda 張老大
Zhang Qin 張欽
Zhang Yuan 張遠
Zhangzhou 章州
Zhao Butang 趙步堂
Zhao Dingxin 趙鼎新
Zhao Jinyi 趙進義
Zhejiang 浙江
Zheng He 鄭和
Zhenjiang 鎮江
zhenzhu 真主
Zhili 直隸
zhisheng 直省
Zhong zhou 忠州
Zhongnanhai 中南海
zhongxiao 忠孝
Zhou 周
Zhu Yuanzhang 朱元璋
Zhuang Cunyu 莊存與
zhuangshu 莊書
zhuangtou 莊頭
zhupi zouzhe 硃批奏摺
Ziyang 紫陽
zong zaitou 總災頭
zongdu 總督
Zou 鄒

INDEX

INDEX

INDEX

GPSR Authorized Representative: Easy Access System Europe, Mustamäe tee 50, 10621 Tallinn, Estonia, gpsr.requests@easproject.com

www.ingramcontent.com/pod-product-compliance
Lightning Source LLC
Chambersburg PA
CBHW021855020426
42334CB00013B/341

* 9 7 8 0 2 3 1 1 5 2 0 3 7 *